Reading New India

ALSO AVAILABLE FROM BLOOMSBURY

Reading New India

Post-Millennial Indian Fiction in English

E. Dawson Varughese

B L O O M S B U R Y
LONDON • NEW DELHI • NEW YORK • SYDNEY

Bloomsbury Academic

An imprint of Bloomsbury Publishing Plc

50 Bedford Square	175 Fifth Avenue
London	New York
WC1B 3DP	NY 10010
UK	USA

www.bloomsbury.com

First published 2013

British Library Cataloguing-in-Publication Data
A catalogue record for this book is available from the British Library.

ISBN: HB: 978-1-4411-8540-2
PB: 978-1-4411-8174-9
PDF: 978-1-4411-3623-7
ePub: 978-1-4411-0556-1

Library of Congress Cataloging-in-Publication Data
A catalog record for this book is available at the Library of Congress

Typeset by Deanta Global Publishing Services, Chennai, India
Printed and bound in Great Britain

For Sabu John
- dil se

CONTENTS

7   Graphic novels 137

Conclusions: New/Old stories in Old/New ways? 145

PREFACE

India has witnessed immense change since the turn of the millennium and 2012–13 celebrates 65 years of independence for India. *Reading New India* explores this new landscape through Indian fiction in English, fiction published within India since the millennium. The book considers this body of fiction against earlier notions of Indian literature in English and against the contemporary socio-cultural backdrop of New India.

The once popular motifs of *Doordarshan*, *Thumbs Up*, and terylene shirts seem to be rapidly fading into an erstwhile India. In 2010 the rupee was given a new symbol, a blend of the Devanagari script 'ra' and the Roman 'r' meant a new symbol for a New India, shiny LPG autorickshaws continue to populate the streets of India's metropolises, Chetan Bhagat muses 'what does young India want', Anna Hazare fasts for an end to corruption, *India's Got Talent* plays on flatscreen TVs and 'home loans' are on the rise.

Reading New India attempts to capture this moment in its analysis of India's new fiction in English, offering insight and analysis of contemporary India and considering what and where India's future directions might be.

The envisioned readerships for *Reading New India* are many but it is acknowledged here that an Indian readership in New India might have particular interest in this book. It is to this readership that the glossary, chronological timeline, authors bios and cultural/historical discussions might prove less necessary and so it is to these readers that I acknowledge their established understanding of the subject and hope that inclusion of such items does not impede their engagement or enjoyment of the text. Thank you, EDV.

ACKNOWLEDGEMENTS

I remember those who backed this book from the absolute beginning. As the plane banked out of the Mumbai monsoon skies of 2009, I had this book in my head and Sabu John was the first to hear of it, he has supported it ever since.

And my sincere thanks to Robert Eaglestone and to David Avital who have embraced this book from the outset. And to Keely for help with the author biographies.

This book acknowledges all that India is, and has been to me, it is a work which embodies many years, many experiences and many people. My thanks therefore are numerous, indeed immeasurable and just as India often proves too big and too diverse to grasp, so too, are my acknowledgements.

It was the poster on the door of the samosa shop on Soho Road that sent me across the road to buy the soundtrack. I left that cassette in a car in New Delhi but I've never forgotten the *taal* of its title track. Mani Ratman's cinematography and A.R. Rahman's melodies have stayed with me ever since, more importantly maybe, so too has the enduring narrative of human relationships against the background of Indian politics.

[station platform, howling wind and rain, ek ladkha aur ek ladkhi]

Dekhiye aap, aap akeli hain,
Mein aap keliye kuch laa sakta hoon?
Ek cup garam chai
Dil Se (1998)

1

Introduction: From postcolonial India to New India

This chapter begins with an overview of the major socio-political reforms since India's independence from British rule in 1947 and how the notion of 'Indianness' has developed in this timeframe, in parallel with these developments. This overview is supported by a chronological timeline (see page 160).

The chapter proceeds to focus on the literary production of this same time period (Section 1.2), presenting:

- key literary figures
- developments and issues in the history of Indian writing in English and, where possible, these will be linked to the developments outlined in Section 1.1
- finally, Section 1.3 focuses on post-millennial Indian writing in English against the backdrop of New India; its post-millennial economical, cultural and societal self

Author biographies support Sections 1.2 and 1.3. and can be found on pages 161–86.

1.1 'Indianness' since independence

India gained independence from British rule in 1947 and the matter of 'Indianness' at this juncture in the country's history was a topic of great debate. Gandhi recognized that Hinduism was part of what it meant to be Indian. However, it was a broad and inclusive sense of Hinduism that shaped his particular idea of India and one consistent with his non-aggressive principles. Despite the presence of militant Hindu nationalists and their desire post-independence for an Indianness to be rooted deeply in Hinduism, it was the European-influenced ideas of what India *should become* post 1947 that helped to form notions of Indianness that followed. At the point of independence, the Indian National Congress, led by Jawaharlal Nehru, looked to create an India that was secular. In accordance with a sense of 'nation' as a hegemonic entity, Nehru pursued a model that was 'committed to protecting cultural and religious difference rather than imposing a uniform "Indianess"' (Khilnani 1999, p. 167). Nehru's monetary policies followed suit and as India's first prime minister, he built an economy around state-sponsored investment. Committed to the importance of state identities, Nehru's idea of Indianness was reflected in his views on India's languages; English was recognized as the language of state and Hindi as an 'official' but not 'national' language – other regional languages were also recognized as 'official'. Of this debate Khilnani writes:

> This technique of compromise refused to anchor an Indian identity to a single trait – an option which, had it been chosen, would have suborned regional cultures to majoritarian definitions of a national one. . . . Indianness was defined not as a singular or exhaustive identity, but as one which explicitly recognized at least two other aspects; Indian citizens were also members of linguistic and cultural communities: Oriyas or Tamils, Kashmiri or Marathi. (Khilnani 1999, p. 175)

Following Nehru's death in 1964, and during the 1970s, Indian politics began moving in very different directions. Regional and caste preoccupations began to invade national politics. Various social groups and movements took precedence over the more hegemonic sense of Nehru's original view of Indianness. The 1970s saw a rise in the birth of political groups and it became increasingly difficult for Congress to maintain its support and strength across India. By the 1980s, demands for regional autonomy grew – such as the cases in Punjab and Kashmir – each looking for more independence and self-rule. This desire for autonomy ostracized the various peoples seeking regional independence as their demands were interpreted as being 'anti-national'. It was to Mrs Indira Gandhi that Congress turned to transform the party into one for the masses, a party that once again, it was hoped, would venerate a secular notion of 'Indianness'. Unlike Nehru, Mrs Gandhi was operating in a different time; there was widespread dissent and deep fissures among peoples of the Indian nation, manifest particularly in their opinions towards central governance. Some of the more controversial decisions influenced by Mrs Gandhi at this time – such as holding political prisoners – have been received variously; indeed, one could suggest that it was the impact of these decisions which led to her death in 1984. In contrast to previous hegemonic strategies of engagement, Mrs Gandhi used associated religious difference in order to garner support and rally voters. The crisis of Congress played out during this period and, in turn, no single political group was able to dominate. General elections in 1991 and again in 1996 produced hung parliaments and coalition governments.

In this political vacuum, the Bharatiya Janata Party was borne out of a Hindu nationalist party – the Bharatiya Jan Sangh. Known as the BJP, the Bharatiya Janata Party's sense of 'Indianness' stood in opposition to Nehru's

India; 'Hinduness' was at its core and its project was to create: 'a culturally and ethnically cleaned-up homogenous community with a singular Indian citizenship, defended by a state that had both God and nuclear warheads on its side' (Khilnani 1999, p. 188). Some thought at the time that this political position would not return India to a Gandhian philosophy of the rural and the village; it did not. Instead, the BJP revisioned a sense of Indianness, claiming that all Indians need not be Hindu to be Indian, but that India be recognized as Hindu. In reality, this political position resulted in little recognition both legally and politically of anything other than Hindu.

Identity politics abound, Ayodhya (see Glossary) found itself at the centre of the Hindu nationalist movement (through the political groups of Sangh Parivar) in 1992, fuelling Hindu–Muslim tensions; a nervousness that reinvoked the days of partition. The Hindu nationalist movement wished to 'reclaim' the ancient city of Ayodhya; for the Hindus, this was the birthplace of Ram and for the Muslims it was the holy site of a sixteenth-century place of worship, the Babri Masjid. The Babri Masjid mosque was destroyed in the violence of Ayodhya and tensions around who was a 'real' Indian reached an all time high. The 'Bombay riots' of December 1992 and January 1993 were fuelled by the Ayodhya violence and many contemporary films make reference to these terrible uprisings, one of the most recent references made in the English-medium film *Slumdog Millionaire* (2008). One of the early scenes in the film shows Jamal Malik's mother washing clothes, when she is hit by Hindu rioters, knocking her into the water where she drowns. Jamal and his brother witness her death and run away from the scene to escape the ensuing violence. This memory is evoked some years later when Jamal Malik is asked a question on the game show, *Kaun banega Crorepati?* Jamal turns to Prem Kumar – the game show host – and says that if it wasn't for Ram and Allah, then he would still have a mother; a reference to the Bombay riots and the legacy of the religious violence. 'Difference and Death', Section 5.2 of this volume, discusses Esther David's *The Man with Enormous Wings* (2010) and Taseer's *The Temple-Goers* (2010); both texts examine communal violence, difference across and within religions and, in David's novella in particular, the Hindu–Muslim unrest in the city of Ahmedabad in 2002.

Despite the religious tensions of the 1990s and the ongoing debates of a secular India versus a religious (Hindu) India, the country was making headway economically. The 1990s benefited from increased domestic consumption and these early fiscal developments put India on a path that has resulted in an increasingly important role in global modernity. Das (2002) explains:

> The notable thing about India's rise is not that it is new – it has been among the best performing economies for a quarter century – but its path is unique. Rather than adopting the classic Asian strategy – exporting labour-intensive, low-priced manufactured goods to the West – India

has relied on its domestic market more than exports, consumption more than investment, services more than industry, and high-tech rather than low-skill manufacturing. (Das 2002, p. 360)

This rise in economic prosperity impacted and shaped the more radical ideas of Hinduism evident in previous years and with this change came a 'rebranding' of India's Hinduism. Khilnani (1999) writes:

For many in India modernity has been adopted through conservative filters of religious piety, moralism and domestic virtue. This has spawned a novel Hinduism, where holographic gods dangle on well-used keychains and cassettes of devotional *ragas* are played in traffic jams: instances of a religious sentiment freed from its original defining contexts, from the subtle iconography of materials and the punctual divisions of the day into sacred and mundane time. (Khilnani 1999, p. 187)

This change in society is further documented by Swaminathan (2007), writing in recognition of India's 60 years of independence in 2007 and of the complexities and challenges that New India is experiencing:

The year 2007 marks the birth centenary of Bhagat Singh. In his last letter before he was hanged, Bhagat Singh mentioned that India would not achieve freedom by merely getting rid of the British because their place would be taken by the *kale Angrez* – the Black English. It is only after the people fight against them and win, will our country be genuinely free. Now, after almost sixty years of "freedom" we not only realize how true his words were, but must also know that those kale Angrez he was referring to, are people like us. (Swaminathan 2007, p. 64)

Swaminathan underscores how India, despite freedom from colonial rule, still suffers at the hands of those in power, and Mondal (2005) reminds us that although India has witnessed leaders who have pioneered secular notions of Indianness since independence, the result has often proved to encode a Hindu majoritarian point of view 'even in the most secular-seeming and tolerant formulations' (Mondal 2005, p. 22). At the heart of many of these secular movements was the idea of 'the composite nation', of which Mondal writes: 'In particular, any attempt to articulate an alternative India by appealing to some "pure" or "uncontaminated" secular nationalism is fraught with particular dangers' (Mondal 2005, p. 22).

As this book will go on to demonstrate, New India faces many challenges and the question of 'Indianness' is only one of many, albeit a crucial one. Emanating mainly from increased fiscal certainty – although the global economic meltdown *has* affected India to some extent – India is now a more confident and adept player in the global economy, and as a consequence of these developments, it is facing new challenges both socially and culturally. The fiction explored in Chapters 2 to 7 talks of and to these changes and considers some of the ways in which New India is being encoded in its contemporary fiction. Ideas of 'Indianness', therefore, run throughout the examination of these texts, as India once again jostles and negotiates (twenty-first century) ideas of what *it is*, and what it *should mean*, to be Indian.

Section 1.2 presents literary developments and the creation of the canon of Indian writing in English since 1947. Where possible, links with the political and societal reforms of India since 1947, outlined above, will be illuminated in the discussion.

1.2 Literary 'Indianness'

India has a deeply established and developed literary scene of writing in English in comparison to other countries of erstwhile British colonial rule. Global economic prominence has inspired a fast-changing literary scene. These literary developments are impacting not only the readership of Indian writing in English within India, but also the genre, forms, voices and modes of artistic expression, engaged with representing this emerging economy. These developments are examined in detail across Chapters 2 to 7 of this book.

In order to understand how Indian writing in English has developed over time, this section offers a brief presentation of early Indian writing in English. Although the focus will be on post-independence writing, it is useful to understand how motifs of 'Indianness' were developed very early on by writers, Indian themselves, as well as those who knew India well through travel and frequent long-term visits to the country. Consequently, some pre-independence writing is discussed initially, followed by a presentation of the post-independence writers.

Empire and Indian writing in English

The first novel written and published in English by an Indian is *Rajmohan's Wife* by Bankimchandra Chatterjee, in print from 1864 (Talib 2002, p. 82). The canon of this period of early writing in English was produced by both Indians and non-Indians. Boehmer writes of the 'British high empire of 1870–1918' (Boehmer 2009, p. xv) and of the colonial writing of that period in which 'India' appeared as a subject and a muse in the writings of non-Indians, as well as in literature written by Indians themselves. From Tennyson's 'The Defence of Lucknow' (1880), Kipling's 'Christmas in India' (1888) and Arnold's The Light of Asia (1879), to Sarojini Naidu's 'Songs of My City' (1912), this era of writing captured the various experiences of the British Raj, in particular. Notably, the poetry of Toru Dutt and her *Ancient Ballads and Legends of Hindustan* (1882) was the first collection of Indian poetry in English to be published by a woman (Boehmer 2009, p. 69).

Kipling's 'Christmas in India' (1888) is infused with sensory experience; the colours of the scene, the smells of the village roads, the sounds of the corn being ground and the parrots calling by the river.

> Dim dawn behind the tamarisks – the sky is saffron-yellow –
> As the women in the village grind the corn,
> And the parrots seek the river-side, each calling to his fellow
> That the Day, the starring Eastern Day, is born.
> O the White dust on the highway! O the stenches in the byway!
> O the clammy fog that hovers over earth!
> And at Home they're making merry 'neath the white and scarlet berry –
> What part have India's exiles in their mirth? (Boehmer 2009, p. 104)

The poem makes a reference to Christmas at 'Home', the capitalized 'Home' rooting Kipling and Christmas to a particular tradition and heritage of Christian life.

Within the body of writing in English discussed here, this book is particularly interested in cultural and societal references to Hindu epics and Sanskrit aesthetics. Section 1.3 explains this interest in more detail. One early example of this relationship between literary production in English and the cultural, religious backdrop of Hinduism is in Sarojini Naidu's 'Song of Radha The Milkmaid' (1912). This poem brings the form of the English Romantic poem together with motifs of Hindu Indian culture. These motifs are embodied in the shrine, the torches and the conch shells found in the following extract of the poem:

> I carried my gifts to the Mathura shrine . . .
> How brightly the torches were glowing! . . .
> I folded my hands at the altars to pray
> 'O shining Ones guard us by night and by day'-
> And loudly the conch shells were blowing.
> But my heart was so lost in your worship, Beloved,
> They were wroth when I cried without knowing:
> *Govinda! Govinda!*
> *Govinda! Govinda!* . . .
> How brightly the river was flowing! (Boehmer 2009, p. 316)

The poem plays on the woman's cry of the name *Govinda!* during her pilgrimage to the place of Mathura, aside the sacred river Ganga, the chief centre of worship for Sri Krishna or 'Govinda' – as this is another name attributed to Sri Krishna, the Divine Cowherd. It is, therefore, not wholly inappropriate for the woman, in bringing gifts to the Hindu shrine to worship her 'Beloved', to call out his name, *Govinda!*; however, her insistence and desire on the calling of his name at various points in the poem are found to be inappropriate. Her actions put into question whether, in fact, she is calling out to the Deity or rather, to a more human form of 'Govinda'. This final verse of the three-verse poem (cited above) is a crescendo of feelings towards 'her' Govinda – as the conch shells blow loudly and the great, sacred river Ganga flows brightly.

In the poem by Sri Aurobindo, 'Hymn to the Mother: Bandemataram' (1909), we read of the Indian 'motherland'. Often found in the Hindu goddesses of Kali, Lakshmi and Durga, the force of the female identity alongside 'Hindustan' in this poem are found in the sacred waters of the Ganga and its 'hurrying streams' and the fertile, green lands and orchards (it would seem) of North India.

> Mother, I bow to thee!
> Rich with thy hurrying streams,
> Bright with thy orchard gleams,
> Cool with they winds of delight,
> Dark fields waving, Mother of might,
> Mother free. (Boehmer 2009, p. 326)

Sri Aurobindo 'hinduises' the poem with his title of 'Bandematram', making strong cultural links to the Hindu goddesses and grounding the motherland in the ancient, the sacred and in a sense of *bharat*. Later in the poem, Sri Aurobindo reveres the motherland further by stating: 'Mother, I kiss thy feet', complementing the equally reverential opening line: 'Mother, I bow to thee'.

In addition to exploring India as a subject or a muse of literature in English, this book is also interested in the role that Indian English(es) play in the 'writing in English' scene. This focus includes the employment of code-switching in Indian literature in English and the following extract from Alice Perrin's prose, 'The Rise of Ram Din' (1906), demonstrates an early example of this. Alice Perrin was born in India and, although educated for the most part in England, she returned to India to marry an Indian and lived out a challenging Anglo-Indian life. In the following extract, we see how Perrin code-switches (using Hindi and Urdu) to recount the story of 'The Rise of Ram Din'.

> My father bought me a white muslin coat, a pair of calico trousers tight below the knee, and a new *puggaree*; and we took seats in the *ekka* and drove out to the part where the sahibs dwell beyond the city. . . . There we heard that a dishwasher was needed, and the *khansamah-jee* said that if my father gave him a *backsheesh*, and I promised him a percentage of my pay, he could get me the palace without any recommendation. He also said that the engineer-sahib was a good sahib, and the service to be desired, and that I should be well treated. (Boehmer 2009, p. 331, original emphasis)

Here, Perrin's writing demonstrates how Indian languages are used alongside the English language and this is a useful benchmark to measure how this intention has changed since the early 1900s when Perrin was writing. As Chapters 2 to 7 will demonstrate, code-switching still takes place in the literary texts of post-millennial fiction; however, unlike Perrin's employment of Hindi or Urdu, contemporary texts code-switch more between 'standard' English and Indian English(es) than with Hindi or Urdu.

Texts from this period of early writing in English speak variously to notions of Indianness of this time. Given that much of the writing was produced by non-Indians (in comparison to the post-independence period and the contemporary period), the notions of Indianness are less centred on the Indian experience of being Indian per se. Despite this, Alex Tickell (2005) reminds us that some early fiction of the pre-independence time written by Indians, albeit outside the country, was particularly interested in Hindu nationalism. In a chapter entitled 'The Discovery of Aryavarta', Tickell discusses two popular romances published in London in the early 1900s (as well as drawing on Sinha's *Sanjogita*). Tickell's consideration of these novels in their historical and political period help to bring together the two areas of interest of this introductory chapter, that of Indianness and of literary expression. Tickell writes: '. . . the rise of Hindu majoritarianism and forms of Hindu nationalism in India is [instead] prefigured in some of the earliest, most popular examples of the form' (Tickell 2005, p. 30), and he goes on to conclude that:

> . . . along with "people" and "nation", "race" seems to have been a unit in this transacted, "replicable" currency of political terms, and could be used as part of the international self-positioning and self-validation of a new Indian intelligentsia, especially where European colonialism seemed to be failing as a global political force. (Tickell 2005, p. 40)

The ways in which Indianness went on to be framed in the twentieth century through the works of writers who have become figureheads of the postcolonial canon of literature in English in India is the focus of the next part of this section. As the nineteenth century became the twentieth century, a generation of New Indian writers was born and their lives were shaped by changing times; World War II, partition and an immediate legacy of British colonial rule.

Forming the postcolonial canon

The canon of writing that started to appear in the late 1930s, 1940s and continuing for some writers until the turn of the century, is framed by the works of R. K. Narayan (b.1906), Mulk Raj Anand (b.1905), Raja Rao (b.1909), Khushwant Singh (b.1915) and Anita Desai (b.1937) in particular, although writers such as Arun Joshi (b.1939), N. C. Chaudhuri (b.1897), Manoj Das (b.1934), Aubrey Menon (b.1912) – of Irish and Indian parentage –, Kamala Markandaya (b.1924), Nisha da Cunha (b.1934) and Ruskin Bond (b.1934) also figure as important writers in the early days of Indian writing in English. These writers have come to be known as authors of 'postcolonial literature'. Gilbert (2001) offers a definition of the postcolonial and I am using it here to understand its role in defining the narratives, plots, characters and voice of 'postcolonial literature' as a recognized body of writing:

> In many contexts, the term indicates a degree of agency, or at least a programme of resistance, against cultural domination; in others, it signals the existence of a particular historical legacy and/or a chronological stage in a culture's transition into a modern nation-state; in yet others, it is used more disapprovingly to suggest a form of co-option into Western cultural economies. What is common to all of these definitions, despite their various implications, is a central concern with cultural power.
>
> For those less interested in staking out disciplinary boundaries, "postcolonial" has become a convenient (and sometimes useful) portmanteau term to describe any kind of resistance, particularly against class, race and gender oppressions. (Gilbert 2001, p. 1)

Put more succinctly, Boehmer (2005) writes of postcolonial literature as 'generally defined as that which critically or subversively scrutinizes the colonial relationship. It is writing that sets out in one way or another to resist colonialist perspectives' (Boehmer 2005, p. 3).

As Chapters 2 to 7 of this book will aim to demonstrate, the defining characteristics of India's 'postcolonial literature' are less apparent in contemporary writing in English. This book suggests that post-millennial fiction in English is less recognizable by the tropes and guises of the body of writing characterized in Gilbert's and Boehmer's definitions. A brief overview of some of the principal Indian postcolonial writers and their works will further help to demonstrate what is meant by postcolonial writing in line with the definitions above. We will return to questions of how post-millennial writing in English, given the backdrop of New India, challenges some of the assumptions, still current, about Indian literature in English and its relationship to the postcolonial canon, as we work through Chapters 2 to 7, closing with specific observations in the conclusions (Chapter 8).

R. K. Narayan

Born in 1906 in Madras (now Chennai) and educated in Mysore, R. K. Narayan is regarded as one of the most prolific writers of Indian fiction in English. His first novel, called *Swami and Friends* (1935), is one of his best-known works and is set in the fictional territory of Malgudi. This fictitious land is synonymous with the author's named series *Malgudi Days* (originally published in 1972), which is a collection of short stories set around the city of Malgudi. Here we encounter an astrologer ('The Axe'), Ramu and his mother ('Mother and Son'), a snake charmer ('Naga'), a dog

('The Blind Dog') and many others. *Malgudi Days* alongside his other novels set in Malgudi made R. K. Narayan one of the founders of writing in English from India.

Mulk Raj Anand

Mulk Raj Anand was born in 1905 and published his first novel *Untouchable* in 1935; it is this novel that most people know him by. *Coolie* (1936) and *Two Leaves and A Bud* (1937) followed *Untouchable* and extended his study of the oppressed through questions of caste and class. The late 1930s and early 1940s saw the publication of the trilogy: *The Village* (1939), *Across the Black Waters* (1941) and *The Sword and the Sickle* (1942). The Punjab is often the geographic landscape of Anand's work and *The Village* follows Lal Singh and his struggle to reconcile village life with progressive, urban India. Anand pioneered the employment of Indian English(es) in some of his literary works, such as 'Duty', 'The Parrot in the Cage' and 'Things Have A Way of Working Out' (Anand 2006). *Across the Black Waters* (1941) is an unusual novel for Indian English writing of the time in the sense that it deals with World War I and a soldier in Flanders. Pre-independence saw most of Anand's best work; post-independence, Anand's work is semi-autobiographical, whether in terms of the geography of northern India (what is now Pakistan) or narratives of the 'peasant' theme and the plight of the underdog. Anand's work is of great importance in terms of the development of Indian writing in English from India as he experiments with social realism. His work is infused with Gandhism, often exploring the struggle between tradition and modernity. Below is the opening paragraph to *Untouchable*, highlighting Anand's commitment to representing the 'other' India:

> "The outcasts" colony was a group of a mud-walled houses that clustered together in two rows, under the shadow both of the town and the cantonment, but outside their boundaries and separate from them. There lived the scavengers, the leather-workers, the washermen, the barbers, the water-carriers, the grass-cutters and other outcasts from Hindu society. A brook ran near the lane, once with crystal-clear water, now soiled by the dirt and filth of public latrines situated about it, the odour of the hides and skins of dead carcases left to dry on its banks, the dung of donkeys, sheep, horses. Cows and buffaloes heaped up to be made into fuel cakes, and the biting, choking, pungent flames that oozed from its sides. The absence of a drainage system had, through the rains of various seasons, made of the quarter a marsh which gave out the most offensive stink. And altogether the ramparts of human and animal refuse that lay on the outskirts of this colony, and the ugliness, the squalor and the misery which lay within it, made an "uncongenial" place to live in. (Anand 1940, p. 9)

Raja Rao

Raja Rao, born in 1909 in Mysore, South India, engaged deeply with the problematic of writing in a language that he perceived as 'not his own'. A Kanarese speaker, Rao wrote in Kannada, French and English; however, his major works are in English. His only novel published in pre-independence India is *Kanthapura* (1932) and it focuses on non-violent resistance to the British occupation of India. Rao's interest in Gandhian philosophy also produced a non-fiction account of Gandhi's life in *The Great Indian Way: A Life of Mahatma Gandhi* (1998). Indian philosophy, Hinduism and questions of identity run through most of Rao's works; in *Cat and Shakespeare* (1965), the Hindu notion of *karma* is symbolized by a cat; in *The Serpent and the Rope* (1960), Rao offers a rendering of the Indian epic *The Mahabharata* as well as exploring the relationship between Indian and Western cultures. The story focuses on an Indian mathematician based in Paris and a married woman; a love affair doomed to failure. These two novels might be considered as examples of literature in English, which draw on ancient Indian and Sanskrit aesthetics.

In *The Chessmaster and His Moves* (1988), Rao uses the analogy of a chessboard to explore characters from different cultures seeking their identities. Rao's interest in French society and culture certainly makes for an interesting combination, particularly at a time when most writers were predominantly North Indian–Anglophone, whereas Rao was South Indian–Francophone.

Khushwant Singh

Partition literature constitutes a large part of the history of Indian writing in English and one author who has contributed significantly to this body of literature is Khushwant Singh. Born in 1915 in the Punjab, Singh experienced the partition of India first hand; in 1947, he was working as a lawyer in Lahore, then part of Punjab. Singh survived the anarchy of the early days of partition because he took his family to Kasauli in the foothills of the Himalayas just days before the trouble started (Singh 2002, p. 112). One of Khushwant Singh's earliest and most famous works tells of the atrocities of partition, *Train to Pakistan* published in 1953. It charts the lives of the villagers of Mano Majra, situated on the banks of the Sutlej, who live in harmony regardless of religious difference, that is, until partition. It is the villagers who remain the heroes of this novel and this is greatly tied to a sense of India itself, the mass of people in whom one can have basic confidence. The following extract is the closing paragraph to the novel.

> Somebody fired another shot. The man's body slid off the rope, but he clung on with his hands and chin. He pulled himself up, caught the rope under his left armpit, and again started hacking with his right hand.

The rope had been cut in shreds. Only a thin tough strand remained. He went at it with the knife, and then with his teeth. The engine was almost on him. There was a volley of shots. The man shivered and collapsed. The rope snapped in the center as he fell. The train went over him, and went on to Pakistan. (Singh 1956, p. 181)

Anita Desai

Anita Desai is also an early voice in writing from India. Born in 1937 in Mussoorie, to a German mother and a Bengali father, she is a novelist, a short-story writer and a children's author. She has written extensively and her books include: *Cry the Peacock* (1963), *Bye Bye Blackbird* (1969), *Where Shall We Go This Summer?* (1975) and *Fire on the Mountain* (1977), all of which follow the very complex emotional lives of female protagonists. *In Custody* (1984) and *Baumgartner's Bombay* (1988) focus on male narratives and *A Journey to Ithaca* (1995) is 'Orientalism' at its most archetypal, as India is perceived by Western eyes as the land of sages, gurus, temples and heat.

G. V. Desani

Another early writer is G. V. Desani, who Indian by ancestry, was born in Nairobi, Kenya, in 1909. Desani's work and the factors that shaped his writing meant that his writing is regarded as highly revolutionary for the time in which it was published. Desani spent most of his life in England until after World War II when he moved to India. Finally, Desani moved to America where he took up teaching religion and philosophy at the University of Texas. Desani's famous novel, *All About H. Hatterr* (1948), was seminal in recognizing a new type of Indian writing in English and this was mainly due to Desani's use of language. *All About H. Hatterr* tells the story of H. Hatterr, son of a European merchant seafarer and a woman from Penang. The story tells of Hatterr's search for 'higher truth', a search that involves encounters with the 'Seven Sins' and seven (false) soothsayers. Despite his travels and worldly experiences between the West and India, Hatterr concludes that the meaning of life is actually life itself; all the confusion, hypocrisy and 'topsy-turvyism' is what makes life, life. Parallels might be drawn, in terms of language, genre and voice, with Rushdie's *Midnight's Children* (1981), which was published 30 years after Desani's novel, demonstrating that Desani's work was groundbreaking at the time.

In addition to the canon of postcolonial writing in English from India, a body of critical writing on Indian writing in English has been published post-millennium and this criticism focuses on writing from the postcolonial canon of writing and on some of the writers noted above. What is significant about this criticism is that it approaches the Indian English writing scene from significant Indian perspectives, focusing on Indian issues from within

India. As examples, in Pathak, the Parsi identity in Indian English literature is examined (Pathak 2003, pp. 104–57, 168–76) and in Prasad, Gandhian ideology is explored (Prasad 2005, pp. 63–86), alongside patriotism (Prasad 2005, pp. 153–61) in Indian English writing.

1.3 New India, a new canon

The 1980s witnessed a new wave of Indian writing in English. Rushdie, born in 1947, made Indian writing in English available to a larger international readership. Rushdie's early works signalled a move towards an expression of narratives in Indian English and this led to increased linguistic diversity in Indian English writing, something that we are still seeing today. Pre-Rushdie, Indian writing in English was generally writing about 'Indianness' through its many cultures and peoples, but it was often expressed through language and forms that were very 'unindian', as we have read above in examples from Sarojini Naidu's 'Song of Radha The Milkmaid' (1912) to Khushwant Singh's *Train to Pakistan* (1956). Anand and Desani's works are perhaps somewhat of an exception to this orthodoxy.

Many of the writers who started to publish during the 1980s were born in the 1940s and 1950s and thus, many of these writers are still publishing today; Deshpande (b.1938), Dhondy (b.1944), Seth (b.1952), Swaminathan (b.1958), U. Chatterjee (b.1959), Gokhale (b.1956), Tharoor (b.1956), Esther David (b.1945), Kapur (b.1948), J. Misra (b.1961), R. Raj Rao (b.1955), Usha K. R., Mistry (b.1952) and Futehally (b.1952–2004) are examples of writers from this generation and they are followed by writers born in the early 1960s, such as Ravi Shankar Etteth (b.1960), Vikram Chandra (b.1961), Amit Chaudhuri (b.1962) and Ashok Banker (b.1964).

Rushdie's impact not only on Indian literature but also on world and transnational literature in English has been widely recognized. Additionally, the Booker Prize winning novel, Arundhati Roy's *The God of Small Things* (1997), has also had ramifications on the Indian writing and publishing scene in English. Roy's novel has shaped both the Indian domestic literary scene as well as the Indian diasporic and international literary scenes (see Lau [2007] for a discussion of Roy's novel). *The God of Small Things* (1997) written in English and Indian English(es) marks a certain turning point, not simply in Indian fiction in English but also in India as a country, its contemporary culture and society, finding itself on the brink of New India.

The God of Small Things (1997) appeared in the late 1990s when India was starting to experience considerable societal change. In 1990, India was drinking 'Thums Up' and 'Gold Spot', and 'Coca-Cola' and 'Fanta' were unheard of; however, by the turn of the millennium, 'Coca-Cola' was everywhere. As India opened its markets in the 1990s under the then finance minister Manmohan Singh (since 2004, the Indian Prime Minister), India embarked on a path that has, in part, led India to where it is now and as Varma (2007) writes,

> The increased space for enterprise that 1991 opened up showed anew what middle class Indians can do if allowed to pursue their natural talent for making money. Many of them were first generation entrepreneurs, and most did not belong to the traditional trading classes – further proof, if any, of the commercial acumen of Indians as a people. The pioneers were risk takers. They had a sense of vision, a belief in themselves, and were exceptionally nimble in seizing the right business opportunity. (Varma 2007, p. xxii)

Roy's novel, *The God of Small Things* (1997), embodies part of this shift that Varma writes about. The risk taking, the vision and the belief alongside the seizing of the right opportunity are manifest in Roy's novel in its linguistic dexterity and its themes. The fact that the novel won the Booker Prize helped to put contemporary Indian writing in English firmly in the international writing scene and this has continued with writers like Adiga, Chandra and Bhagat.

By the mid-2000s in India, it was clear that life for many Indians was changing rapidly. 'India Shining', a party slogan of the BJP in 2004, was part of a campaign that included glossy adverts, banners and plenty of television exposure. The 'India Shining' campaign accentuated the benefits of Indian life in the mid-2000s – access to car and house loans, a growing tourist destination and a steadily growing economy due, in part, to India's home-grown IT professionals. The BJP campaign's core audience was the upwardly mobile and professional classes of New India; Brosius (2010) writes: 'New professional groups, new leisure sites and practices are the most obvious markers of "India Shining" . . . globalised capitalism, in particular since the new millennium, has produced a large and heterogeneous middle class that is distinctly different from the "old" middle class' (Brosius 2010, p. 2).

The 'India Shining' slogan was picked up by the opposition – the Indian National Congress party – who stated that the BJP was neglecting most of the country with its 'India Shining' campaign. The Congress highlighted in particular the regrettable spate of farmer suicides that had befallen agricultural communities at that time – a social preoccupation that was taken up by the India Bollywood actor and film director Aamir Khan in his comic satire film, *Peepli Live* (2010) some years later.

The Indian National Congress party's 'India Rising' was deemed a better slogan to represent India. For all its show and grandeur, the BJP's 'India Shining' campaign did not win the election, instead the Congress party won comfortably, resulting in Manmohan Singh as the prime minister of India from 2004. Varma (2007) suggests that it is this prime minster, with his background in finance, who continues to allow India to develop; he writes: 'With the new Manmohanomics, there are many more opportunities to make money and even more avenues to spend it' (Varma 2007, p. 185).

As part of India's growth, October 2010 saw New Delhi host the Commonwealth Games. Controversy ensued as questions of corruption, land clearing and unlawful working and living conditions of the thousands of labourers at the Commonwealth Games village were brought to the fore. Such tensions of New India – caught between old ways and new ideas – beleaguer India as it continues to move forward at a fast rate despite feeling the effects of 2008 and the slump of the global economy. As recently as 2011, India was dogged by an anti-corruption debate around the passing of the Lokpal Bill (see Glossary) and the August fast by Anna Hazare at the Ramlila grounds in New Delhi saw Indians unite across the country in support of the Lokpal Bill. Jalan (2012) highlights two issues regarding the impact of corruption on society. These issues are the larger economic effects of corruption and the 'systemic' nature of supply and demand for corruption in India (Jalan 2012, p. 289). The latter is a well-rehearsed point in Anna Hazare's fight for the passing of the Lokpal Bill. For corruption to be stamped out completely, *everyone*, whatever their position in society, must be held responsible for their involvement in corruption. Chetan Bhagat's novel *Revolution 2020: Love Corruption Ambition* (2011) tackles head-on some of the issues around corruption in society, in particular the impact on young people who aspire to grasp the opportunities of New India and who face issues of corruption.

It is too simple, of course, to suggest that Roy's book, *The God of Small Things* (1997), is the touchstone to a canon of work that epitomizes New India, a canon of work that is unrecognizable to the literature in English from India, which has preceded it. Rather, fiction from the turn of the millennium demonstrates new departures in writing in English, often in genre, form and voice and some of these new departures are seen in contemporary film too. Although the quintessential Bollywood or 'masala film' continues to sell well at the box office, a growing number of films are exploring New India, indeed some of these films are adaptations from Indian fiction in English, such as *Slumdog Millionaire* (*Q&A*, Swarup 2005), *Three Idiots* (*Five Point Someone*, Bhagat 2008) and a forthcoming film based on Bhagat's novel *2 States* (2009). In 2011, the Aamir Khan produced film *Delhi Belly* caused some commotion as its 'young India' narrative took its audiences in new and challenging directions. The Indian English narrative (the film was produced in Indian English with very little Hindi) is set in a contemporary Delhi of advertising companies and journalism. The main character's air hostess girlfriend works for one of India's newly created airlines and life seems to be full of opportunity. The lifestyles and opportunities of the young people in the film confirm that India is changing both socially and culturally and the fact that a leading Bollywood actor and director produces such a film for a supposed mainstream Indian audience is equally noteworthy.

'Young India' is a considerable part of the identity that is New India, but so too is the growing middle class(es) of India's urban populations in particular. Radhakrishnan (2011) talks of the revised senses of 'middle-classness' in India experienced today, when she writes:

> Claims to middle-classness also overlook entrenched caste divisions that have historically segregated India's educational system, as well as public life more generally. Class and caste have a complex relationship, and this relationship varies greatly among different regions of the country. (Radhakrishnan 2011, p. 8)

Thus, for Radhakrishnan, a sense of Indian middle class is better understood as a series of middle class*es* given the factors of the urban, the rural and the Indian caste system as well as the religious groups within India too. Complex notions of New India's middle class arise when we look at configurations of being Indian in this social strata. As an example, a Keralite Christian Indian might be Catholic or Orthodox, (s)he might be English medium having been educated in India or the Arabian Gulf and (s)he might be living in Kerala or in other parts of India. A Tamil might live in Bangalore as an IT professional, Hindu, and India educated, and be of a 'middle caste' background, (s)he might be socially mobile and living away from his/her family. As these configurations of a New India Indian demonstrate, the factors are myriad and in a fast-paced economy like India's, it begs the question as to the shape and constitution of India's (immediate) future of the 'middle classes'. Despite these myriad manifestations of middle-classness and Radhakrishnan's reiteration for the need to understand India's middle classes in the plural, she does suggest that the 'new middle class' is not as complicated as might first be thought:

> In the earlier Nehruvian model of Indian nation building, the "old" middle class was made up of government workers who served the nation by working for it. In a globalized model of the Indian nation, the middle class engages in a global economy of work and consumption, serving the nation by, ironically enough, directing itself away from it. (Radhakrishnan 2011, p. 42)

Radhakrishnan (2011) goes on to say:

> This "new" middle class is most often described as compromising those who are employed in high-end service sector jobs. What appears to be "new" about this class, however, is *not* its composition. Most of those who make up what has been dubbed as India's "new" middle class had parents who were part of the "old" one. (Radhakrishnan 2011, p. 42)

Chapters 2 to 7 of this book consider these questions of Indianness through Radhakrishnan's markers of class, caste and religious identities within

New India and are explored through the following works in particular: Adiga's *Last Man in Tower* (2010), Bhagat's *One Night @ The Call Centre* (2005), Trivedi's *Call Me Dan* (2010), Taseer's *The Temple-Goers* (2010), David's *The Man with Enormous Wings* (2010) and Sanghi's (2010) *Chanakya's Chant* (2010), as well as passing references in other texts that engage with these questions.

The growth of post-millennial Indian fiction in English has predictably witnessed an increase in publishing house production; Penguin India (including its Metro Reads series), Rupa & Co, Hachette India, Tranquebar, Zubaan Books, Roli and HarperCollins India have all increased their publishing lists in the last ten years. The rise in publishing has also been seen in other Indian languages and in translation. Chennai-based publishing house, Blaft Publications, is an example of high-quality publishing in translation such as its *Tamil Pulp Fiction* anthology (from Tamil into English) and this company in partnership with Tranquebar has launched the republication of Ibne Safi's detective stories (Urdu into English).

The themes of published post-millennial Indian novels in English are diverse. Some have narratives set in the 1960s and 1970s where narratives of 'the Emergency' (see Glossary) are present, there are other political narratives such as Maoist rebellion, terrorism and imagined political revolution, and there are also stories of making your wealth in New India, alongside narratives of the corporate world. There are growing 'trends' in this body of post-millennial fiction and these developments can be found in the genres of the new writing, such as Indian chick lit, youth narratives such as narratives in corporate settings or call centres, narratives on cricket (which I term 'crick lit' here), sexuality and a significant body of crime writing/murder mystery. There are also departures in science fiction (SF), fantasy and graphic novels, and a boom in publishing novels that draw on Hindu epics (see Section 6.2). It is these trends and departures in the new fiction that constitute the focus of this book.

1.4 How the book is organized, its interests and focus

The analysis of the fiction that follows in Chapters 2 to 7 will interrogate questions of Indianness as outlined in this introductory chapter. As the book moves through a discussion of narratives set in particular urbanscapes, to young India, and questions of chick lit, crick lit (my term), call centre narratives, crime writing, fantasy and finally, graphic novel departures in post-millennial Indian fiction in English, so the analysis of these narratives will focus on the relationship of this body of fiction with the idea of New India. Thus, the main thread of enquiry running through the analysis of these texts is that of New India, how it might be defined and how, concurrently, the body of post-millennial Indian fiction in English is shaping and forming identities of being Indian in New India.

A sociology of literature

The analyses of the fiction texts in Chapters 2 to 7 engage (albeit differently) with a sense(s) of living New India today. Given the interest in how these fiction texts speak of, and speak to, ideas of New India, this book engages with the idea of a sociology of literature; that is, the interface between the literary text and its reflection of the society(ies) from which it is produced. Writing on the topic in the early 1970s, Laurenson and Swingewood (1971) stated:

> Imaginative literature is a reconstruction of the world seen from a particular point of view, and while the writer may be aware of literary tradition, it is the non-conscious reworking of experience, fused with his values, which produces the fictional universe with which the sociology of literature is concerned. (Laurenson and Swingewood 1971, p. 80)

Similar to modes of reading such as New Historicism, Cultural Materialism and Marxist criticism, this book is interested in the society(ies) from which the literature of New India is produced; specifically, the (often changing) cultures and contemporary political situations, as well as the interest in the production, consumption and status of the literary texts within New India. Throughout the book, reference will be made to the various Indian publishing houses and their ever-growing catalogues of new fiction in English, as well as current political and cultural flashpoints, such as the Lokpal Bill and the fast of Anna Hazare, post-millennial India media and news channels, the politics of New India and its ideas of Indianness, and the IT sector and its growing industry in major metropolitan hubs such as Bangalore, Mumbai and New Delhi.

The interface between literature and the society(ies) from where it is produced, is a complex one. The social study of literature has been of interest to sociologists and cultural studies scholars particularly since the mid-1900s through sociolinguistic and structuralist methods of inquiry in particular, and for Filmer (1998) the two principal approaches to the social study of literature can be termed as 'the extrinsic' and 'the intrinsic' (Filmer 1998, p. 277). He writes:

> The extrinsic approach is designed to provide sociological knowledge *about* literature; the intrinsic approach is to analyse the sociological knowledge to be found *within* literary texts. The extrinsic approach involves the view that, because literature is produced in a societal context, it is determined by society and so can be treated as a reflection of the social conditions of its production. It is, in a sense, a mirror of social life which presents society with some image of itself. (Filmer 1998, p. 278, original emphasis)

Filmer goes on to explain that a characteristic of the extrinsic approach is that it devotes very little time or attention to the literary text itself. Indeed, literary critics argue (against the extrinsic approach) that the idea of the production of literature is not in any way focused on 'representing' society, but rather the characters we encounter when reading a literary work are subjective minds, created by and from the writer's own mind, experiences and imagination. Characters in a literary work are, therefore, elements of the narrative structure and thus viewed invalid as agents who might capture or speak of 'society' in a larger sense. Although the intrinsic approach recognizes that literature is indeed produced in and from society, it counters the extrinsic position by advocating that the literary text is one which engages in critical reflection on social practices; the literary text is not to be accepted as some kind of illustration of society per se. Filmer (1998) reminds us though that since both approaches emphasize different aspects of the society–literature interface, both approaches – extrinsic and intrinsic – can be applied to any one text simultaneously.

The analyses of the texts in this book will apply this very idea, both extrinsic and intrinsic approaches. The analyses are interested in the intrinsic, the features and stylistic elements of the literary text while being equally interested in the extrinsic, and how the body of fiction presented here talks to New India in societal and cultural terms. The manner in which the post-millennial body of fiction has been selected and organized for the purposes of this book also reflects this extrinsic approach. The body of fiction published since 2000 is broad and various.

In the early stages of planning for this book, the broad base of new writing was surveyed in order to identify trends *across* this body of new writing. This keen methodological element to the planning of the study exemplifies this interest in the social study of literature as it seeks to learn from recently published fiction, assessing it through a comprehensive and yet large-scale methodology.

The large-scale assessment leads then to a more careful, close reading of the individual texts, looking at how the characters, narrative plots, genres and voices construct the work, which is of the contemporary, New India writing scene, and Chapters 2 to 7 demonstrate this activity. The close readings of the texts in this book hold two objectives: (1) to explore the interface between language and literature *as well as* (2) to offer insight and understanding into new Indian society through the explanation of key cultural terms, practices and events.

In order to explore the language–literature interface, I draw on the field of literary stylistics, as this framework allows analysis from a linguistic level, up to more interpretative levels, as Verdonk (2002) writes:

> Whereas generally speaking, literary criticism directs attention to the larger-scale significance of what is represented in verbal art, stylistics

focuses on how this significance can be related to specific features of language, to linguistic texture of the literary text. (Verdonk 2002, p. 55)

Jeffries and McIntyre (2010) remind us that 'literary stylistics' aims to use linguistic techniques to assist in the interpretation of texts (Jeffries and McIntyre 2010, p. 2); moreover, Jeffries and McIntyre (2010) go on to detail stylistics and its relationship between author, text and reader:

> Stylistics has no settled view of the relationship between author, text and reader, but constantly evolves new theories and models of this dynamic relationship, in order to elucidate ever more clearly the processes by which meaning comes about. (Jeffries and McIntyre 2010, p. 3)

Gregoriou (2009) states that: 'Stylistics was, initially, born out of a reaction to the subjectivity and imprecision of literary studies, and in short, attempted to put criticism on a scientific basis' (Gregoriou 2009, p. 3). This approach to the fiction presented in this book is befitting since it recognizes the 'newness' of post-millennial fiction and allows space for interpretation from the linguistic level upwards. This effectively means that the analysis of this new body of fiction is not predestined to be analysed by a certain framework of 'reading' (or criticism) such as 'the postcolonial', but rather the fiction might be explored through a more transparent and less ideologically situated vehicle of interpretation. Indeed, although scholars within literary studies agree on the existence of textual effects in literature, traditionally very little has been offered concretely in its recognition and formulation. Stylistics offers both the terminology to look at texts in this way and the non-insistence of reading a literary text for the 'ideas' it encompasses (Jeffries and McIntyre 2010, p. 4).

Linguistic and cultural interests

In essence, the analysis of the literature in the post-millennial body of fiction presented in Chapers 2 to 7 is grounded in a literary stylistic approach, although the analyses vary considerably in stylistic detail and depth and are not akin to some of the most detailed stylistic studies in the growing field of literary stylistics. Sadana (2009) echoes this interest in the linguistic in Indian literature in particular when she writes:

> This way of reading texts, focusing on place and linguistic context, illuminates a process of indigenisation of the English language itself. And it is this process that tells us something essential not only about society and politics, but about the creative process and impulse itself. What is required, therefore, is a new politics of reading Indian English literature that is grounded in the very languages that it seeks to represent, and most centrally, that English itself has become. (Sadana 2009, p. 15)

The close readings of the texts also look to offer insight and understanding into new Indian society through the explanation of key cultural terms, practices and events. The body of post-millennial fiction in English examined here is fiction published within India; very few of these texts are readily available outside India (or the wider 'subcontinent' region – some books are available in Singapore, Malaysia and the Maldives as examples). An objective of the close readings of these texts is to offer some interpretation (and reading) of the cultural and societal references which are found within these texts.

A further interest and thus recurring topic in this book is one that explores ancient literary and aesthetic Indian traditions, such as Vedantic traditions, the Indian epics such as *The Ramayana* and *The Mahabharata*, as well as the aesthetic attitudes grounded in *The Natyasastra* – considered in some traditions as an additional Veda. (This volume will always refer to these three works using the definitive article, although it is acknowledged that the practice is sometimes found otherwise.)

Where possible, this book will assess if, and then, how, these literary forms and traditions are being revisited, reinvented and are newly manifest in the Indianness investigated in the new post-millennial writing.

The Natyasastra, a compendium of performed arts – drama, music, dance – the authorship of which is attributed to Bharatamuni, is described by Devy (2010): 'The Natyasastra was used through the fifteen hundred years of Sanskrit literary thought as the bedrock of literary theory' (Devy 2010, p. 3). As influential as *The Natyasastra* has been and continues to be on Indian literary production, it is also important to acknowledge other Sanskrit influences, such as Dandin's *Kavyadarsa* – one of the earliest texts in literary theory, in which epic poetry features. The *Kavyadarsa*'s explanation of epic poetry includes:

> . . . a great and generous person as the hero. It is embellished with descriptions of cities, oceans, hills, the seasons, the moonrise, the sunrise, of sports in the garden and sports in the waters, of drinking scenes, of festivals, of enjoyment (love), of separation (of lovers), of (their marriage) and their nuptials and birth of princes, likewise of consultation with the ministers, of sending messengers or ambassadors, of journeys (royal progress), of war and the Hero's victories: dealing with these at length and being full of *Rasa* and *Bhava* (flavour and suggestion): with *sargas* (chapters) which are not very lengthy and which are well formed with verse measures pleasing to the ear; everywhere dealing with a variety of topics (in each case ending each chapter in a different metre). (Devy 2010, p. 27)

Although a description of epic poetry and not of narrative, the description of *Kavyadarsa* is manifest in contemporary works such as Omair Ahmad's *The Storyteller's Tale* (2008), a blend of Persian, Urdu and Sanskrit literary aesthetics. In Chapter 6 of this volume, a discussion of some of the fantasy departures in post-millennial writing in English also demonstrates how they draw on the ancient aesthetics of Dandin's *Kavyadarsa* and Bharatamuni's *The Natyasastra* and so we will return to this discussion later in the book.

The book's focus

Overall, *Reading New India* is concerned with post-millennial Indian writing in English from within India and not works in translation or diaspora writing. The majority of texts discussed in Chapters 2 to 7 are published in India or 'the wider subcontinent'; a few exceptions include Joseph's *Saraswati Park*, Taseer's *The Temple-Goers* and Adiga's *Last Man in Tower*. In analysing the fiction in Chapters 2 to 7, insightful links with other Indian language writing will be made where appropriate. Correlation of trends with other cultural forms of artistic expression such as film will be made against the backdrop of New India.

This book offers not only a detailed survey of the broad and various body of post-millennial fiction in English from India, but also detailed, close readings of a careful selection from this body of fiction. These close, stylistic readings explore the language–literature interface of the texts, offering a transparent and less ideologically situated reading of the new fiction. Naturally then, attention to the employment of Indian Englishes in the texts (where appropriate) is given, understanding how Indian English(es) forms part of this body of new writing. 'Interpretation' (and reading) of the cultural and societal references is a large part of this book's project, in particular how these references are made in relation to New India and how ancient literary traditions and Hindi epic narratives are drawn on for this body of new fiction. A glossary of terms pertaining to cultural, religious, political and societal points of reference is included in this volume.

Chapter 2 explores post-millennial fiction in English and the New Indian urbanscapes of Bangalore and Mumbai.

Further reading

Boehmer, E. and Chaudhuri, R. (eds) (2011), *The Indian Postcolonial*. London: Routledge.

Dalrymple, W. (2009), *Nine Lives*. London: Bloomsbury.

Das, G. (2002), *India Unbound: From Independence to the Global Information Age*. New Delhi: Penguin India.

Deshpande, S. (2003), *Contemporary India: A Sociological View*. New Delhi: Penguin India.

Gupta, S. (2009), *Globalization and Literature*. Cambridge: Polity Press.

Jalan, B. (2012), *Emerging India: Economics, Politics and Reforms*. New Delhi: Penguin/Viking.

Khilnani, S. (1999), *The Idea of India*. New Delhi: Penguin India.

Kothari, R. and Snell, R. (2011), *Chutneyfying English: The Phenomenon of Hinglish*. New Delhi: Penguin India.

Mehrotra, A. K. (ed.) (2003), *A History of Indian Literature in English*. London: Hurst & Company.

Narayan, R. K. (2001), *The Idea of India*. New Delhi: Penguin India.

Pande, I. (ed.) (2007), *India 60*. New Delhi: HarperCollins.

Rao, R. (2003), *The Meaning of India*. New Delhi: Vision Books.

—(2004), *The Great Indian Way*. New Delhi: Vision Books.

Sen, A. (2005), *The Argumentative Indian: Writings on Indian Culture, History and Identity*. London: Penguin.

Tully, M. (1995), *The Heart of India*. London: Viking.

—(2007), *India's Unending Journey: Finding Balance in a Time of Change*. London: Rider.

Varma, P. K. (2007), *The Great Indian Middle Class*. New Delhi: Penguin India.

—(2004), *Being Indian*. London: William Heinemann.

Vohra, R. (2000), *The Making of India*. New Delhi: Vision Books.

2

Urban scapes

A dominant motif of New India is India's urban centres. It is often the sprawling metropolises of Mumbai and New Delhi, although more recently, Bangalore, the country's IT hub and growing centre of biotechnology industries. The idea of the metropolis has influenced one publishing house in its decisions on what and how to publish contemporary fiction. The 'Metro Reads' were launched in 2010 by Penguin India and the design idea behind 'Metro Reads' is that they are easy to read, lightweight books that can be read while commuting or travelling around a city. The series carries the tag lines 'Fun, feisty, fast reads' and 'For the reader on the go!'. The books are marketed at 150 rupees (around £2.00) and, to date, the series has published:

Dreams in Prussian Blue (2010)
Love Over Coffee (2010)
No Deadline for Love (2011)
Losing My Virginity and Other Dumb Ideas (2011)
Where Girls Dare (2010)
The Premier Murder League (2010)
Jack Patel's Dubai Dreams (2011)
What Did I Ever See in Him? (2011)
Love on the Rocks (2011)
With or Without You (2010)
Close Call in Kashmir (2010)

Although the name of the series Metro Reads appeals to the life of the metropolis most broadly, the Metro Reads series is somewhat concurrent with actual developments in metro transport systems across India. The Delhi Metro began operation in the early 2000s, constructed in phases and some of the metro lines were completed in 2010 in order to support the Commonwealth Games. The metro system of Bangalore ('Namma Metro') began operation in late 2011 and is being built in phases throughout 2012 and 2013. The metro system of Mumbai ('Mumbai Metro') starts work in 2012 with a ten-year proposed term of construction. Construction of the

'Kolkata Metro' started as early as the 1980s, but the system is now being updated and expanded with a view to having much bigger metro operations in the near future. The construction of the metro systems in these urban centres will continue to change the landscape of these cities, especially as many people currently travel by autorickshaws, pushbikes, scooters and buses to get to work; cities will experience significantly less of this kind of traffic, which in turn, will significantly impact the street life of India's metropolises as well as people's lifestyles.

Penguin India's Metro Reads series might be seen as catering to a market that uses or will use these metro systems in the future, most likely as commuters who might spend 150 rupees on a book to read to and from their workplace. A further tag line on the books underlines the importance of the 'popular' in its market; it reads: 'Every life has a story'. This market is, and will most likely continue to be made up of young professionals travelling to their places of work on the metro and the stories of the already published Metro Reads series echoes such a demographic. Titles in the series include the chick lit genre, which we will look at in Section 3.1, and the crick lit narrative *The Premier Murder League* (2010), which is explored in Section 3.2, as well as crime thriller and murder mystery, for example: *Close Call in Kashmir* (2010). There are several corporate narratives, such as *Jack Patel's Dubai Dreams* (2011), a Dubai-based story set in the world of corporate finance hit by global recession; *With or Without You* (2010) by Partha Sarathi Basu is set in the corporate world of B2Y, the 'emerging market' Gurgaon-based office, sister to the Seattle-based office headquarters, managed and mismanaged by Aarav who is married to Raika; and *Love Over Coffee* (2010) by Amrit N. Shetty is a story of Anup who works for an IT company and Rajni who works in the same office. Rajni is the love of Anup's life but her family and the office gossip machine prevent the two from developing their relationship. It is only at a life-changing moment that Anup can finally pursue his goal to marry Rajni. This novel, alongside Basu's *With or Without You* (2010), are the only two love stories to date that are narrated from a male perspective within this particular series.

More generally, Bangalore, New Delhi and Mumbai feature as city backdrops in this new fiction and of Bangalore, Nair (2005) writes: 'Bangalore, . . . has struck a metropolitan path that is remarkably different than older cities such as Calcutta or Bombay. In this sense, it may indeed be the city of the future' (Nair 2005, p. 21). The focus of Bangalore as a 'new city' appears later in this book in the analysis of Usha K. R.'s *Monkey-man* (2010) in Section 6.1, as well as alongside the analysis of *Neti, Neti, Not This, Not This* (2009) by Hasan, in Section 2.1. In her Bangalore novel, Hassan writes of the three cities, Mumbai, New Delhi and Bangalore:

> . . . Bombay, where the bombs could go off any time and the commuter train rides were interminable; Delhi, in whose buses girls carried open

safety pins to ward off lecherous, groping men; Bangalore, where too many people killed themselves and where everyone was on his way to getting rich. (Hasan 2009, p. 33)

Although Hasan highlights the differences across these urban centres, the role of the residents' associations as a key middle-class component of urban living in India appears in several of the fiction texts analysed in this book. Adiga's *Last Man in Tower* (2011) explored in Section 2.2, is a narrative built around the complexities and dynamics of a residents' association 'Vishram Society – Tower A'. Another author of the post-millennial fiction scene is Swaminathan and her novel *The Gardener's Song* (2007) also features a residents' association, one where she investigates a murder in 'Utkrusha building'. Varma (2007) writes of the residents' associations:

Of course, the class is still powerful, but it realizes now that in order to get what it wants it has to compete with other erstwhile quiescent constituencies. It is this realization that is forcing some of its more percipient members to engage with society im their own self-interest. The newfound activism of some Resident Welfare Associations in the metropolitan cities is a good example of this development. (Varma 2007, p. xxix)

Various parts of Anjali Joseph's *Saraswati Park* (2010), which is analysed in Section 4.2, Choudhury's *Arzee the Dwarf* (2009) and Uttam's *Dreams in Prussian Blue* (2010) as examples, deal with the challenges of accommodation in Mumbai and the impact this has on their lives and characters. Choudhury in *Arzee the Dwarf* (2009) writes:

He passed the grey building which was his home – he could hear the television blaring all the way up from the second floor, because Mother listened to all her soaps on full volume – and then the empty school, its blue gate being locked by the watchman. (Choudhury 2009, p. 12)

Sampurna Chattarji's novel *Rupture* (2009) also deals with the 'urban' as the novel moves across five cities in India. Bombay and New Delhi feature as two of the five cities and although the book focuses on the nine characters across these five cities, the urban and the metropolitan are imposing and necessary scapes to the narrative.

This chapter will now focus on fiction texts from the two urban centres of Mumbai and Bangalore, namely, Adiga's *Last Man in Tower* (2011) and Hasan's *Neti, Neti, Not This, Not This* (2009). Additional chapters in this book discuss texts that have other urban centres as their backdrop, such as New Delhi; see Advaita Kala's *Almost Single* (2007) in Section 3.1, Chetan Bhagat's *One Night @ The Call Centre* (2008) in Section 4.1 and Taseer's *The Temple-Goers* (2010) in Section 5.2.

2.1 Bangalore

Neti, Neti, Not This, Not This (2009)

Anjum Hasan's novel *Neti, Neti, Not This, Not This* (2009) charts the life of 25-year-old Sophie Das, born to Bengali parents and brought up in Shillong. Having moved from Shillong a year previously, Sophie Das has acquired a job in a Business Process Outsourcing company (BPO – see Glossary) 'Star Titles', producing the subtitling for American films. She has also secured rental of a small flat, a boyfriend named Swami, and she has integrated into a group of free-spirited friends who also work variously in BPO activities.

Rukshana, the girlfriend of one of Sophie's friends, Ringo Saar, ridicules Sophie's job at 'Start Titles' and on one occasion when the friends are all watching a film together, Rukshana says:

> "You work in that company that does these subtitles right. They're so crappy. They make a complete hash of what a person's saying," said Rukshana. Though she was baiting Sophie, there was also, Sophie realized to her surprise, a desire to make up.
> "These are all done in the sweatshops in Hong Kong or somewhere," said Sophie. "The films we caption for never get released in India. They're for Europe and the U.S. And they're absolutely accurate. We get hauled up even if there's a comma in the wrong place." (Hasan 2009, p. 117)

When Sophie first started working at 'Star Titles', she enjoyed the captioning and the challenge of the various systems of subtitling that she encountered. She was quick to recognize various cultural references to brands and supermarkets in the US and was mindful of American spelling. As her time at 'Star Titles' continues though, Sophie sees the job as 'repellently mindless' (Hasan 2009, p. 41), she becomes increasingly bored, distracting herself by reading blogs. Despite her apathy towards the job, Sophie knows of the global BPO hierarchy in film subtitling and, in confronting Rukshana above, explains how Bangalore's subtitling BPO activity is of a high calibre, catering only for the European and US markets. Sophie explains that the subtitling that India has on its films is outsourced to Hong Kong 'sweatshops'. This curious hierarchy of BPO activity makes the job that Sophie does (despite her apathy towards it) somewhat 'better' than that which Rukshana has stereotyped her as doing. BPO activity in *Neti, Neti* takes on a strange, almost 'unreal' persona given its multifarious nature and the quirky business processes with which it engages. It is this diversity of BPO activity which underscores the reliance of the US and Europe on India and, particularly, on its young workforce.

Bangalore, a city awash with BPO activity, results in a struggle for identity and Sophie is not alone in this struggle, as it is also evident that other characters of Hasan's novel are struggling with the same issues. Sophie's boyfriend, Swami, works in a call centre, managing calls from America, problem-shooting credit card terminal and payment service failures. Here, Swami laments the 'unreal' life of BPO activity in Bangalore:

But I *want* their damned credit card terminals and their payment services to work. I want no one in America who calls me to feel like – heck, this guy is useless. The rotten thing is that if there's a real problem, we can't fix it. We can only tell them to wait while the technical guys do their bit. It's not real, what we're doing. That's why it's frustrating – because it's not real. (Hasan 2009, p. 66)

Alongside the assortment of the city's BPO work, another dominant motif of Hasan's novel is the 'unrealness' of Bangalore and its identity as a transient city. Hasan (2008) writes of Bangalore:

And all the while, the little and large squares of land filling up like an animated film with beauty salons, game parlours, jewellery shops, bakeries, clothes stores, cafes, apartment buildings and then, often in just the space of a year, morphing into something else – bungalows torn down to make way for office blocks, gift shops becoming travel agencies, internet parlours converted to coffee shops, everything succumbing to this fantastic flux. (Hasan 2009, p. 80)

The catalogue of buildings, services and occupations listed here describe a temporary, often ephemeral Bangalore, an idea that is also embodied in the characters of the novel. Sophie, Swami, Ringo Saar, Maya and Anu are all looking for something in their lives and living in Bangalore is part of this quest. Sophie battles with an unhappy family life in Shillong and a sister who self-harms; Swami is looking for a better life with money and cars; Ringo Saar, son of an alcoholic father, is angry and unpredictable and in a tumultuous relationship with Rukshana; Maya is always dreaming of leaving for America; and even the free-spirited Anu would leave Bangalore given the chance. The lives of these characters are in themselves transitory, in the sense that they do not live, settled, routine-like lives. Most BPO activity is synchronized with the time zones of America and the UK, which means that the characters' days begin in the evening in India, resulting in their sleeping through most of the Indian day. In one scene, Sophie asks Rukshana why she is eating cornflakes at night: 'Because my day is just beginning, darling', she said, touching her face pack gingerly. 'I do the midnight to eight in the morning shift' (Hasan 2009, p. 117).

The transitory reality of Bangalore is captured in other parts of the narrative too; at Sophie's employment 'Star Titles', if an employee performs consistently well, they can be promoted to the position of coordinator, a role that is often unoccupied. Hasan (2009) writes:

> . . . the coordinator positions were often vacant; coordinators routinely quit because there was no room for them to move up (if they tried they would bump into Maya). And they were too smart to be content with their positions for more than a year or two. All these girls and boys were set to apply to universities abroad; in their minds they were already in Boston or New York or Berkeley . . . (Hasan 2009, p. 41)

This longer quote below, further demonstrates Bangalore's inherent commitment to the identity of a changing city and as Nair (2005) writes: '. . . the city of Bangalore has, over the past forty years, been swiftly remapped as a territory for accumulation of economic power on an unprecedented scale' (Nair 2005, p. 345). The diversity of Bangalore is not simply in its various BPO activities, the peoples and cultures are equally varied and diverse. Moreover, so are the objectives for arrival in Bangalore as Hasan (2009) writes:

> Boys from smaller towns in the state coming to study in engineering and medical colleges; girls from the Northeast coming to work as waitresses or run tiny beauty parlours; men and women from one or another big city moving here because Bangalore seemed to urgently need designer boutiques and five-star hotels and architectural firms and advertising companies; couples from the North relocating for software jobs; whole clans moving from neighbouring states to work on construction sites and live in their flimsy plastic tent homes; wave after wave of people arriving and at once establishing their own passage through the city. And the city, as if it were a living thing with a generous heart, taking them all in uncomplainingly. (Hasan 2009, p. 163)

The 'Indianness' created in the Bangalore of *Neti, Neti* might be contrasted to the Indianness of the Bombay novel or the New Delhi novel. The Bangalore sense of 'Indianness' is more grounded in the contemporary and the transience than the city has known in recent times. In one scene, Shiva, studying a map of Bangalore with Anu and Sophie, exclaims: 'Do you realize what a huge brown cancer of a city this is?' (Hasan 2009, p. 263). As Shiva moves around the map of Bangalore, its tightly fixed boundaries of Cubbon Park, the slum areas – marked out in neat fawn-coloured boxes (264) – the areas of Malleswaram and Lal Bagh, Shiva's finger passes by the north of the city through to the east and in doing so, encompasses Cox Town where Anu lives and from where they are looking at the map. Hasan writes (2009): '. . . and Sophie felt cheated again. She could not put herself onto this map and yet there it was right under their gaze – the road on which Anu's apartment stood' (Hasan 2009, p. 264).

Sophie's inability to see herself as part of Bangalore's map further confirms her sense of being misplaced in the city and yet, as Hasan (2009) writes, Sophie is bound to the city in an emotional sense: 'Sophie took the map from Shiva once he had completed his cartography; she looked at her enormous, churning city made humble by a picture and for the first time felt something like love for it' (Hasan 2009, p. 263). Here, Sophie 'owns' the city, calling it '*her* enormous, churning city' and this is connected to the moment when she sees the city as a whole without 'the messiness, the noise, the shops [and] the people' (Hasan 2009, p. 264).

Sophie's identity and connection with Bangalore is also caught up with her identity with India. Born to Bengali parents with a father who refused to speak Bengali at home, Sophie is raised Hindi and English speaking in Khasi-speaking Shillong. Sophie compares her one year spent in Bangalore to the decades spent in Shillong and how her parents, having lived there longer than herself, had 'added not one extra word to their stock of half-a-dozen phrases in Shillong's local language, Khasi – phrases they threaded into their conversations with maid-servants and taxi-drivers' (Hasan 2009, p. 11).

Sophie's life in Bangalore often entails revealing to people that she is from Shillong, a place often regarded as dangerous, and according to Shiva, 'tragic' (Hasan 2009, p. 124). Sophie's sense of India is 'the girls who oiled their hair and worried about exams' (Hasan 2009, p. 125) and more specifically:

Amar Chitra Katha comics, the 9 o'clock news on TV, diyas on Diwali, the gaudy colours of idols during Durga Puja, the Republic Day parade, the mithai shop from where they always bought their sweets, where the flies floated without drowning in the basin of rosogullas and the laddoos were so sweet they gave Sophie a head-rush – all of these were uniquely and indisputably India. *Swami and Friends* was India. (Hasan 2009, p. 125)

Bangalore is a world away from Sophie's Shillong. In Bangalore, Sophie mixes with a group of friends whose activities are mainly visiting malls, drinking in pubs, smoking grass and holding house parties. The pub scene in particular is a large part of Sophie and her friends' lives. Sophie's favourite pub, where she often meets Swami, is decorated with posters of Pink Floyd's *The Wall* in Berlin in 1990, The Who in London, as well as portraits of Bob Marley smoking a joint, and an outline of the Beatles on the low ceiling (Hasan 2009, p. 59).

Sophie has lived in Bangalore only a year and yet her life has been transformed considerably. In Bangalore, she is 'free' in the sense that her life is her own. Hasan (2009) writes:

Sophie possessed all this – the view from the window, the tiny flat and every particle of air in it. She could cook what she liked, smoke to her heart's content . . . For the first time in her life she was free. She stopped pacing around and stood under a fan, sweating and still. (Hasan 2009, p. 30)

But as the novel progresses and the murder of Rukshana by their friend Ringo Saar takes place, Sophie begins to rethink life and the choices that she made in leaving Shillong for Bangalore. She has been 'free' and financially independent while in Bangalore but at what cost?

Now when she had the sharp rectangle of the credit card pressing against her thighs, now when pleasures were graded for her and lay stretched out in every direction like some version of paradise, all she got was suffocation, death, people screaming. (Hasan 2009, p. 74)

And again, later in the novel, Sophie laments the overwhelming nature of living in Bangalore:

There were just too many people – it was a kind of calamity, the sheer number of them. Every year more arrived with the kind of idiotic hope in their hearts Sophie had first felt when she saw her brightly lit office cubicle. (Hasan 2009, p. 163)

The title of the book *Neti, Neti* takes its name from Hindu sources, as a chant or mantra and also as a saying found in the Vedic texts (the Upanishads). 'Neti, neti' as a philosophical process, looks to identify something by looking at what it is not, and this is particularly true when understanding the Divine in Hinduism. As human beings, we are unable to capture and express in words exactly that which is divine. We might be able to say what the Divine is *not*, but not necessarily say what it *is*.

Sophie's character in the book is at the heart of the philosophy of 'neti neti' in different ways. In moving to Bangalore, Sophie is, like many of the other characters in the book, on a quest or journey to find herself; to be independent and to be free is part of this journey. Throughout the narrative, Sophie experiences life in ways of 'neti, neti', in that she understands what her sense of life is *not* but she is unable to express what it *is*. At various points in the story, Sophie is 'lost in life' and wonders about her existence and her place in it all. In the following example, Sophie finds herself with her usual group of friends, watching a film:

And Sophie, standing there blinking, was suddenly overtaken by a powerful sense of disorientation. *Who were these people and what place was this and why was she here?* For a moment she had no clue. (Hasan 2009, p. 119)

Struck as Sophie is here, by a sense of disorientation, the big questions of 'who', 'what' and 'why' hit her. She is with a group of friends she knows very well and they are socializing as usual, nothing is new or strange here for her, yet she is overtaken by a strong and impactful sense of estrangement.

A year in Bangalore has set in place certain rhythms of work and play and Sophie is struck by this routine, a routine that for most people would not be a 'routine'. As discussed above, Sophie and her friends inhabit an unreal 'BPO world', functioning on a different time zone and engaged in various, and at times, *odd* BPO activities. This routine, yet non-routine, troubles Sophie. On one occasion, Sophie and Swami are talking about this issue, prompted by Swami's father's comments on their lives:

> "I called my dad and told him what had happened and he said – it's because you people don't sleep and eat at regular hours. The old man's got it all figured out."
>
> "Has your dad ever not woken up at 5 o'clock, ever not drunk coffee at 7.30 a.m.?"
>
> "It's not just the routine. It's the whole tradition and progress funda. His great grandfather probably had the same idea of life. It's kinda okay. You don't have to worry about whether what you're doing makes sense because so many people have done it before you." (Hasan 2009, p. 143)

The lives of Sophie, Swami and their friends in Bangalore are testament to New India and their topsy-turvy living is part of this urban scene. It is not an India that Swami's father or Sophie's parents have ever known, because even though they are living in India, they are not part of the India that Sophie and Swami are experiencing. What the extract above puts into question is whether it is possible in this New India to continue 'the whole tradition and progress funda' (Hasan 2009, p. 143), or whether India has morphed to the degree that it is now impossible to say that 'so many people have done it before you' (Hasan 2009, p. 143).

Sophie's religious and philosophical views on life are often drawn back to three literary texts – *Vivekananda: Awakener of Modern India*, *Madame Bovary* and *Swami and Friends*. As Hasan (2009) explains: 'Her father was an atheist and her mother's God was transcendental – he was everywhere and nowhere. Mrs Das never went into temples and only occasionally reminded her children about the invisible divinity she believed in' (Hasan 2009, pp. 75–6). Moreover, Sophie's parents had a 'love marriage' going against their parents' wishes, a result of which being that Mrs Das was cut off from her family. Mr and Mrs Das moved to Shillong and we learn that Mr Das refused to socialize with the Bengali community in Shillong. This family situation might well be regarded as 'unusual' given the love marriage, the atheism and Mr Das's disinterest in his ethnic heritage as a Bengali living in Shillong; thus, later in the novel, when Sophie's mother talks to her about the Hindu notions of '*dharma* and *karma*', Sophie is somewhat taken aback:

> You can't have everything. You can't be happy all the time, but you can do your duty. But what one tends to forget in this blind pursuit of dharma is that all the time your karma is also building up. What about that? Muku is in this state because of our bad karma – his and mine. My God! I thought that my duty to my family is over. I was thinking about the straight line of dharma and I forgot about the crooked line of karma. (Hasan 2009, p. 258)

Sophie is not totally disinterested in religion, despite her parents' indifference towards matters of faith and belief. Sophie's flat in Bangalore is rented from a Mr Bhatt who lives in the same building with his wife and their extended family. Similar to Adiga's setting for his novel *Last Man in Tower*, Sophie, too, lives as part of a residents' association. Mr Bhatt and his wife appear throughout the novel as archetypal Hindus, exemplary in their customs and conduct. Mr Bhatt, as a landlord and as an inhabitant of the block of flats, is at the mercy of the Residents' Welfare Association secretary, Chinnappa. Early on in the novel, we read that Mr Bhatt is called to speak to Sophie about her underwear:

> "Madam, please remove your underwear," said Mr Bhatt, the landlord.
> "Huh?"
> "Underwear, underwear," said Mr Bhatt urgently. For a few moments, the impatient Mr Bhatt and the incredulous Sophie stared at each other. It was only when he gestured in the direction of the balcony that she understood. He had peeked out of the window on the landing and was objecting to the panties she had hung out to dry. (Hasan 2009, p. 16)

The scene is rendered comic with Mr Bhatt's use of 'remove your underwear' (rather than a request to 'remove the underwear from the balcony'), especially as Mr Bhatt is a very proper and correct family man. Throughout the novel, Mr Bhatt, despite liking Sophie and wanting to keep her on the straight path (especially as she is 'alone' in Bangalore), is forced to reprimand Sophie for her (and mostly her friends') behaviour.

Three major incidents damage the relationship between Sophie and her landlord, namely, the friendship group's insistence on smoking grass in the apartment, the group's 'barbeque incident' where Mr Bhatt's young grandson, Mani, is caught eating a sausage (the family is strictly vegetarian), and the most public of the three incidents happens at a temple where a Baba Sampige satsang (see Glossary) is being held.

Having been to the shops before coming to the temple, Sophie arrives laden with heavy bags. At the entrance to the satsang, she considers that:

> . . . it might be vaguely sacrosanct to enter with the beer she had in the bag. It was too late to do anything about it, however. She kicked off her sneakers, clasped her bags to herself to prevent the bottles from clinking and went in. (Hasan 2009, p. 80)

Sophie falls asleep during the satsang and is woken by the crashing of bottles behind her. While she was sleeping, Mani, Mr Bhatt's grandson had managed to get hold of the shopping bags and empty them, sending the bottles of beer crashing. Sophie is met by a very angry Chinnappa – the Residents' Welfare Association secretary – exclaiming: 'Oh, ho, ho, ho, ho! Madam, what is this? Why you are insulting our guruji?' (Hasan 2009, p. 82). Sophie is then addressed by the priest and to everyone's surprise, in English he says: 'What are you thinking? People are doing holy things here. Satsang, satsang' (Hasan 2009, p. 83). Sophie runs out of the satsang, in a bid to flee the wrath of Chinnappa and the others.

This ousting of Sophie from the satsang and the wider (Hindu) community – Mr and Mrs Bhatt, Chinnappa and other residents of the building in which she lives – means that Sophie is further isolated in her already confused position within Bangalore. Questions of 'Indianness' are found throughout the course of this novel; in particular, questions of Indian identity in modern urban centres such as Bangalore and the myriad manifestations of such an identity. Caught between a Shillong upbringing in a Bengali family, a complex religious background of atheism, Hindu and Christian belief systems (to varying degrees) and opportunities of New India in the ever-changing city of Bangalore means that Sophie is the victim of feelings that leave her without a sense of direction and although she is able to ascertain what and who her life should *not* contain, it is more challenging for her to work out what her life *does* and *should* contain; she is caught up in eternal questions of 'neti neti'.

2.2 Mumbai

Last Man in Tower (2011)

The residents of Vishram Society (Tower A) are such an essential part of Adiga's *Last Man in Tower* (2011) that the novel begins with a plan of the tower and its various residents from the ground floor to the fifth floor. The tower is in Vakola, in the vicinity of the airport and for most Bombaywallahs, Adiga tells us, anything in or around Vakola is 'slummy'. Vishram Society, however, stands as a respectable, middle-class housing cooperative, built in 1959 with a three-foot-tall polished black-stone cross. Adiga (2011) writes:

> ... a reminder that the building was originally meant for Roman Catholics. Hindus were admitted in the late 1960s, and in the 1980s the better kind of Muslim – Bohra, Ismaili, college-educated. Vishram is now entirely "cosmopolitan" (i.e ethnically and religiously mixed). (Adiga 2011, p. 5)

Testament to this 'cosmopolitan' residency is the door of flat 3B:

> An eczema of blue-skinned gods, bearded godmen, and haloed Christs covered the metal door of 3B . . . so that it was impossible to know if the present tenant was Hindu, Christian, or a member of a hybrid cult practised only in this building. (Adiga 2011, p. 15)

In Adiga's descriptions of Vishram Society it is clear that the residents identify themselves as middle class. Adiga offers touchstones of this middle-classness as he describes the dress codes observed within the tower: 'checked polyester shirts over white *banians*', 'the older women wear saris, salwar kameez, or skirts and the younger ones wear jeans', the men's hair styles: 'oiled and short', and as a marker of their place and responsibility to society, Adiga writes: 'All of them pay taxes, support charities, and vote in general elections' (Adiga 2011, p. 9).

This urban sense of middle-class living in post-millennial India is taken up by Radhakrishnan, who talks of the revised senses of 'middle-classness' in India today:

> Claims to middle-classness also overlook entrenched caste divisions that have historically segregated India's educational system, as well as public life more generally. Class and caste have a complex relationship, and this relationship varies greatly among different regions of the country. (Radhakrishnan 2011, p. 8)

Vishram Society is a microcosm of Indian society – the evolution of the building itself, from Roman Catholic accommodation to a now, 'cosmopolitan' building, the 'eczema of blue-skinned gods' on the door of Flat 3B, are witness to this development – and yet, *difference* is underscored throughout the narrative.

Interestingly, the lines along which difference is drawn are further complicated by a sense of New India. Mrs Puri of Flat 3C is concerned by the presence of a 25-year-old 'single' woman, Ms Meenakshi, who works at various hours of the day and night as a journalist. Moreover, it is the lifestyle of Ms Meenakshi, her boyfriend-visitor and the item that the cat found in Ms Meenakshi's rubbish that are of most concern to Mrs Puri. Talking with

Masterji (a retired school teacher, recently widowed) of Flat 3A, Mrs Puri expresses her concerns, to which Masterji replies:

> "When this building first came up, there were no Hindus allowed here, it is a fact. Then there were meant to be no Muslims, it is a fact. All proved to be good people when given a chance. We don't want to become a building full of retirees and blind people. If this girl and her boyfriend have done something inappropriate, we should speak to them. However. . ." He looked at Mrs Puri. ". . . we have no business with her rubbish." Mrs Puri winced. She wouldn't tolerate this kind of talk from anyone else. (Adiga 2011, p. 26)

Masterji is mindful here that both himself and Mrs Puri (and her family) are Hindus and he gently reminds Mrs Puri that as Vishram Society was intended only for Christians in the first instance, her residency in Tower A is one formulated on 'being given a chance'. This tolerance and open-mindedness on the part of Masterji (at the age of 61) is central to the novel's concerns with societal change and New India. The lines along which Mrs Puri further draws her sense of 'difference' are developed later on in the narrative, in particular through a conversation with Mrs Rego, another of the tower's residents.

Mrs Puri's position seems to be constructed through her fear of a difference that she does not know, nor understand. This is, in principle, her issue with Ms Meenakshi in Flat 3B. Referred to as 'the modern girl' (Adiga 2011, p. 22) and her lifestyle described by Mrs Puri as 'the modern shame-free way of living' (Adiga 2011, p. 22), Mrs Puri's lines of difference are drawn along those of modernity (versus tradition) of an unmarried, single woman (versus a married woman) and a working woman – a journalist – (versus a family-orientated woman) and are not, in this case, drawn along the lines of religion. Indeed, we read later in the novel that Mrs Puri, eternally in turmoil over her son's Down syndrome, seeks out *all* places of worship in Mumbai in a bid to 'remove the stone that blocks Ramu's mind':

> When it came to places of worship in Mumbai, Mrs Puri was an expert; Muslim, Christian and Hindu, she had been to each of them for he Ramu. Haji Ali, Mount Mary, Siddhi Vinayak, Mahalakshmi, you name it, she had prayed there. (Adiga 2011, p. 73)

Adiga's narrative is constructed around 'the offer'. On the announcement of 'the offer', the three-foot-tall polished black-stone cross at the front of Vishram Society is centre stage as the secretary, Ajwani and the 'strange man' (Adiga 2011, p. 75) stand before it with folded palms. 'The offer' to buy out the residents of Vishram Society, in order for redevelopment of the site on which the housing colony stands, is received as being 'a miracle' by

Mrs Puri. Her husband attributes this miracle to the building's steadfast middle-class lifestyle, he exclaims:

> "We've paid our taxes, and we've helped each other, and we've gone to Siddhi Vinayak and Mount Mary church and Mahim church. . ."
> "Yes?"
> ". . . and now all of us in this building, all of us good people, have been blessed by the Hand of God."
>
> . . .
> Mr Puri watched his wife. "Well? What do you think?"
> "If this is really true," she said, "it will be the first miracle of my life."
> (Adiga 2011, p. 75)

'The offer' from the development company is seen as a 'miracle' of New India, its growing economy, opportunities and rise of the new middle classes. For Mrs Puri though, it is not simply the middle classes who benefit from this miracle, for Mrs Puri who was born in Bombay (although her parents are from Delhi), it is only those people who are from Bombay who should enjoy what the city is offering in New India. In the following exchange, Mrs Puri and Mrs Rego argue over what it is to be *of* Bombay:

> "Too many people come into the city, it's a fact," Mrs Puri said. "Everyone wants to suck on our . . ." She touched her breasts.
> The battleship turned to her.
> "And did you drop to Bombay from heaven, Mrs Puri? Isn't your family from Delhi?"
> "My parents were born in Delhi, Mrs Rego, but I was born right here. There was enough space in those days. Now it is full. The Shiv Sena is right, outsiders should stop coming here." (Adiga 2011, p. 39)

Mrs Puri's reference to the Shiv Sena (see Glossary) is an incendiary one to make, especially to Mrs Rego who is Christian, and given the heritage and origins of Vishram Tower's construction, Mrs Puri's statement is very misplaced. Mrs Rego goes on to defend the migrants who come to the city of Mumbai, providing labour that keeps the city running. Mrs Puri can only think of 'outsiders' to Bombay as beggars and suggests to Mrs Rego that she has more time for the beggars outside Victoria terminus (VT – see Glossary) than for the developers who are trying to improve life in the city. Mrs Puri's incendiary statement about the Shiv Sena is rebuffed with an argument by Mrs Rego equally anchored in religious doctrine: 'I am Christian, Mrs Puri. We are meant to care for the poor' (Adiga 2011, p. 39). The two ladies are interrupted by Mrs Puri's son, Ramu, and Mrs Puri silences him by saying: 'Quiet Ramu. Mummy is speaking to Communist Aunty' (Adiga 2011, p. 40). Mrs Puri's words further extend the malice, as she politely refers to Mrs Rego in front of Ramu as 'Aunty' while at the same time, insulting her with the political slur: 'Communist Aunty' (communism in India has its particular historical and contemporary overtones). The conversation between the two women moves through various kinds of difference, drawn first along the lines of those who *belong* to Bombay and those who don't belong, to the religious politics of Hinduism versus Christianity and finally to politics per se. Adiga's novel explores the physical upheaval that Mumbai faces today as well as the personal challenges of identity within the city's communities against a backdrop of New India.

3

Chick lit to crick lit

Chapter 3 investigates the rise in chick lit and crick lit (my term) narratives. Advaita Kala's chick lit novel *Almost Single* (2007) is a seminal work in the evolution of chick lit within the Indian publishing scene. Her book explores what it is to be young and female in India today and this novel is analysed along with Chauhan's *Battle for Bittora* (2010), a novel that brings the chick lit genre together with a political narrative and contemporary boy-meets-girl plot. Section 3.2 considers the recent body of fiction on cricket, 'crick lit' as I term it, and this presentation includes analysis of *The Premier Murder League* (2010) by Geeta Sundar and *The Zoya Factor* (2008) by Anuja Chauhan.

3.1 Chick lit

Today's body of writing that we might call 'chick lit' is mainly written by women, with a female protagonist who, in various ways, faces challenges, questions and changes in contemporary Indian society, these narratives often include a 'love' or 'romance' element and are often narrated humourously. However, there are a few exceptions, see: *With or Without You* (2010) by Partha Sarathi Basu, *Love Over Coffee* (2010) by Amrit N. Shetty and *Chocolate Guitar Momos* (2011) by Kenny Deori Basumatary. These male-authored narratives, although stories of 'romance' (in various guises), have less emphasis on the female protagonist as they are told from the male perspective.

Today's canon of chick lit might be considered alongside female narratives that have been published earlier in the history of writing in English in India. The work of Shashi Deshpande, Anita Desai, Shama Futehally, Temsula Ao, Nisha da Cunha, Kamala Markandaya as well as other women writers with recent novels in publication such as Jaishree Misra and Manju Kapur, all have engaged with female narratives. Lau (2006) writes of the emotional and domestic territories which are so often explored in the fiction of these writers, stating: 'their writings frequently include detailed descriptions of the interior spaces of home, the negotiation of roles and hierarchies, and the emotional lives played out against a background of the bedroom and the kitchen' (Lau 2006, p. 1098). This sentiment is echoed in Deshpande's words when she states:

> Yes, I did and I do write about women. Most of my writing comes out of my intense and long suppressed feelings about what it is to be a woman in our society, it comes out of the experience of the difficulty of playing the different roles enjoined on me by society, it comes out of the knowledge that I am something more and something different from the sum total of these roles. My writing comes out of my consciousness of the conflict between my idea of myself as a human being and the idea that society has of me as a woman. All this makes my writing very clearly women's writing. (Bhalla 2006, p. 1)

This position taken by Deshpande is useful in setting a benchmark by which we might consider post-millennial chick lit in English from India. As Section 3.1 will go on to demonstrate, the narratives of post-millennial chick lit, like Deshpande's works, also explore 'what it is to be a woman in our society' and to further quote Deshpande: 'the conflict between my idea of myself as a human being and the idea that society has of me as a woman' (Bhalla 2006, p. 1). Anita Desai's work has also often interrogated 'what it is to be a woman in our society', to take Deshpande's words. Desai's novel *Where Shall We Go This Summer?* was first published in 1975 and is an intense story of Sita, who struggles with the monotonous life of her married, middle-class existence. One of the most striking scenes in the novel is when Sita, seven months pregnant, prepares to leave for an island, Manori, which she knew as a young girl. Her husband warns that the journey to the island is too difficult; he considers the monsoon's raging heat and the boat ride across the monsoon sea at seven months pregnant as out of the question. Sita believes that the island can work miracles and that the madness of the everyday that she has been observing for so long now, can disappear if only she can make it to Manori. Sita is terrified to bring her fifth child into the world and she is at odds with her husband, who she claims, has no idea of her suffering:

> "But you were always so pleased about the babies, Sita," he said, closing his fists, unclosing them, uncertainly. "They always pleased you."
> "I'm *not* pleased, I'm frightened," she hissed through her teeth. "*Frightened.*"
> "Why? Why?" he spoke gently. "Everything will go well. I thought it grows easier and easier."
> "It's not easier. It's harder – harder. It's unbearable," she wept. (Desai 1982/2001, p. 32)

The analysis of the new chick lit fiction contrasts the narratives of Deshpande, Desai and others against the post-millennial chick lit narratives of Kala, Chauhan, Jain and Vadya. What remains in these new narratives is certainly questions of being a woman in society and 'playing the different roles enjoined [. . .] by society', as Deshpande writes, but what we might speculate as 'different' in the new narratives of post-millennial chick lit is the decision-making processes that the female protagonists face. Chapter 2 has narrated how the lives of women in India today can play out and Sophie Das in *Neti, Neti: Not This, Not This* (2009) is one such example. The character of Aisha in Kala's chick lit novel *Almost Single* (2007) examined here, is another such protagonist, both women characters finding themselves alone in Indian urban centres, with an independent working life, a group of friends and a boyfriend. In these novels, as with other chick lit narratives, it is the decision-making processes around the lives of these female protagonists that create a marked difference from the narratives of Desai or Deshpande. Both Hasan's 'Sophie' and Kala's 'Aisha' face moments in their lives when they stand back and ask what decisions they have taken and why. What is it that these characters want in their lives and how will they achieve it? Perhaps the best example of this is Kala's 'Aisha' when, faced with the man she loves, who is handsome, successful, independent and wealthy, and moreover, who has asked Aisha to marry him, Aisha's response is not 'yes' but rather, a request to spend time together so that they might know each other better. Aisha's position here foregrounds the independence of decision-making that shapes many of the female characters found in the chick lit narratives of post-millennial fiction.

Metro Reads

Chapter 2 has already discussed the 'Metro Reads' series of fiction from Penguin India, but it is worth noting that a considerable amount of titles in this series are told from a female perspective and can be classified as chick lit. The narratives are very 'real' in the sense that they speak of contemporary young India: *No Deadline for Love* (2011) takes the life of Megha, a career woman working long hours and meeting unreasonable deadlines, with her mother who is all out to get Megha on the 'marriage market' and makes life even more complicated when a new creative consultant arrives in the midst of Megha's own dearth of creativity, turning her world upside down. *Love on the Rocks* (2011) is a romantic thriller where newly wed Sancha is put to the test when her husband is implicated in a murder enquiry, with the narrative made up of diary entries by Sancha, Aaron, First Engineer Harsh Castillo and Raghav, the investigating officer. *Losing My Virginity and Other Dumb Ideas* (2011) introduces the reader to Kaveri who is single and a gifted interpreter. On her thirtieth birthday, Kaveri decides that it is time for her lose her virginity with or without love and the novel charts this journey. *Dreams in Prussian Blue* (2010) details the life of Naina as she decides to 'live in' with Michael. Smitten by him, she learns to see the other side of him in time, a side which is selfish and temperamental. Things only get more difficult after an accident that leaves Michael blind and Naina is forced to support him even more. Finally, *Where Girls Dare* (2010) is a light-hearted story about a group of 52 women who train as lady cadets in the army, alongside 400 male cadets.

The Metro Reads presented here all engage with a 'young India' through characters in their twenties and thirties, through urbanscapes such as Mumbai and in the IT corporate worlds of New India's industries that are helping to grow the economy. The characters often find themselves at crossroads with modern day India, a family's expectations, the challenges of juggling a career and a relationship as well as finding a life partner on their own initiative. Many of these themes are found in Kala's *Almost Single* (2007) discussed below, as well as other chick lit novels such as *Keep the Change* (2010), *A Break in the Circle* (2010), *Priya In Incredible Indyaa* (2011), *The Zoya Factor* (2008) and *Battle for Bittora* (2010). Another publisher of chick lit novels or novellas Srishti Publishers and the books retail at around 100 rupees, which means that they are cheaper than the Metro Series books. These include: *The Thing Between U & Me... When Life Goes Filmy* (2010), *It Happened That Night: A Tale of Love, Deceit and Murder* (2010) and *It's All About Love: Matters not Whom You Fall in Love With!* (2011).

Ravinder Singh's *I Too Had A Love Story* (2008), also published by Srishti Publishers, proved a bestseller within India. The autobiographical story tells of the death of the protagonist's girlfriend five days before their engagement. The two had met on one of the most famous matrimonial websites – www. shaadi.com. Singh's second novel *Can Love Happen Twice* (2011) is not based on real-life events although it is a sequel to *I Too Had A Love Story* (2008) and is proving a popular read.

This chapter will now examine one of the earliest and most influential texts in the development of post-millennial chick lit from India, Advaita Kala's *Almost Single* (2007).

Almost Single (2007)

Advaita Kala's *Almost Single* (2007) is a landmark in the burgeoning scene of Indian chick lit. The novel concerns the lives of three close friends, Aisha, Misha and Anushka, who are 'on the wrong side of twenty-nine' (Kala 2007, p. 4). Aisha and Misha are single and Anuskha is going through a divorce. Although the novel follows the lives of these three women, it focuses on Aisha and is narrated from her perspective. Aisha Bhatia works as the 'Guest Relations Manager' at the Grand Orchid Hotel in New Delhi. She tolerates the job even though the salary does not reflect the rates of the hotel, the hours she has to work are often unsociable and she hates her boss. Away from her parents, living in New Delhi, she spends most of her time with her two girlfriends and together they shop, drink coffee, hold parties and look for love. It is Misha's desire to meet a non-resident Indian (NRI – see Glossary) that results in the women registering on a shaadi website:

Did I mention that Misha's one and only ambition is to net the perfect NRI? It is in pursuit of this goal that she moved from Bhatinda to New Delhi. And now, she's decided it's a grand idea to register with desivivaha. com – the One-Stop Site for an NRI to Hold Tight. So, we logged on and spent the next forty-five minutes thinking up glowing adjectives to describe our assets and ambivalent ones to dodge the iffy bits. (Kala 2007, p. 5)

The shaadi website results in a couple of dates for the women but nothing very serious and Misha, in particular, begins to think that her idea of 'netting an NRI' will remain a dream. Aisha is somewhat preoccupied by her age, that is, nearing 30, but is heartened by the fact that street urchins or peddlers refer to her as *didi*. For Aisha, this is a clear indicator of ones market value, as you move from *baby* when you are young to the respectful *didi* as a young woman, followed by, Aisha says 'the most traumatic transition, from *didi* to the dreaded *aunty*' (Kala 2007, p. 11), finishing the progression with *mataji*. Fortunately, Aisha is still addressed as *didi* on the streets and therefore believes that 'she's still good to go' (Kala 2007, p. 11). It is Aisha's mother who, if anyone, puts pressure on Aisha to find someone and get married. The novel is interspersed with telephone conversations between Aisha and her mother, Mrs Bhatia, and one such call is to inform Aisha that the neighbourhood catch, 'Deepak', is getting married. Deepak, Aisha says, is generous on cash but not on good looks or personality, to which her mother replies: 'Beta, when it comes to boys like that, who looks at the face . . . Money does conquer all. Someone should update the old adage' (Kala 2007, p. 12). Aisha's reaction is one of disinterest and this, in turn, provokes her mother's response: 'Everyone is getting married now. Chalo, it's all karma at the end of the day' (Kala 2007, p. 12). Her mother's remark leaves Aisha anxious. Her mother's philosophical attitude to Aisha's singleton position in life is in stark contrast to all the effort her mother has made until now in looking for a husband for Aisha. Distressed by this turn of events, Aisha decides to call Shastriji, her astrologer, to see if her wedding is imminent. Shastriji commits to very little but concludes that there are 'indications'.

As with fiction explored in other chapters of this book – *Neti, Neti, Not This, Not This* (2010) in Section 2.1, *Call Me Dan* (2010) and *One Night @ The Call Centre* (2008) both in Section 4.1, narratives around ideas of young New India often involve city nightlife and drinking.

I reach the bar early and snag a nice booth by the window. TGIF is mostly a watering-hole for young working people to assemble post work and grab a couple of beers. It's a cool environment for single women: no looks, no come-ons, no free drinks. Okay, the last bit isn't the really cool part, but sometimes a girl just wants to buy her own drinks. (Kala 2007, p. 57)

Aisha suffers numerous hangovers in *Almost Single* (2007), one of which coincides with a date with Karan Verma, an attractive and single, financial analyst. In addition to Aisha's friends, Misha and Anuskha, Aisha has two close friends called Ric and Nic. Ric is her 'party hag' (Kala 2007, p. 101) and the person she phones an hour before she is due to meet Karan. Aisha looks terrible, her hangover has resulted in a puffy face and bags under her eyes. Ric instructs Aisha to wear her Jackie O glasses all day because concealer will not help with the 'eye problem', given the extent of the bags under her eyes. Ric tells her: 'No, darling, you need really dark glasses, no tints. So, find the Jackie O. ones, and remember, even if he takes you into a cave, don't take them off' (Kala 2007, p. 102). The date with Karan takes place at a dimly lit Chinese restaurant. Having already nearly fallen over on some steps inside the restaurant, Aisha takes the opportune moment, while Karan is away from the table, to phone Ric for some 'Diva Intervention' (Kala 2007, p. 106). Aisha explains to Ric how difficult it is to see in the restaurant and that she can't read the menu while wearing the Jackie O glasses. She asks Ric if she might remove them: 'Don't you dare. If you take them off, then never ever call me for advice. You don't want to look like a bag lady' (Kala 2007, p. 107). As Aisha decides to order from memory, the waiter brings a candle to the table and Karan explains: 'Terrible lighting. I thought we might need it' (Kala 2007, p. 108). Karan winks and leans back in his chair, his eyes 'sparkling with amusement' (Kala 2007, p. 108).

This is the beginning of a relationship that grows between Aisha and Karan. Aisha finds it hard to accept that a relationship might be developing between them even when Karan's mother comes to stay with him in Delhi, where Aisha is invited to have dinner with them. The novel charts their somewhat tumultuous dates, ending with Aisha finally deciding to commit to a 'serious' relationship with Karan.

The novel revolves around matters of 'acceptability' and this works on various levels. At times in the novel, Aisha as a character is used to challenge and push the boundaries of societal 'acceptability' in New India and this often takes place around her role as a female. One such occasion involves her 'uniform' at the Grand Orchid Hotel. On arrival in the locker room to change into her saree, Aisha decides to wear her red Reeboks because her first task of the day is to walk around the corridors to ensure that all the breakfast order cards have been picked up and it will be much more comfortable to do this in trainers. According to Aisha, her Reebok trainers are 'flat, comfortable, well worn and cleverly disguised by the uneven fall of my saree' (Kala 2007, p. 27). Not only does the wearing of the Reebok trainers instead of her 'regulation heels' contravene the hotel's dress code, but the fact that her saree is also 'uneven' further demonstrates Aisha's disinterest in the uniform and the societal norms of wearing her saree correctly. This nonconformity is further manifest in the scene which follows, as Aisha, losing an important piece of paper to the wind, hitches up her saree to retrieve the paper from across a partition separating the corridor from the lawn: 'I hold my saree up to my knees and sprint towards the offending piece of paper, and am about to scoop it up with my free hand, when I see a flash of white' (Kala 2007, p. 28). The flash of white is the guest's towel as he removes it from his waist, revealing 'all his morning glory' (Kala 2007, p. 28). The man sees Aisha who bolts 'Reebok, saree, paper and all' (Kala 2007, p. 28). Her unacceptable behaviour as 'Guest Relations Manager' – she was, after all, in his private space, outside his hotel room – further emphasizes Aisha's non-conformist character.

Later in the novel, Aisha has another problem with her saree as she forgets the petticoat, meaning that she has to tie her saree over her jeans. Aisha dislikes having to wear a saree, referring to it as the 'male repellent':

People always wonder why I have not met a nice young man at work yet. It's because of the saree – I call it the male repellent. Yes, I know a lot of women look stunning in it. I am not one of those women. On a good day, I look like a well-draped potato. And there are bad days when I end up wearing it over my jeans. It's a basic design flaw, sarees should come with a stitched-on petticoat. (Kala 2007, pp. 182–3)

Aisha and her friends conduct lives that are judged as 'unacceptable' by neighbours in particular. Misha's neighbour, Mrs Mukherjee, is one such example. After a dreadful date with Sameer, Misha arrives back at her flat somewhat drunk: 'She stumbled into her apartment and Mrs Mukherjee, her nosy neighbour, watched and tut-tutted with a look of disdain splashed across her face. Right, some more grist for the neighbourhood gossip mill' (Kala 2007, p. 69). Aisha discloses that 'Mrs Mukherjee has a very fixed notion of "bhadralok" and Misha just doesn't cut it. It has become her life's ambition now to get Misha evicted' (Kala 2007, p. 81).

Mrs Mukherjee's sense of 'bhadralok', a Bengali expression meaning a well-mannered person of a middle-class background is not how Misha and Aisha understand the idea. We understand from this extract that Aisha considers herself to be of the same class as Mrs Mukherjee and although different from Mrs Mukherjee, she is not rude or offensive in her manners, she has a respectable job and earns a very good salary and, therefore, considers herself, like Misha, as middle class. Misha comes from a well-to-do family in Bhatinda and works as an insurance advisor, a job that was secured by her Papaji (her father). She works because she wants to and not because she has to as Misha is financially independent. Mrs Mukherjee's notions of middle-classness, female behaviour and conduct are not in line with how Aisha, Misha and Anuskha understand them and herein lies the tension.

On another occasion, Aisha, Misha, Anushka, Ric and Nic decide to carry out a havan (see Glossary) on the roof of Misha's block of flats. The havan is conducted to rid themselves of past misdeeds and Aisha states that despite the usual presence of a pandit (see Glossary), *their* havan requires no pandit, only a fire. The havan quickly morphs into drinking and discussion around a blazing fire with an overstocked bar at hand. Mrs Mukherjee rouses the neighbours in protest of the 'party' on the roof. As Mrs Mukherjee arrives to address the crowd, the group have managed to extinguish the fire, remove all alcohol from view and Anushka is standing amidst the group with a bottle of coke in her hand:

> Mrs Mukherjee's disappointment was palpable. She hoped to find a flaming orgy, preferably with alcohol, and if possible, some hash thrown in. She probably rehearsed her outraged civilian call to Aaj Tak about the *asheel* youth of today. (Kala 2007, p. 86)

Following the 'havan' incident, in a bid to reintegrate with Misha's colony and as an effort towards finding a husband, the girls decide to keep the Karva Chauth (see Glossary) fast. This involves staying at Misha's flat in order to carry out a short ceremony in the middle of the night, to then fast the whole of the next day. They contribute money to the association and the secretary purchases the various sundries for the event. Their efforts result in 'good PR for Misha, an opportunity for her to reintegrate with the bhadralok in her neighbourhood' (Kala 2007, p. 111). As the ladies assemble for the ceremony, Mrs Mukherjee arrives. Anushkha whispers: 'Isn't she Bong? Do they fast as well?'. This slang term for Bengali, 'Bong', asserts the girls' identities as 'northern' (and not Bengali) and this, in turn, creates a sense of ownership over the Karva Chauth proceedings. It is the cultural heritage of Northwest India that is centre stage here and the girls feel that they have a right to attend the fast given their cultural heritage (despite their reputation according to Mrs Mukherjee). This importance of 'acceptability' is echoed in Aisha's statement: 'There's something about these community thingies that makes you want to feel "decent", a part of normal and accepted community' (Kala 2007, p. 112), but the event results in unease for Aisha as, at the heart of the fast, is the sacred union of marriage; she laments:

> I feel like a wannabe, a poseur. I have no man and resuscitated wedding lehenga to wear. Story of my life: every time I feel I've reached a stage where I actually fit in somewhere, I suddenly find myself in an unfamiliar place again. (Kala 2007, pp. 113–14)

Misha, on the other hand, is very much enjoying the event, revelling in all its tradition. Aisha says of Misha: 'She is made for this stuff, and if our traditions are to withstand India's sprint towards the western way, women like Misha have to get married' (Kala 2007, p. 115). Once again, Aisha's position of 'acceptability' is under question, as she, compared to Misha, does not really feel part of the proceedings. On the continuum of 'acceptability', where Mrs Mukherjee's 'bhadralok' ideas lie at one end and Aisha's at the other, Misha, one of her closest friends and adversary of Mrs Mukherjee, is closer to Mrs Mukheerjee's end of the continuum, than Aisha's. These uneasy feelings that Aisha experiences are explained away by her mother: 'According to my mother, whenever something is not right with me, it's because I live in a big, bad city on my own, and did not get married when I was supposed to' (Kala 2007, p. 98). Everything in Aisha's life, it seems, comes back to marriage.

The fast comes to an end as they wait for a sighting of the moon. Aisha's mobile rings and it is Karan. His flight to Mumbai is delayed and the two talk until his plane lifts off the tarmac. As she puts the phone down, the moon is sighted and the fast comes to an end. The appearance of the moon so close to the ending of the phone call with Karan makes Aisha think about him and the possibility of a relationship. As the ladies come together to break the fast, Ric and Nic turn up with a picnic hamper full of food and they all relocate to Misha's roof:

> Ric and Nic, with the sensitivity that is the reserve of gay men, have brought a hamper with the ultimate Moët and Chandon, Boursin cheese, shepherd's pie, garlic bread, a tossed salad and brownies, not to mention linen serviettes and real silverware. Not exactly religious fare, but then, we aren't great on religion either. (Kala 2007, p. 119)

Traditionally, the fast is broken with water and usually something sweet administered by the husband. A simple, Indian meal then follows. Aisha, Misha and Anushkha do not follow this protocol, breaking their fast with alcohol, rich 'European' foods and a gay couple. Aisha, on the sighting of the moon is thinking of her 'nicotine fix', so we can assume that she also breaks her fast with a cigarette. The young women's breakfast takes place on the roof without the presence of husbands, instead they are 'fed' by Ric and Nic, their gay friends, and moreover, the food is markedly different from the food being consumed at the bottom of the block of flats by Mrs Mukherjee and the other ladies. The Karva Chauth fast is a religious occasion, in the sense that it is part of Hindu (and Sikh) religious custom and yet Aisha says 'I just have to look at this as a detox thingy. People spend thousands to go to fancy places to purge themselves; I am getting to do it for free' (Kala 2007, p. 114). Moreover, as we read in the quote above, 'Not exactly religious fare, but then, we aren't great on religion either' (Kala 2007, p. 119).

Aisha's willingness to take part in the Karva Chauth fast is a negotiated one, she does it because Misha wants to and she rationalizes it as a 'detox' and the 'breakfast' as a time to hang out with friends, drink alcohol and eat rich food. The real significance of the fast, however, is caught in her chance phone call with Karan and the sighting of the moon as she hangs up from speaking to him. She also experiences the community 'bonding' and the breaking of the fast with her close friends, who, as a single woman living in Delhi, are as close to her as her family is. This experience of the fast is, however, divergently different from its 'traditional' intent, where the women of the family come together, a husband is present to break the fast and the food is prepared at home, a traditional home-cooked meal, all in a religious context. This display of various female worlds, inhabited by women of different generations and different life experiences is a strong motif in Kala's novel.

As the novel comes to an end, Aisha's mother is so concerned about her daughter that she goes to see Swamiji who phones Aisha to say that her mother is there with him:

> "*Bacchi, tumhari ma hamare saath hain.* She is very worried about you." A squeaky voice comes over the phone.
>
> "*Namaste Swamiji*" I whisper. I don't know if he heard me, for he continues with his ramblings. I guess godmen are prone to monologues even on the phone.
>
> "*Ab chinta band karo.* The time has come." It's almost as if he is predicting an apocalypse. "*Samay ab theek chalega. Ab relax karo. Bahut aashirwaad, beta.*" I stare on in silence for a few moments. (Kala 2007, p. 265)

Swamiji announces that the time has come, all is going to be well and that Aisha has many blessings. Aisha is rendered silent as she listens to Swamiji and thinks to herself:

> The *Hinglish* godmen are a boon for our nation, thank god for their easy accessibility. They're like your neighbourhood kirana seth who speaks the English of a department store clerk and the Hindi of a thelawala. A very comforting combination. Plus, of course, he stocks everything from Indian veggies to face bleach. And he does home delivery. (Kala 2007, p. 266)

This extract demonstrates how the godmen figures, so bound to Mother India and so integral to Indian society, have morphed and changed into godmen of the twenty-first century; as Mrs Bhatia is not able to take Aisha to Swamiji, so Swamiji takes himself to Aisha by calling her mobile phone to deliver divine guidance and encouragement. Swamiji speaks English as well as a 'department store clerk' and Hindi as well a man who works on the streets carrying and fetching goods (a *thelawala*) – for this, Aisha describes him as 'Hinglish'. Swamiji also diversifies his business activity, as in addition to divine teaching, he is able to deliver all household commodities to your door.

As Aisha is wondering what to do about the situation with Karan, Misha meets up with a childhood friend, Guru (Gurinder). Misha's father pushed her to meet him as he is visiting from Canada and alone in Delhi before he makes his journey to Bhatinda. Misha remembers a very nerdy, short

Gurinder and is unhappy at the idea of having to meet him. She dresses in a very 'prim salwar kameez and leaves the cigarettes behind' (Kala 2007, p. 269). As Misha leaves her flat, 'Mrs Mukherjee takes in her new look and gives her the thumbs up' (Kala 2007, p. 269). Misha waits at the hotel for Guru to appear and is surprised when, on feeling a tap on her shoulder, she turns around to find a gorgeous Gurinder who has had 'more than one growth spurt' (Kala 2007, p. 270). Misha follows Guru off to Bhatinda the next day and that evening she calls Aisha to inform her that she has decided to sleep with Guru in order to know if they are sexually compatible. Aisha replays the conversation in her mind as she lies in her bed:

> Sexual compatibility is important, but is it sufficient? These days, it's like the last bastion to be conquered before one travels down the aisle. A betrothal is a visa to a pre-conjugal tryst and most people are keen to make the trip, which makes me wonder just how many virgins brides are there in the world. (Kala 2007, p. 273)

The idea of 'sex before marriage' in order to work out 'sexual compatibility' is set up here as an accepted norm between Aisha and her friends (and the wider generation of twenty-somethings/thirty year olds we might assume). Interestingly, Aisha uses the phrase 'travels down the aisle', which, apart from the relatively small community of Christians in India (comparatively), is not something that Hindus (or Sikhs – given the setting of this novel in North and Northwest India) perform as part of the marriage ceremony. The equivalent 'walking down the aisle' is found in the circling of the fire (agni) seven times for the seven steps or vows (saat phere).

The novel ends as Aisha decides to tell Karan Varma how she feels. She makes this decision while she is on a 22 hour train journey to Nashik. She gets off the train at Bhopal, takes a taxi to the airport and then a flight to Mumbai as Karan is on business in the city. Kala writes: 'The Celine Dion version of the song *I Drove All Night* keeps playing in my head as I fasten the seat belt and close my eyes, refusing to think about what I will do once I get to Mumbai' (Kala 2007, p. 277). Aisha arrives at Karan's hotel but misses him by 5 minutes. At the bar and three Screwdrivers later, Aisha decides to go to the reception desk, proclaiming that she is Karan's wife and wishing to surprise him for their anniversary. 'The world loves a lover and I am soon led up to his room' (Kala 2007, p. 178). Aisha is met sometime later by Karan's boss as she stands in her towel at the bathroom door. Karan had booked both rooms in his name – his own room and his boss's room – and this explains how Aisha finds herself in the incorrect suite. With nothing to lose, Aisha says:

> "Karan, please, I know this sounds weird, but can we put off marrying for a bit and like really get to know each other?" . . .
> Karan walks over to me slowly and takes my hands in his. "Aisha, I can't claim to understand you, but I do love you."

"So we are together then? Together because we love each other's company? Not because we're bound to do the right thing or what's expected?"

"Meaning?" he asks, looking really confused.

"What I'm trying to say is that I'm okay being the oldest bride in India just as long as when I do get to be a bride it is the right man." (Kala 2007, p. 281)

Thus, *Almost Single* finishes with a scene where once again Aisha challenges the orthodoxy, looking for ways in which her life in New India might be made more meaningful to her, more sincere and, most importantly, more in line with how *she* understands life and love in the twenty-first century.

Battle for Bittora (2010)

Anuja Chauhan's second novel, *Battle for Bittora* (2010), follows her popular first novel, *The Zoya Factor* (2008). Just as her first novel marries the genres of chick lit and crick lit (*The Zoya Factor* is discussed in Section 3.2), so her second book marries chick lit and politics. The protagonist, 25-year-old 'Jinni', whose full name is Sarojini Devi Pande, hails from Bittora, Pavit Pradesh in North India. As a graduate of animation design from Canada, she takes a job in 'Pixel Animation' in Mumbai, and here she works with her friend Gaiman Tagore Rumi. 'Rumi' takes his name from 'mixing the names of three creative artists he admires the most – Neil Gaiman – the dude who wrote the Sandman comics, Bengali litterateur Rabindranath Tagore and the mystic Sufi poet Rumi' (Chauhan 2010, p. 4). The novel opens as the two friends debate the sexual orientation of their favourite superheroes. Jinni makes the case for Spiderman as a 'straight' male:

> Rumi gave a throaty laugh. "But that constant *fssssskkch fssssskkch* spurting of sticky grey stuff into the air is thoda sa phallic, don't you think?"
>
> I gasped. "Those are *webs*!"
>
> He shrugged his thin shoulders. "Then they're symbolic of his desire to entrap as many men as possible into the sticky web of his want."
>
> "Or women," I replied doggedly. (Chauhan 2010, p. 2)

As Rumi goes on to argue the next case, that is, the gayness of Superman, Jinni orders pizza as they have a long night ahead with all the work they must complete. Once they hear someone arrive in the reception area of 'Pixel Animation', Rumi assumes it's the pizza delivery, so he goes to the reception to collect it. He returns, without a pizza, saying that there is someone for a 'Sarojini Pande'. Rumi, never having heard Jinni addressed by this name, is somewhat dumbfounded. Jinni makes her way to the reception lobby to find her maternal grandmother waiting for her. Her grandmother or 'Amma' is the famous 'Pushpa Pande' of 'Pragati Party' (PP). Rumi is overwhelmed by this revelation as he has followed PP for some years. As they sit down in the lobby with the pizza, Rumi learns how Jinni belongs to 'a political family' or 'dynasty' and that Amma is actually 'Pushpa *jiji*, a hard-core, three-time Lok Sabha MP, an MP3 so to say, hailing from the dusty badlands of Pavit Pradesh, one of north India's most populous states' (Chauhan 2010, p. 9). This is the reason Jinni has kept her 'dynasty' roots secret from her recently made Mumbai friends, especially Rumi, as Jinni says: 'I mean, Rumi's seen *Rang De Basanti* thrice. He even thinks the ending made sense. And he's still wearing those black armbands in remembrance of the victims of 26/11!' (Chauhan 2010, p. 9).

Although *Battle for Bittora* (2010) is essentially a chick lit narrative (between the two main characters of Jinni and Zain, childhood friends who meet some years later back in Bittora), the novel also observes the contemporary and young 'political' India of the noughties. The film reference *Rang De Basanti* (discussed again in Section 4.1, see Glossary) is one film of a body of post-millennial Indian films that explore politics, justice, corruption and contemporary 'Indianness'. The 2010 box office smash hit *Dabaang* with the Robin Hood-type protagonist (he is addressed thus in the film), police inspector 'Chulbul Pande', played by Salman Khan, is another example of a film which explores these themes, as is the 2011 film *Singham*, with the protagonist Ajay Devgan, also playing a police inspector, Bajirao Singham, who fights corruption and menace from local gangs. Also released in 2010 was the political film *Raajneeti*, which follows the lives of a 'family dynasty' not unlike the lives and fate of an authentic Indian political family still active in politics today. Chauhan's novel makes a reference to *Raajneeti* when Rumi suggests that Jinni 'assassinate' those who are running for the 'ticket' (Chauhan 2010, p. 33). Moreover, Chauhan takes this idea of a film production about a 'dynasty' a little further as Amma (Pushpa *jiji*) tells Jinni that a film is to be made about their own 'PP' family. Amma insists that an actress named 'Katrina' is not to play 'her' in the planned film. When asked why, *jiji* says it's not because she is *Muslim* but rather because she is *fat* (Chauhan 2010, p. 342). These references are highly cultural and contemporary; the fact that a film is planned to be made about the 'dynasty' speaks directly to the 2010 film *Raajneeti* and, moreover, the lead actress in *Raajneeti* was played by Katrina Kaif. Other film references further locate Chauhan's novel in New India as Jinni happens 'to know all the steps to the Dhan-ta-nan song from *Kaminey*' (Chauhan 2010, p. 118), a popular Bollywood film from 2009. Jinni's mother makes references to contemporary television, media and culture when she says:

And you *cried* when you saw that Airtel ad, the one where Saif carries a photo of his childhood sweetheart around for years, and searches high and low for her, and then, when he finally finds her, dumps her for Kareena Kapoor. (Chauhan 2010, p. 78)

All these features of the novel situate the narrative in a very contemporary and young India; however, it is the romance between Jinni and Zain which makes this novel a particular chick lit read. Jinni grew up in Bittora as did Zain, they were childhood friends, thrown together because their respective grandfathers were close friends. At the age of 13, sitting on the branches of a mango tree, Zain kissed Jinni on the back of her neck and this was the start of a special friendship which lasted until they went their separate ways; Zain to a school in England and Jinni, later to Canada for her studies. Despite the connection between the two families' grandfathers, there is deep rivalry and resentment between the family of Zain Altaf Khan and the family of Sarojini Devi Pande; the divide is drawn along religious and ethnic lines – by Amma (Pushpa *jiji*) in particular – as well as along political lines, as the two families hold different political views. PP, led by Pushpa *jiji*, a Brahmin, is portrayed as a Hindu-led party, traditionally focusing on the votes of Hindus of all castes, particularly the poorer parts of society. Pushpa *jiji*'s religious prejudice is portrayed early on in the novel when she journeys to Mumbai to fetch her granddaughter 'Sarojini'. Rumi calls Sarojini by her 'Mumbai name' *Jinni* to which Amma scornfully exclaims that 'Jinni' is a Muslim name:

> Toh kya *Jinni* kahen? She said disdainfully, leaning back in her chair, her eyelids all wrinkled and tissue-papery over her closed eyes. "Mohammedan sa name hai. You sound like a poor carpenterj fourth wife." (Chauhan 2010, p. 11)

And Amma's prejudice does not stop at ethnic and religious identities, she also refers to Rumi in pejorative terms: 'Who ij this Article 377, Sarojini?' (Chauhan 2010, p. 11), referring to the recent penal code and debate around homosexuality in India.

Zain's family, on the other hand, leads the Indian Janata Party (IJP) and attempts an 'all India' inclusivity where 'minorities and backwards will be well-represented' (Chauhan 2010, p. 68), all this, despite the Muslim background and privileged 'nawab' heritage Zain's family has known.

Fate (and some help from Pushpa *jiji*) conspires to render Jinni the PP candidate for Bittora in the upcoming general election and Zain, as the IJP candidate. The two childhood friends are pitted against one another along both political and ethnic lines. Their shared motivation is belonging to 'young India' and the desire to improve life in Bittora and in Pavit Pradesh for all. In their own ways, both Zain and Jinni flout the norms and conventions of their parties and they especially contravene their ethnic/religious backgrounds. Zain stands for the IJP and as this, historically, is *not* an all-Muslim party, rather a Hindu party, this fact plus the strong standpoint of 'inclusivity' which he is taking, means that Zain is received with scepticism across all communities, but especially across the poorer, Muslim communities. Zain works hard to stress that his IJP is a 'new party', with a focus on representation for all. Jinni, too, flouts convention as she pulls away from the more Hindutva-focused, populist Hindu reputation that PP has fostered over the years, looking instead to garner votes from across the communities, despite being a high-caste (Brahmin) Hindu. These unconventional political positions are captured in Chauhan's fiction-newspaper article included in the novel as it reads:

> So is this the new, post-26/11 India? Genuinely concerned, young educated people-like-us, coming to a head at the hustings? Or is it just a sordid continuation of dynastic politics? Whatever else it may be, it is certainly a piquant situation when a Brahmin girl from the Pragati fights a Muslim ex-royal from the IJP. (Chauhan 2010, p. 68)

And it is this situation, the diametrically opposed Zain-and-Jinni, which plays out as the two fight and refuse, only to rejoin again (and again) in their love for each other. As candidates for their respective parties, Zain and Jinni meet at a community event. Zain makes sure that he sits next to Jinni.

> I glared at him, thinking it was disgraceful how the V-neck of his kurta left the golden skin at the base of his throat freely visible to all. Didn't he realize it was blatantly soliciting kisses? "And can't you go sit somewhere else?" I added. "This is stupid". (Chauhan 2010, p. 161)

Throughout the narrative, Jinni is physically attracted to Zain, which transforms their 'innocent' childhood friendship into something more, and for Jinni at various points in the novel, she wonders if their 'relationship' is one based on lust and a sexually charged rivalry. Jinni reveals that she didn't have sex until she was 20, losing her virginity to a 'cute, sensitive banker' (Chauhan 2010, p. 57), and a second sexual encounter with a 'dark, sarcastic music engineer which had gone nowhere fast' (Chauhan 2010, p. 57). When Jinni and Zain meet for the first time after 9 years, they find themselves at a wedding party, a select gathering whose invitation list is politically motivated, and an event that will help to decide Jinni and Zain's immediate fortunes of standing for their respective parties in the forthcoming general election. Unbeknown to the two, who, kissing on an 'overstuffed sofa' (Chauhan 2010, p. 56) in a quiet side room, lies an imminent future of politics and division. Jinni, brought back to her senses by a noise in an adjoining room, takes stock of what she's involved in: 'And here I was, behaving like some feisty, get-on-the-carousel-boys chick and unbuttoning achkans like I did it every day of my life' (Chauhan 2010, p. 57). She wonders whether they have laced the drinks with some kind of aphrodisiac and then escapes to the veranda. Zain joins her and asks 'Can we just talk?' (Chauhan 2010, p. 57). Jinni replies:

> "What about?" I snapped, trying desperately not to remember how he'd looked with the achkan off. (Lean, taut, chiselled and honey gold.) Zain made a vague gesture in the air.

"About . . . anything. Like, what you're doing here for instance. I thought you lived in Canada?"

"I did," I told him. "I went to cartoon college there."

He looked a little startled.

(Lean, taut, chiselled and honey gold.)

"What I mean to say," I continued, babbling moronically . . . (Chauhan 2010, p. 58)

Amma is concerned about Jinni's friendship with Zain. She knows of their childhood friendship and of the great bond between Zain's grandfather and Jinni's grandfather, since the latter was Amma's husband. Amma had married at the age of 13 when Jinni's grandfather or 'Bauji' was 33. Bauji's name was Pandit Madan Mohan Pande and when he passed on, Amma, after watching and studying his political life for years, took on his political role.

Amma, talking across Jinni to Gudia aunty, warns of the relationship with Zain:

See doesn't realize that all musalmaan men think this way about Hindu women – that we are all nympho. See thinks all this is a game, with rules and *times-please* and good manners. Arey bhai, this is politics! It ij free-style fighting! No holes barred! (Chauhan 2010, p. 269)

Amma's warning comes at a point in the narrative where pamphlets have been issued defaming Jinni's character, suggesting that she had secured 'alliances' in order to attain her place in the general election. Amma and the PP campaigning team suggest that the pamphlet is Zain's doing. Jinni dismisses the suggestion: 'Amma, Zain couldn't have done this' . . . 'Because, well, he's my childhood friend . . . Surely Zain wouldn't stoop to something like this?' (Chauhan 2010, p. 268). The doubt in Jinni's mind stays and resurfaces at various points in the story, demonstrating how their relationship ebbs and flows according to the political landscape, its challenges, but mostly in response to its dirty politics. But Jinni and Zain are not alone in all the political mess; both candidates are surrounded by their campaign teams, especially Jinni's team as it is led so forcefully by Amma. Zain and Jinni's resistance to demonstrating any kind of affection for each other in public is tested beyond measure when Amma dies. Chauhan reveals that the reason Amma had travelled to Mumbai to fetch Sarojini was to settle her into the political scene in Bittora as Amma knew that she was dying. As Sarojini stands at her Amma's funeral pire, Zain arrives:

"Sarojiniji," he said formally, a tiny pulse jumping at the base of his throat. "I just wanted to offer my condo-"

But I didn't let him finish.

> With an exquisite sense of relief, of laying down a burden, of bursting out of a cold, dark well into hot, bright sunshine, I threw myself into his surprised but incredibly steady arms, laid my head against his superbly muscled chest, and sobbed like my heart would break. (Chauhan 2010, p. 337)

This public display of affection and need is all over the newspapers and television the next day. Jinni comforts herself in the knowledge that 'in the rural areas, mercifully, there had been power cuts . . . almost all day long, so none of them had seen the damaging footage of me at the funeral' (Chauhan 2010, p. 359). The funeral happens shortly before the elections and the counting of the votes reveals a very close contest. Jinni wins by a small margin of 600 votes, but her success is tainted. Jinni is told by one of her campaign team, Gudia aunty, that she, Gudia aunty, in a fit of rage, took their expense bills to Zain in order to expose PP, Pushpa *jiji* and Jinni for all the expenditure on the PP campaign – some of which was 'questionable'. Gudia aunty had decided to take this action after Jinni had accused her of stealing. Zain had been given evidence enough to expose the PP party and win the elections through Gudia aunty's behaviour. Zain, however, did not expose the PP party because with Amma dying 'it would've been . . . indecent' (Chauhan 2010, p. 408). Zain had also come to hear of how Jinni had played out one of their childhood fictions, that of saving someone from their death, something she had actually done in between her campaigning despite putting the PP at great risk of losing votes. For Zain, this display of courage meant that Jinni was destined to win the campaign. The narrative closes as Jinni and Zain 'consummate' their childhood friendship, their now adult relationship, Jinni exclaiming worriedly: 'Suppose this is just unfinished business? Suppose once this is done, we get totally *over* each other?' (Chauhan 2010, p. 414).

The novel finishes with an epilogue. Zain drives Jinni to Delhi in order 'to be sworn in'. As she gets out of the car to a sea of media personnel asking how it feels to be the youngest MP, Zain is offered a pass into Parliament House to watch Jinni being sworn in. He takes the pass happily and Jinni says to herself: '*Huh?* I know, I know. I don't deserve him. I almost hugged him in public again, but managed to stop myself in the nick of time (Well, to tell you the truth, I kind of half-lunged into the Sumo but then TB's hand closed warningly over my arm.)' (Chauhan 2010, p. 420).

Chauhan's novel brings together the genre of chick lit with a political narrative, setting the story against the backdrop of New India. Although, a very different narrative from Kala's *Almost Single*, Chauhan's novel asks similar questions about female experiences in New India, that is, looking for love and, most importantly, the independence of decision making in contemporary society.

3.2 Crick lit

Cricket in India can be considered a national obsession, particularly post-millennium; a motif of New India. In 2008, the Twenty20 cricket league was launched in India, namely, the Indian Premier League (IPL), a professional league for 'Twenty20 cricket' and not the formation of a league for (the rather slower game of) 'Test cricket'. Test cricket, it can be argued, anchors international cricket to London and although Indians were passionate about cricket pre-IPL, Test cricket was never going to be able to foster the kind of following that league cricket in India has created since its launch in 2008. The inauguration of Twenty20 cricket in India has changed the face of cricket immensely. As Sundar in her novel *The Premier Murder League* (2010) reminds us, Twenty20 league cricket is built around the American model of sporting events and tournaments, meaning that cricket games morph from the 'Test game' of slow, patient play, to an energized, fast-paced game with regional, state teams pitted against one another and all the hype that comes with prime-time entertainment. Writing in 2006, Bose (2006) postulated the future of Indian cricket:

> With India's growing economic muscle, and an insatiable appetite for the one-day game, this is a market that cricket administrators round the world want to cultivate. . . . Commercial sponsors see such events [as ICC, World Cup] as a wonderful way to reach the growing Indian market for whom cricket, particularly one-day cricket, is now the great marketing tool. (Bose 2006, pp. 245–6)

Bose was correct in his statement and in the years since his publication, the market for one-day cricket has exploded. In this sense, IPL and the appetite for the 'one-day game' is a motif of New India, emerging in the late, first decade of the noughties and very much in line with the economic boom that India has been enjoying. IPL talks directly to the growing middle classes of India, their desire for 'Indian cricket' per se, consumerism and the advertising and celebrity hype that accompanies it. Televised cricket has been at the heart of this boom, Bose (2006) writes: 'This television age has made Indians realize that because of India's location it is India, not England, which is at the centre of the cricket world' (Bose 2006, p. 259). Bose goes on to explain how Indians might choose to watch an Australian game live, early morning in India and as the Australian day comes to a close, Indians can then switch to watch cricket in South Africa and even a late night can be spent watching a match in the West Indies. This ability to follow cricket (other sports, alongside news, etc.) is a relatively new phenomenon given that it was only in 1991 that television and satellite viewing entered the Indian market and the state broadcaster Doordarshan was sidelined for the plethora of other viewing possibilities. During this time, under pressure from the World Bank, India opened up its economy, allowing foreign investment into the country and Indians started to buy televisions and satellite dishes a habit that grew in immense popularity, particularly in the metropolitan centres. Today, Twenty20 is watched on televisions in homes, in bars, cafes and restaurants across the country and is much more than a 'game', it is an 'event'. Twenty20 attracts Bollywood celebrities, business moguls, much sponsorship and advertising. Mishra (2009) recognizes the multifaceted self that is Bollywood when he writes: '[it] is at once a fad, a taste, an Indian exotica, and a global phenomenon growing out of, as it so happens, the cultural and political economy of a film industry based primarily in Mumbai' (Mishra 2009, p. 440). The Bollywood support of Twenty20 is a reciprocal, rewarding relationship and it is financially supported by many Indians who enjoy seeing their favourite film celebrities involved in their favourite sporting event.

The Indian national cricket team is made up of some of India's most popular, contemporary cultural icons, including Sachin Tendulkar, Yuvraj Singh and Mahindra Singh Dhoni; these three cricketers were part of the team that saw India win the International Cricket Council (ICC) World Cup in 2011, propelling them to iconic cultural status. In Chauhan's *The Zoya Factor* (2008), cultural iconic status is at the heart of the narrative. Zoya is 'a mid-level client-servicing executive in India's largest ad agency' (Chauhan 2008, p. 3), who inadvertently ends up spending time with the Indian cricket team and experiences first hand, the celebrity status, almost God-like prominence of the cricketers, especially when they are winning.

It is not only post-millennial fiction in English which is registering the interest in fictional cricket worlds, the post-millennial Bollywood (Hindi) film scene has also produced cricket-orientated narratives, including the 2007 film *Hattrick*, *Jannat* (2008) and its narrative on match-fixing, as well as *Dil Bole Hadippa* (2009) starring Rani Mukherjee as a talented, female closet cricketer who manages to star in a heated Pakistan–India annual cricket match, disguised as a young, male Punjabi. *Patiala House* (2011), also a Punjabi-orientated film, set in Southall, London, the protagonist Gattu, played by Akshay Kumar, is prohibited from following his dream of playing cricket for the England team due to his father's experience of racial aggression in Gattu's early years, resulting in the death of Gattu's uncle. The film explores the tension between Gattu's dream and talent for cricket, and his loyalty to his father and the wider community. Another father–son cricket film appeared in 2012, *Ferrari ki sawaari*. The film follows the trials and tribulations of a talented young Parsi cricketer, Kayo, and his devoted father, Rusy, who will stop at nothing to find the necessary funds to send his son to Lords to train. The film includes a strong 'Sachin Tendulkar' plot line, it is Sachin's Ferrari that dominates much of the film, even if Sachin never actually appears on screen. Mumbai and India as a cricket-loving nation is at the heart of the film's narrative.

One of the most famous cricket films in Bollywood is also a post-millennial production; *Lagaan: Once Upon a Time in India* (2001) starring

Aamir Khan. Set in the late 1800s, during the days of colonial British India, this period film revolves around a game of cricket on which rests the annulment of high taxes (*lagaan*) imposed on the poor villagers by British rule. If the villagers, led by Bhuvan (Aamir Khan), win the cricket match, then the taxes will be waivered for three years. The classic Bollywood motif of boy-meets-girl is explored in the triangle of affection between Bhuvan, Gauri (a local woman) and an English woman, Elizabeth Russell, sister to Andrew Russell who is an important member of the British-led administration in the area. Andrew has a dislike for Bhuvan; however, despite this, it is Elizabeth who trains Bhuvan and the villagers in the details and rules of English cricket.

Although the body of crick lit in English from India is small compared to the proliferation of chick lit by example, post-millennial crick lit is certainly a growing body of fiction and since 2008, a number of crick lit fictions have been published. Interestingly, many of the works in the crick lit genre also draw on a second genre, such as Chauhan's *The Zoya Factor* (2008), whose narrative around cricket is also of the chick lit genre; Sundar's *The Premier Murder League* (2010), which explores the murky world of an Indian cricket board where reputations and crores are played for, even if it means murder, thus the novel marries crick lit with detective fiction; *Bowled and Beautiful* (2009) by Das brings together cricket and a love story; whereas, *Run, Romi, Run* (2010) by Raheja and one of the popular novels by Chetan Bhagat, *The 3 Mistakes of My Life* (2008), both write of cricket in the Bildungsroman genre.

Other books in the crick lit genre look at corruption and match-fixing, including Rajendra's *Doosra* (2011), which delves into the corrupt practice of match-fixing and the protagonist experiences first-hand what it is to ride and fall from the crest of the celebrity cricket wave; Sinha's *22 Yards* (2008) introduces the protagonist Mayank, who is under pressure to manage the team's morale and above all to find out if the Twenty20 World Cup has really been fixed. The blog novel, *The Gamechangers* (2010) is inspired by the events of the 2009 IPL season when an anonymous blogger posted controversial revelations about the tournament. The blogger's identity was never revealed. *The Gamechangers* (2010) is organized as a blog, comprised of 36 'day entries' on the 'IBL', the Indian Bollywood League, and the blogger promises to bring you 'the "aankhon dekha haal", the stuff they never report, the stuff that gets edited out. The stuff you always suspected but couldn't confirm about the world of cricket. And cricketers' (Anonymous 2010, p. 5).

The Sri Lankan author Shehan Karunatilaka's novel *Chinaman* (2011) also brings together some of the themes evident in India's body of crick lit as he examines contemporary Sri Lanka through the game of cricket, evidence perhaps that some of the trends in genre and theme in new Indian writing in English from India are also demonstrative in wider (South Asian) regional fiction, in English and otherwise. Moti Nandy's work in Bengali should not be forgotten either. Evidently a precursor to the newer writing on cricket albeit not written in English, Nandy created a whole oeuvre of fiction focused on sports, including football, tennis and cricket.

The Premier Murder League (2010)

Geeta Sundar's novel *The Premier Murder League* (2010) is set around a fictional IPL involving a criminal cricket board which 'disposes' of anyone who might get in the way of the board running as the boss dictates. The novel brings together the genres of crick lit and detective fiction and her novel opens as S. N. Rao, Union Sports Minister and, more importantly, cricket board member, dies after eating two poisoned paans (see Glossary), following his evening meal. His death is both painful and slow, slow enough for him to write on the wall of his living room: 'cell phone taken, door locked' (Sundar 2010, p. 10).

From the crime wing of the police, Ravi Sharma, deputy commissioner of police and Rahul Singh, assistant to the deputy commissioner, are in charge of the case. The two have worked together for some time when the death of Rao is set to be investigated and Sundar (2010) writes: 'Rahul and Ravi had become so close professionally that they seemed to operate on the same wavelength, often understanding each other without a word having been spoken' (Sundar 2010, p. 6). The death of Rao is followed by the death of the cricket board treasurer, Sunil Mane. Mane is also poisoned; the same poison used in Rao's paan is also used in Mane's drink. With the deaths of two prominent members of the cricket board, Rahul is not surprised to discover that the dynamics between the members of the board were not always harmonious. The root of the discordant board, Rahul finds out, is the 'T20 League'. The launch of the T20 League of India (TLI) is the brainchild of Rao, Mane and Ramesh Patel – owner of Ex-el TV – and it results in countless problems for the cricket board. The idea of a more succinct, fast-paced game would, the official cricket board argue, mean less interest in the full matches. Sundar (2010) writes:

> Though cricket purists were horrified, to many youngsters in the country, Twenty20 cricket was thrilling, pulse-racing stuff that was about to catch the nation's imagination. . . . A youngster working for a BPO said, "Who wants to spend five days following a game that seems to run in slow motion? It 'tests' my patience." There was a roar of appreciative laughter from his friends at the intended pun. (Sundar 2010, p. 20)

Misfortune and mishap hit the TLI and despite its enthusiastic beginnings, the league falls apart bit by bit, public interest dwindles, and by the end of the tournament, the TLI is no more. Seizing the opportunity, another member of the cricket board, Rajeev Kabra, gets together with a man he refers to as the 'boss' to set up their own league: Indian Twenty League (ITL). The 'boss' elects Manik Jindal as the ITL's president and Jindal's rousing speech at the inaugural meeting in Mumbai reveals that:

> Our aim should be to become *the* richest sporting body in the world. And we can easily reach a figure of 2 billion dollars next year if we launch the ITL. That would translate to an eight-fold increase in revenue since 2005! . . . Now about the ITL – it will comprise eight teams, eight franchise owners and sixteen players in each team to begin with and the matches will be played over one and a half months. . . . Let me end by saying that the future looks very bright and rosy for Indian cricket and for the board! (Sundar 2010, pp. 28–9)

In their investigations into the dynamics of the cricket board, Ravi and Rahul decide to question Vineet, the son of Rao. Rao and Vineet had been on bad terms for some time before Rao's murder and Vineet's addiction problems had fuelled the numerous arguments he had been having with his father. As a suspect in the murder case, Ravi is interested to question him:

> Astute policeman that he was, Ravi could figure out that Vineet's responses to a few questions did not ring true. To the question, "Did you know that relations between your father and the other members of the cricket board were strained," Vineet came out with a markedly loud and firm "no". Again, when Ravi asked whether Vineet himself had any dealings with the cricket board, the answer was a vehement "of course not!" (Sundar 2010, p. 90)

The police duo turns to Rao's wife, Vineet's mother, and her responses to their questions confirm that the bad feelings between the father and son were very real. Mrs Rao, however, is more forthcoming with her thoughts on the cricket board:

> I did get the feeling that there were some serious issues between my husband and some members of the board, and that my husband was not acknowledging them. . . . . . . the problem was that he was probably privy to a number of secrets, and they could not let him leave easily. (Sundar 2010, p. 95)

As Sundar weaves together a web of intrigue and mystery around the murders of Rao, Mane and two other murder cases from 2007 – which increasingly seem to be connected – the narrative captures the New India of the noughties through its engagement with advertising, television, media and celebrities. The novel tells of the closing ceremony of the ITL and the fifty thousand-odd spectators. Sundar (2010) writes:

> For over a month, the nation, and half the world, had either watched the tournament "live" or its highlights, and had been as involved in the

league matches as the thirteen players on the ground or the nine sitting in the dugouts with the reserve players.

As for the franchise owners, they too had given up their money-making ventures to be "one with the boys". Not that they didn't expect to make money out of these matches. In fact, many of them were physically present, but mentally plotting how to generate more wealth out of their latest acquisition! (Sundar 2010, p. 217)

Sundar's narrative foregrounds the sense of 'opportunity' produced from the cricket frenzy and that any kind of scandal only enhances the sense of (financial or business) 'opportunity'. She writes: 'Any scandal to do with the cricket board was enough to ensure the highest TRP ratings and all the channels tried to outdo each other in their reporting' (Sundar 2010, p. 168). This media obsession is echoed in the narrative of Basu's *Turbulence* (2010) discussed here in Section 6.1, where political events are followed minute-by-minute by eager media companies who wish to be the first to bring the story to light. Basu carefully renames the media companies in his narrative, referring to one television news station as 'DNNTV' (Basu 2010, p. 84). One of India's biggest news broadcasters launched 'NDTV India' and 'NDTV 24 × 7' in the early 2000s, the former a Hindi language medium news channel and the latter an English language medium channel. Although NDTV exists among competitors, this news channel is an insightful example of post-millennial news reporting, supported by its online presence: www. ndtv.com.

Other internet-based news reporting, such as online newspapers, for example *The Times of India* (TOI), which have comprehensive sports sections, have also impacted the growth and interest in IPL cricket in India. Both satellite – in particular the English medium news channels – and online newspapers have meant that Indians abroad and diaspora Indians can follow news and sport more easily, that is, in terms of an Indian-produced media, and not a US- or UK-mediated news channel. Sundar's description of the media frenzy around the Rao and Mane deaths captures something of the reporting styles seen in post-millennial news channels today, when Sundar (2010) writes:

They carried mainly this news the whole day and speculations were rife as to the fate of the other members of the board. Anyone remotely connected to cricket or politics had become an "expert" on the topic. There were innumerable talk shows, SMS polls, and panel discussions to do with the case – all good fodder for twenty-four-hour news channels. (Sundar 2010, p. 168)

As we move now to explore Chauhan's novel *The Zoya Factor* (2008), similar themes of media attention, celebrity and 'opportunity' in New India will become evident despite the differences in genre and style exhibited in Sundar's and Chauhan's works.

The Zoya Factor (2008)

Zoya Singh Solanki of Chauhan's *The Zoya Factor* (2008) is, until she meets the Indian cricket team, a 27-year-old 'mid-level client-servicing executive in India's largest ad agency' (Chauhan 2008, p. 3). Her meeting with the Indian cricket team changes her life considerably as she becomes the Indian cricket team's lucky charm.

Zoya, Chauhan reveals, was born on the day that India won the World Cup, 25 June 1983, and this, alongside the fact that Zoya once had breakfast with the team in order to gain a 'No Objection Certificate' for an advertising company (and this very 'breakfast with Zoya' resulted in India winning the day's match) translates into Zoya being the team's lucky charm. Nikhil Khoda, the captain of the team, sceptical of Zoya's fortune, is mindful of the propensity India has for all things 'lucky'; he says: 'Ours is a superstitious country and a precedent like this could lead to chaos in the future' (Chauhan 2008, p. 114). Here, Khoda tells the media that their win is down to skill, not to a 'lucky Zoya'; however, as the breakfasts continue and they are all followed by winning games for the Indian team, members of the team become more and more convinced of Zoya's ability to bless their play, resulting in wins for India.

Chauhan (2008) writes of the cricket obsession in India:

> It's a Great Indian Disease, I tell you. Worse than dengue or polio or tuberculosis. They should vaccinate us against it when we're born, I thought gloomily as I queued up behind the long line of Dhaka-bound cricket freaks. One shot at birth, a couple of boosters over the years and you're immune to cricket for life. No heartache, no ulcers, no plunge in productivity during the cricket season and no stupid bets that make you lose money and lead you to commit suicide. (Chauhan 2008, p. 24)

Moreover, when Zoya is quizzed on her general knowledge of the Indian cricket team, her colleague is disappointed to find out that Zoya doesn't even know the name of the captain of the team: 'How can you not know *Khoda*? He's *God*, dude, he's a *King*!' (Chauhan 2008, p. 25). Chauhan comments on how cricket in India permeates Indian lives, depicted as viral in its nature, compared to some of India's most prevalent diseases of polio or dengue fever. Moreover, Chauhan likens the cricket obsession with medical problems associated with stress, reinforcing the individual's fixation with cricket as well as the wider, national fixation with the cricket season as the nation's level of productivity slumps due to the distraction of the cricket being played. Unlike Sundar's novel *The Premier Murder League* (2010), which focuses on the murky world of league cricket and the board that is supposed to regulate it, Chauhan's novel concentrates more on 'young India'. This focus becomes apparent in the worlds of the advertising company and the cricket league celebrity (Bollywood) activity that the novel inhabits. Not only is the cricket team itself young in its composition, the other characters in the novel, namely, Zoya and her colleagues at the advertising company, are also, for the most part, in their late twenties or early thirties. At the beginning of the novel, we meet one such colleague, Neelo Basu, who is described as: 'a lean, mean cadaverous machine, in a SICK MY DUCK tee shirt who lives to smoke joints and download South Indian sleaze off the Net' (Chauhan 2008, p. 21). Neelo is particularly keen on delivering scripts to his boss, Sanks, for potential, televised advertisements:

> ... The dude grins a crooked grin and rides through and then he comes up to this high mountain pass in fucking Ladakh, okay? And these massive boulders roll open magically too. He grins, again, like this happens everyday for him, you know? And then passes this green meadow where these babes are doing yoga, okay? They're really hot, stacked types. Solid mutton-*shutton* happening, in skin tight leotards, okay. And as he approaches them, they do this fucking *mandook aasan*, the *frog position*, okay, basically all hundred of them go up on their hands, raise their butts in the air and spread their legs out, like *fully* man. Then this Hollywood-trailer type voice-over says: "THE WORLD OPENS WIDE FOR THE NERO-TASHA TERMINATOR." (Chauhan 2008, p. 22)

Advertising in India has developed in tandem with the economic growth. As the middle classes have emerged, televisions have become more available (and affordable) and satellite has opened up the vistas for myriad viewing possibilities. Bollywood stars endorse products often with massive advertising campaigns; skin-whitening products, clothes' brands, soft drinks and chewing gum to name only a few, and televisions often play out such advertisements in bars and restaurants in India's cities.

Neelo's advertisement pitch to his boss is designed with a certain audience in mind; an audience grown out of New India. Neelo's script blends elements of Western cinema culture (he makes reference to The Terminator before this excerpt as well as in the name of the 'Nero-Tasha Terminator'), a typical Western advertising scape of a 'sexy fucking highway' (Chauhan 2008, p. 21) – although many of the main highways in India are being redeveloped in cities that are experiencing heightened revenue – and 'babes' in skin tight leotards practising yoga (yoga practice in India is traditionally in loose-fitting, cotton clothes). These images are placed alongside more Indian, *desi* motifs, the mountainous Ladakh region, the *mandook asana* and the motif of the motorbike – the 'Nero-Tasha Terminator', the product that is being advertised here. The motorbike, in particular, talks to contemporary ideas of Indian masculinity, essentially through a subtle, cultural reference to the post-millennial 'Hero Honda' advertising campaign, which has been endorsed by several Bollywood stars. Neelo's pitch also demonstrates that the advertisement looks beyond the boundaries of India as he states that 'the world opens wide for the "Nero-Tasha Terminator", recognition of the global possibilities of Indian products and its trade interests today. Neelo's pitch, however, is not well received by his boss, Sanks: '"It's the Nero-Tasha *Terminator*, you fuck," he spat out balefully. "Not the Nero-Tasha *Fornicator*. When are you going to get your mind out of the gutter?"' (Chauhan 2008, p. 22).

Later on that day, when Neelo is driving Zoya home, he tells Zoya his theory of successful advertising: 'In fact . . . that's the only way to sell *anything*, man! Bikes, televisions, insurance, cold drinks . . . Buy *this*, get laid! Buy *that*, get laid! Buy fucking *anything*, get laid!' (Chauhan 2008, p. 23). Neelo's theory might seem a little zealous given that Bollywood films have only recently screened the more 'intimate scenes', but his idea that 'sex sells' is not completely misplaced in this New India. A reference to a nightclub called 'Bed' in Gurgaon is made in both Chauhan's *The Zoya Factor* (2008) and in Bhagat's *One Night @ The Call Centre* (2008). 'Bed' according to Bhagat or 'The Bed Lounge' according to Chauhan, is described as having a plush interior with 'beds' arranged around the bar-cum-nightclub. Chauhan (2008) writes:

> It really *was* shady. The kind of place where Dawood and Monica would have partied in the good old days. The[y]re were all these huge four-poster beds everywhere, with curtains drawn around them, so you couldn't see what the hell was going on inside. It was very, very dodgy. (Chauhan 2008, p. 117)

Bhagat writes (2008): 'The interior design of Bed was a cross between Star Trek and a debauched king's harem. Ultraviolet bulbs and candles were the only sources of light' (Bhagta 2008, p. 197). And he writes of the flatscreen televisions that accompany the 'beds':

> There were two flat LCD screens in front of our bed, one tuned to MTV, and the other to CNN. A Bollywood item number was being played on MTV, as part of its "Youth Special" program. A girl stripped off successive items of her clothing as the song progressed. The breaking news on CNN was that the US was considering going to war with Iraq again. (Bhagat 2008, p. 199)

As with Neelo's pitch to Sanks, the nightclub that is 'Bed' places (and juxtaposes) the two worlds of India and 'The West' (America, in the case of Bhagat's novel), the 'positioning' in the extract from Bhagat's novel is very real as the two flatscreen televisions sit side-by-side, the two worlds almost existing in one space. Neelo's advertising idea, however, only brings the two worlds together notionally and as Sanks' reaction demonstrates, the worlds struggle to coexist in the same cultural milieu. The two flatscreen televisions of Bhagat's novel depict some of the challenges of New India – when and what to take from one television, when and what to take from the other television. This challenge of 'choice' is also demonstrated in Sundar's novel discussed above in this chapter section, where ideas of 'league' cricket (IPL) are imported from 'outside' (elsewhere), while ideas of 'Indianness' (Bollywood celebrities, film soundtracks, national flags and dhol playing) anchor IPL and the cultural event that it is, to Indians and to New India.

Zoya's own journey in the novel is focused on her growing awareness that she might actually be responsible for the Indian team's successful games. At first, Zoya's presence at the breakfast table is something that she agrees to go along with and her evident lack of general knowledge on cricket and, more strikingly, the Indian cricket team, reinforces the idea that Zoya is being pulled along with little control over the events. As the narrative progresses, more games are won after breakfast with Zoya and on the occasions she doesn't meet the team before their match, they lose their game. The media attention grows as the games are won and this impacts Zoya and her perception of the role she is beginning to play. As Zoya lies ill in her bed in the hotel room, a fever raging, Swami Lingnath Baba is brought to her bedside: 'Clad in three delicious shades of saffron, tinkling gently with various charms and amulets, his hairy halo aglow, Swami Lingnath Baba stood in the doorway, smiling benignly' (Chauhan 2008, p. 360). Zoya is taken aback by the very fact that Swami Lingnath Baba should be in his ashram in Uttar Pradesh, India, and not at her hotel door in Australia; how important is Zoya in this entire game of 'cricket luck'? It is during this visit from the swami that Zoya is confronted with the idea of her God-like status. The swami refers to her as a 'Devi' and reaches into the deep pocket of his saffron sarong choga for some medicine for her.

I looked at him in horrid fascination, fully expecting him to produce some crumpled little paper parcel full of human ash, or dried cow dung, or something. Instead, he pulled out a crisp silver strip of multi-vitamin tablets from his pocket and handed it to me. (Chauhan 2008, p. 361)

As the swami takes his leave, he addresses Zoya: '. . . stay vigilant in your post as the celestial guardian who will lead our team to victory'. And he adds: 'Pressure is building. I see much conflict ahead. Stand strong Devi!' (Chauhan 2008, pp. 361–2). The swami's entreaty invokes images of the strong Hindu Goddess Durga whose immense feminine power sees victory over evil. Durga is a form of Devi and like the swami's entreaty to Zoya suggests, Durga is celestial in her patience, compassion and fearlessness. As we read in Chapter 1 of this volume, Aurobindo's 'Hymn to the Mother: Bandemataram' (1909) invokes similar images of female 'shakti', anchoring the female to *Bharat* and to a particular sense of Indianness.

Zoya, up until this point in the narrative, has dismissed the superstition and urban myth-making about her cricket luck, but the presence of the godman compromises this conviction and she asks the swami if it is indeed true that giving all her luck to the team will mean that she will be left with only bad luck in her personal life. As the relationship, albeit a tumultuous one, between Zoya and Khoda has recently developed, Zoya is keen to know – even from the swami – if her personal life is set to suffer. The swami's answer is grounded in the Hindu philosophy and belief that is befitting of 'Zoya Devi': 'Balance is what keeps the cosmos in motion, Devi' (Chauhan 2008, p. 362).

Troubled by the swami's visit, Zoya turns to the internet to read www. crickindiya.com in order to find out what Indians are saying about her presence in Australia with the team. The comments swing from positive to negative and the positive following is clearly grounded in superstition and worship while the negative comments attack such beliefs and India's potential for corruption in sport (and otherwise):

> "Jogpal Lohia has prepared an army of eunuchs. A hijron ki baraat. They are all useless without this girl. They should all put on bangles and sit at home, rolling chapattis."
>
> . . .
>
> "There is no such thing as co-incidence. Zoyamata ki jai."
>
> . . .
>
> "Very soon Nikhil Khoda will be sacked and this girl – who cannot tell batsman from Batman – will become captain. Wah, wah, mera bhaarat mahaan. It happens only in India!"
> (Chauhan 2008, pp. 375–6)

The comments on the internet include one in particular which talks to some of the themes in this chapter as well as some of the broader themes and challenges of New India already introduced in this book. As Chapter 1 has already cited, Khilnani (1999) writes of the 1990s rebranding of India's Hinduism and how modernity has spawned a novel Hinduism, where holographic gods dangle on well-used keychains and cassettes of devotional *ragas* are played in traffic jams (Khilnani 1999, p. 187). This idea of 'worship' together with the ideas of New India providing a market for all, is embodied in the following internet comment/advertisement for Zoya Devi:

> Aarti of Zoya Devi performed daily every morning and evening. For Zoyadevi amulet, saamagri and autographed photograph visit my website at www.zoyadevikachamatkaariballa.com. All are welcome. (Chauhan 2008, p. 375)

Here, prayer (aarti) is offered for Zoya alongside the more commercialized 'autographed photograph', clearly a counterfeit item, given that Zoya has not entered into any agreement to produce such merchandise. The irony is further suggested by the website's statement: 'All are welcome'.

As the final game of the tournament approaches, Zoya becomes more philosophical about her role as the team's 'lucky charm'. Through the course of the novel, Zoya has held several theoretical positions on her role, moving from disbelief at the suggestion of her 'lucky charm' status, to an acceptance that maybe she does have a 'gift' – after all, she was born on the day that India won the World Cup – to a position somewhere in between the two which embodies confusion and bewilderment. On the eve of the final, Zoya finds some peace of mind in her decision to leave the team to play the game without her presence at the breakfast table:

> If I *was* the Goddess of the Game, born at the very moment of India's greatest cricket victory if my purpose in life was to help them win, if my hand was *supposed* to hover over them in constant benediction, wasn't it part of my job description to keep Indian Cricket from harm? By going back to spoon cornflakes and slimy papaya slices into my face with the team before they played the Final, all I'd end up doing was erode their faith in their own ability.
>
> Even if they won, they would never be sure of the real reason behind the victory. (Chauhan 2008, p. 470)

As the Swami Lingnath Baba had told Zoya: 'Balance is what keeps the cosmos in motion, Devi' (Chauhan 2008, p. 362), and so, in a move towards this idea, Zoya decides that 'balance' might be found in *not* being present and she decides to support the team in her intrinsic belief that they *can* win the game without her. This mediated allocation of support ('benediction') empowers both the players and Zoya herself as, after battling with cultural and societal pressures, Zoya takes charge of her situation and most importantly, is at one with the decision.

4

Young India

4.1 Call centres and corporate lives

The notion of New India is often grounded in a sense of economic growth and prosperity. Such enhanced fiscal activity has meant that India is increasingly a 'global player' in the world's economies and part of this growth is due to its dexterity in BPO activity. BPO activity ranges from call centres, film dubbing, business process analysis, academic journal proofing and editing, to IT support for some of the world's biggest brands and corporations. According to Radhakrishnan (2011):

> The economic and social transformations of the 1990s and beyond have fuelled new kinds of job opportunities for an educated, English-speaking group of mostly urban Indians . . . . Talented urban Indians with the appropriate technical training can today enter the IT industry and realistically hope to advance far enough in their firms to travel far and wide. (Radhakrishnan 2011, p. 5)

A growing body of new writing explores these new lives of New India, of call centre existence, IT support and corporate living. The narratives are namely about young Indian lives, English speaking and often 'immigrants' to an urban centre. Hasan's novel *Neti Neti: Not This, Not This* (2009) discussed in Chapter 2 is such a narrative. Set against the urbanscape of Bangalore, the narrative follows the life of Sophie Das, an 'immigrant worker' from Shillong in north-east India, and her troop of friends, all of whom are thirty-something. Similar interests can be seen in other Indian fiction, such as the Bengali language novel *Sikandar* (2011), which charts the lives of ten players over 68 days in a reality show called 'Sikandar' where the ten contestants are locked inside a house 'Jatugriha' all hoping to win the title of 'The Sikandar of Bengal'. As Section 3.2 has already demonstrated, and Section 4.2 will also demonstrate, the role and impact of television on Indian society – cricket games, reality shows, Western sitcoms and music videos (such as those of MTV) – particularly since the turn of the millennium is significant. Television, satellite and the film industry have all helped shape the senses of Indian youth culture today.

Call Me Dan (2010)

Trivedi's *Call Me Dan* (2010) captures the call centre lifestyle so often cited as indicative of New India. The protagonist's life is in sync with UK and USA time zones, thus asleep through most of India's working hours, impacting on his family life – his parents and sister – while equipping him well for long night-hours spent in the bars and clubs of Mumbai when not at work. The narrative is peppered with difficult moments with his parents; in the following extract, his father reprimands him for his 'call centre lifestyle':

> Whole day you're out. Whole night you're out. You think I don't know what goonda giri you're doing? I told you, from the start I told you when he was born, he will turn out to be like your brother. (Trivedi 2010, p. 38)
>
> ['goonda giri' a type of hooliganism, street-based involving petty crime and harassment, often involves types of money extortion]

The protagonist is 'Dan' at work, and 'Gautam' at home, brother to Pooja and son of Gujarati, Ahmedabadi parents who moved to Mumbai before he was born to make a better life. Gautam is in a relationship with Michelle and has been for the past 4 years. Gautam is Hindu and Michelle is Christian (Catholic). Throughout two-thirds of the narrative, Michelle is pushing for Gautam to commit, that is, to marry her:

> ". . . I'm telling you it's time we made a decision about moving on. You can't spend the rest of your life living with your parents. I can't spend the rest of my life living with mine. I want to live with you. Do you want to live with me?"
>
> "Just like that?" The morals of the middle class, occasionally misplaced, never quite absent.
>
> "No. We have to get married first. What the hell do you think I meant?" Middle class and Catholic.
>
> " Let's talk about it."
>
> "We are talking about it."
>
> "I mean let's think about it."
>
> "I have been thinking about it."
>
> "I meant me."
>
> "What the hell have you been doing for four years? You haven't been thinking about it too?" Bloody men.
>
> "Of course I have." You bring it up once a month.
>
> "What did you say?" Did he really say that last bit aloud? (Trivedi 2010, p. 43)

Throughout the book, Trivedi plays with the outer and inner voices of Gautam's character and, at times, Michelle's outer and inner voices are part of the narrative too. In the case of Gautam, these often contradictory statements of his outward self and his inner self further confuse his identity. Indeed, 'identity' in this novel, set in emerging India is central. The title of the novel *Call Me Dan* sits against the book's front cover image of a man's face. One half is 'Dan' with eye sparkling, snappy shirt collar, spiky, well-gelled hair and slightly more light-skinned than the other half of the face which is 'Gautam' with darker skin, flat 'parted' hairline and a less fashioned shirt – this image sets the question of identity, and the question of two worlds from the beginning.

The worlds of 'Dan' and 'Gautam' are explored, extended and shaped as the book unfolds. Gautam also negotiates generational worlds – the young, youth-filled 'call centre' world versus the world of his home, his parents and their steady lives, his father having worked for a 'reliable' Swedish firm for as long as Gautam can remember. In addition, Gautam negotiates the world of 'the Michelle relationship', a relationship started just before his work at the call centre began. Since then, his life has changed but their relationship has not developed accordingly. As the novel develops, it becomes increasingly difficult for 'Gautam' particularly in his most 'Dan' moments to hold on to the relationship that he has with Michelle. Part of his transformation (or confusion, depending on how this the novel is read) is the character 'Cassandra' or 'Sondra' as she calls herself, an American working at the call centre and living with two other girls in a flat in Juhu. Meeting often at the coffee machine in the call centre, Dan arranges a date, to which Sondra says:

"You got yourself a deal, Danny boy"
"This weekend?"
"This weekend."
She smiles. He smiles. He has five days in which to get Michelle and her friends to another country. He can do it. He can do anything. He is Daniel. His friends can call him Danny. (Trivedi 2010, p. 91)

So here we see that Gautam, having chosen the name 'Daniel' once appointed at the call centre (to use with the UK and USA clients on the phone) adopts the name more widely, using it here as his *name* with the other employees at the call centre. We learn later in the novel about the choice of the name behind 'Daniel' as Michelle asks Gautam:

"Why did you call yourself Daniel? Why not John or Jack or Jim?"
"It was your favourite song."
"What?"
"Elton John. *Daniel*. It was your favourite song." (Trivedi 2010, p. 262)

From Daniel, it becomes 'Dan' and finally we see in the extract above 'Danny' once Sondra makes the reference to 'Danny Boy', and it is with each name change that Gautam seems to change just a little bit more and his confidence (and excitement) in this new life he is experiencing, increases. This is not to say that Gautam is 'lost' in his existence in New India, he is very aware of the changes, particularly the economic ones that India has experienced, especially since he is now living them and benefiting from such. Trivedi gives over a page to Gautam as he tries to explain to Sondra what the last 40 years in India have meant:

> For him [Gautam] the change is economic, beginning a life in the scarcity of the '70s and leapfrogging to the surfeit of choice he now has, not as much as Sondra is used to in her Californian town, but choices no generation before his has had, not just in what he can buy, but in how he can earn it. . . . Gautam had lost two jobs before he was thirty, testament not to turbulence, but perhaps to the fact that there are jobs to lose. (Trivedi 2010, p. 147)

To read Gautam as a misunderstood, misplaced young Indian, chasing an American girl at work and unconsciously caught up in all New India has to offer would be a misreading of this work. At the end of the novel, Gautam loses Michelle, his parents (they move back to Ahmedabad), his sister Gopi (she marries) and even Sondra, as she returns to America; however, Gautam is not without, he has his life and his place in New India, earning good money at the call centre (he is promoted), meeting new girls at the bar he frequents and benefiting from the flat his parents have left him in charge of in Mumbai. All in all, Gautam's future looks bright and full of opportunity, but in ways that previous generations (his parents included) have not ever known. Therefore, to read 'Gautam' as 'old India' and 'Dan' as New India would dilute this narrative considerably, rather the novel, its series of identities and the fluidity of Gautam's life in particular, is more in line with how both 'Dan' and 'Gautam' might be best considered as being part of New India.

One Night @ The Call Centre (2008)

As with Trivedi's novel, Bhagat also explores the life of the call centre in *One Night @ The Call Centre* (2008), first published in 2005. Here too, the protagonist is assigned a call centre name; 'Sam Marcy' at work and 'Shyam Mehra' otherwise. We read early on of his daily transformation:

> There was no hot water in the kitchen, and my face froze as I washed it with cold water. Winter in Delhi is a bitch. I brushed my teeth and used the steel plates as a mirror to comb my hair. Shyam had turned into Sam and Sam's day had just begun. (Bhagat 2008, p. 15)

Shyam, although not officially recognized as being so, is the team manager of six employees, the 'Western Appliances Strategic Group' (WASG) and they work in a bay. They deal with customers of home appliances and specialize in 'troublesome and painful customers' (Bhagat 2008, p. 37) They are: Shyam, Military Uncle, Radhika, Esha, Vroom and Priyanka. Like Shyam, they all, with the exception of Military Uncle as he does not work on the phones, hold call centre names. Radhika Jha becomes 'Regina Jones', Esha Singh becomes 'Eliza Singer' and Vroom – Varun Malhotra, obsessed by anything on wheels – becomes 'Victor Mell'. They work for *Connexions*, a call centre based in the burgeoning business district of Gurgaon near New Delhi and all travel together in a *Qualis* with their driver to the call centre. At work, the characters slip between identities:

> I looked around; people were busy with calls. Radhika helped someone defrost her fridge; Esha assisted a customer in unpacking a dishwasher. Everyone was speaking with an American accent and sounded different from how they had in the Qualis. (Bhagat 2008, p. 40)

In her book *Appropriately Indian* (2011), Radhakrishnan writes of the importance of learning 'culture' for IT professionals when she states:

> In corporate hallways and cross-cultural training sessions, culture becomes something that can be apprehended and absorbed, something transferable and strategically deployable. Corporations are invested in fostering a "global work culture" because it offers the promise of better efficiency and productivity, which improves their bottom line. (Radhakrishnan 2011, p. 55)

The WASG team's boss is called Mr Bakshi and he is not well liked, he speaks call centre jargon-laden English, is generally lazy and addresses the call centre employees as 'agents' and always by their non-Indian, call centre names. During the course of the night at the call centre, 'Bakshi' emails a copy of the recently authored (by Shyam and Vroom) 'guidance manual' over to Boston, USA, for perusal and ratification; Bakshi 'forgets' to copy in Shyam and Vroom. On their insistence, Bakshi forwards the email over to them and Vroom, already suspicious of Bakshi's character, opens the attachment of the guidance manual to find that Bakshi has replaced their two names as authors of the document, with his own name. Vroom is livid and Shyam is further dismayed with his life and prospects at the call centre. Other dramas ensue; Vroom pretends to be a radio jockey and calls Radhika's husband in Kolkata to offer him the chance to send a bunch of red roses to someone special. Radhika's name is not the name he gives, rather he chooses to send the flowers to 'his girlfriend', Payal (Bhagat 2008, p. 157). Esha is found in the conference room by Shyam, box cutter in hand, blood dripping from her leg. Shyam, unsure of how to handle the situation, finds that Esha has been self-harming for some time, tortured by her failing modelling career and a recent incident in which she agreed to sleep with someone in order to win a modelling contract. When Shyam attempts to stop Esha from cutting herself further, with warnings of potential gangrene or tetanus, Esha says:

> This is tame. I'll tell you what is dangerous. Your own fucked up brain, the delusional voice in you that says you have it in you to become a model. (Bhagat 2008, p. 152)

The group's troubles are further developed through the ongoing tension between Shyam and Priyanka who were together as a couple for some years. As with Trivedi's *Call Me Dan*, Bhagat's narrative also explores the dynamics of a couple who are 'together' yet 'apart'. Bhagat's novel also involves the family in the relationship, with Priyanka's mother being vehemently against Shyam ('Are you still talking to that useless call centre chap, what is his name . . . Shyam') (Bhagat 2008, p. 133), and we are told through a series of 'My Past Dates with Priyanka' (Bhagat 2008, pp. 44, 81, 96, 136, 171) of the issues their relationship faced. The unresolved issues – and the fact that they are basically still in love with each other – are brought to the fore as Priyanka's mother finds a match for her daughter and begins to arrange the wedding. Priyanka, in principal, is in agreement and 'Ganesh' a Microsoft employee, based in the US seems quite a catch given his NRI (see Glossary) status, and his house with a pool in a nice area of Seattle.

The night at the call centre is not only problematic with people issues, it is also problematic technically as the phone lines go down and the 'IT guys' have difficulty in repairing them. The tension builds until around 3 a.m. when Vroom suggests that he 'borrow' the *Qualis* and they go for a drink at a nearby bar called 'Bed' in Gurgaon. Shyam, annoyed by Bakshi and his latest dirty trick over the guidance manual, agrees that they should take a break. On the way back from 'Bed', Vroom driving and slightly drunk, attempts a short cut to the call centre as they are running late (and shouldn't really have left the call centre at all). However, in taking the short cut, the *Qualis* slides off the road and into a construction site where the car precariously lands on some rods used for setting the foundations of the new buildings. The car hangs there in limbo, no one daring to move for fear the car will fall off and plunge them all to their deaths. They check their phones – no one has a signal – and just as they are wondering how they will ever get out of this mess, Shyam's phone rings. It is God calling. What happens then inside the *Qualis*, is a conversation which involves each of the team members, probing in turn, their situations, fears and anxieties. But there is one question God asks them all:

> "Let me ask you a question. How many phone calls do you take everyday?" God said.
> "A hundred, on busy days two hundred," Vroom said.

"Okay. Now do you know which is the most important call in the world?"

"No," Vroom said. Everyone else shook their heads.

"The inner call," God said.

"The inner call?" everyone said in unison.

"Yes, the little voice inside that wants to talk to you. But you can only hear it when you are at peace – and then too it is hard to hear it. Because in modern life, the networks are too busy. The voice tells you what you really want. Do you know what I am talking about?" (Bhagat 2008, p. 217)

In order for the *Qualis* to be saved from a very possible death, each member of the team promises to God (and to themselves) to alter the situation that they are facing which is currently making them unhappy. Vroom vows to leave the call centre in order to build a more satisfied life and to leave his anti-American sentiments in the WASG bay; Priyanka promises to choose a life (and a life partner) for herself and not for her mother; Military Uncle promises to build bridges with his estranged family in order to be part of his grandson's life again; Radhika vows to leave her cheating husband, Esha, to leave her dreams of modelling in an attempt to find a more fulfilling career; and finally, Shyam, who also decides to leave the call centre, to become more self- assured and to become worthy of a partner like Priyanka.

Interestingly, all the characters' aspirations mean that they must move on from the call centre job and lifestyle they are currently involved in, the call centre becomes transitory, an income but not a career, a place to take stock and from which to move on. The call centre becomes a place of limbo, mirrored in the event at the construction site. The near-death experience with the *Qualis* (which they manage to manoeuvre out of the construction site – with God's help) is the catalyst the characters need to move on with their lives. In this sense, 'the call centre' might be read as a metaphor for New India on several levels. The call centres that have sprung up around India, especially in New Delhi, Mumbai and Bangalore, are a motif of India's role in global business and communications. Call centres and BPO activity, as we read of in Hasan's *Neti Neti* (2009) in Section 2.1, underpin business activity in the UK, US and other parts of the world. In this sense, there is a reliance on New India and its labour market. If it is that India continues to grow, it might be that 'the call centre' becomes more and more of a transitory occupation and that BPOs might become less-valued employment as India moves to a stronger, more self-reliant and self-servicing economy. This relationship between the service provider (India) and its customers is a tension that weighs heavily on Vroom. Out of all the characters in Bhagat's novel, Vroom struggles the most with the relationship that the call centre has with America. Shyam intervenes at various parts of the story to warn Vroom not to 'act like a hero' as Vroom's temper is quick and petty violence comes easily (he breaks myriad pens and a computer screen in one scene), his source of frustration is usually Americans and America:

> "Americans are sick," Vroom said, as he pointed to a US politician who had spoken out in support of the war. "Look at him. He would nuke the world if he could have his way."
> "No, not the whole world. I don't think they'd blow up China," Priyanka said, sounding high. "They need the cheap labor."
> "Then I guess they won't blow up Gurgaon either. They need the call centers," Radhika said.
> "So we are safe," Esha said, "that's good. Welcome to Gurgaon, the safest city on earth." (Bhagat 2008, p. 199)

Vroom is almost politicized over the matter of the call centres 'serving' the West. He goes on to say how he would be ready to commit to work which resulted in road building, power plants and airports and yet states:

> But the government doesn't believe in doing any real work, so they allow these BPOs to be opened and think they have taken care of the youth. Just as this stupid MTV thinks showing a demented chick do a dance in her underwear will make the program a youth special. Do you think they really care? (Bhagat 2008, p. 201)

Vroom also takes issue with the advertisement of a cola company that uses a Bollywood actress to sell the product:

> "You see her?" Vroom said, pointing to the actress.
> I nodded.
> "There she is, looking at us like she is our best friend. Do you think she cares for us?"
> "I don't know. She is a youth icon man," I shrugged my shoulders.
> "Yes, youth icon. This airhead chick is supposed to be our role model. Like she knows a fuck about life and gives a fuck about us. All she cares about is cash. She doesn't care about you or me. She just wants you to buy this black piss," Vroom said, pointing to the cola bottle. (Bhagat 2008, p. 204)

Vroom's unrest with India's governance is reminiscent of the themes explored in Rakeysh Omprakash Mehra's 'youth film' *Rang De Basanti* (2006). This film title has been translated as *Colour of Saffron*, saffron being a colour associated with the idea of India as a nation – the colour features in the flag – but also a colour associated with Hindu nationalism (the Saffron Brigade). (Section 6.1 mentions another of Mehra's socially minded films: *Delhi 6* (2009), a film that engages with India's religious communities in Delhi). Although a different narrative from Bhagat's *One Night @ The Call Centre*, *Rang De Basanti*'s nexus of questioning youth and revolution is echoed in Bhagat's novel, manifested mainly in the character of Vroom. The film impacted India's youth by instigating debates around the idea of 'citizenship', political responsibility and social awakening. As an example, *Rang De Basanti* (2006) includes a candlelight vigil at India Gate in New Delhi as part of its story, and this idea of a vigil was re-enacted in New Delhi over a high profile murder investigation – the Jessica Lal case – as a sign of civil protest (The Bollywood film *No one Killed Jessica* was based on this true story, released in 2011). Furthermore, the Jessica Lal case rallied the middle classes into public expressions of outrage. Varma (2007) describes this response when he writes: 'the middle class – perhaps for the first time in such an intense and pervasive manner – gave public expression to its outrage' (Varma 2007, p. xxix). The middle-class response was galvanized through SMS messaging in response to public polls, set up by the news channels and media.

The media sometimes uses the phrase 'RDB effect' (Rang De Basanti effect) to describe youth-orientated civil uprising. In the closing scenes of Bhagat's *One Night @ The Call Centre* (2008), Vroom instigates a type of call centre revolution against America, an act that might be described as being 'RDB' orientated. The plot that Vroom designs is one which results in the call centre remaining open (it had been facing possible closure) by 'capitalizing on Americans being the biggest cowards on the planet' (Bhagat 2008, p. 244). Vroom's 'Operation Yankee Fear' plays on America's weakness – that their nation is at risk from 'evil forces' (Bhagat 2008, p. 244) which will enter as a virus into everyone's computer. According to Vroom, all the Americans need to do – to be safe – is to phone *Connexions* every 6 hours. Vroom writes a new phone script for the 'agents':

Tell them [the Americans] you can save them from this virus as a) you are from India, and all Indians are good at computers b) India has faced terrorism for years and c) they are valued clients and you believe in customer service. (Bhagat 2008, p. 245)

Bhagat's novel, although interested in the personal lives, hopes and dreams of the WASG team, essentially questions the role of India as a service-provider economy in today's world. In politicizing the day-to-day activity of the seemingly banale goings-on of the call centre, managed by everyday people with their own problems and issues, the novel raises questions about globalization and the very 'shared' world that we live in.

The Incredible Adventures of Robin 'Einstein' Varghese (2010)

The 'Dork' series, published by Penguin India and authored by Sidin Vadukut, chart the life adventures of Robin 'Einstein' Varghese. The first book is entitled: *The Incredible Adventures of Robin 'Einstein' Varghese*

(2010) and the second book is entitled *God Save the Dork* (2011), where Robin 'Einstein' Varghese is 'dispatched' to London to manage the Lederman account.

The Incredible Adventures of Robin 'Einstein' Varghese (2010) is prefaced by an 'Author's Note' in which Vadukut reveals how Robert 'Einstein' Varghese's life adventures came to be recorded in the novel. Vadukut, in moving into a new apartment in Delhi, discovers an old Domino's Pizza box wedged under the kitchen sink near a mouldy drainpipe. In the pizza box, seven CDs were found; three of them with porn on them, one CD on 'ball bearings', another CD full of Wikipedia pages and one CD with hundreds of pictures of dogs downloaded from the internet. The seventh CD had three years of diary entries on it, typed and saved as MS Word Files. The 'Author's Note' to *The Incredible Adventures of Robin 'Einstein' Varghese* (2010) goes on to say how Vadukut, struggling for ideas for his new book, took the diary entries into the Penguin India office, and although the staff at Penguin India had been sceptical of Vadukut's proposals previously, he exclaims 'they instantly knew we had a winner with the diaries on CD no. 7' (Vadukut 2010, p. 4).

Vadukut's dry humour, which runs throughout this novel, is framed by his note to the 'real' Varghese (which also appears in the 'Author's Note'):

> Varghese, I hope you enjoy this book as much as I enjoyed cutting and pasting the text and changing the font to Georgia (Comic Sans? Really?) Also Varghese, remember that a good book is seldom about the royalties or the rights to the story, but about the story itself. The joy of storytelling is what is paramount. (Vadukut 2010, p. 4)

The novel is arranged as a diary, meaning that the text appears as a series of date and time entries running from April 2006 to January 2007 (Vadukut's second novel *God Save the Dork* (2011) is also a series of diary entries, found on a USB stick, discovered in a conference room by a co-worker of Robin and sent to the author, Sidin Vadukut).

The diary opens with Varghese's celebration of securing a job as a 'Business Process Analyst – Trainee' at Dufresne Partners. Varghese's arch nemesis is Rahul Gupta and the diary entries frequently make reference to him. As Varghese sent out his resume to consulting firms and investment banks, Rahul Gupta's exact words (we are told in Varghese's diary) were: 'Einstein, you are a complete idiot'. Varghese invokes this memory, writing on 2 April 2006 at 4 p.m.:

> IN YOUR FACE, RAHUL GUPTA! PODA PATTI
>   Bastard. Just because you topped the batch does NOT mean you can screw around with Einstein.
>   Phew. Wow. I need to hold my breath. This is a big moment – my first job. And that too a Day Zero job. Wow. (Vadukut 2010, p. 9)

The novel follows Varghese's time at Dufresne Partners, his inability and lack of skills at work, his accommodation nightmares in Mumbai and his love life, which is mainly a hypothetical activity. The surname 'Varghese' is known within India to be a Keralite name and, as 'Robin Varghese', we understand that the protagonist is most likely Malayali Christian. The diary entry above, the first entry we read in the novel, includes Malayalam, the derogatory phrase 'poda patti' (Get away, dog!), thereby confirming the idea that the protagonist is Keralite.

As Robin Varghese sits waiting to be interviewed by J. P. Morgan, he is given a folder of documents in preparation, his name is printed in bold letters across the top of each page: ROBIN WERE GEESE. His surname, spelt phonetically, further ridicules a character who has a tendency to ridicule himself through his 'mishaps'. As Robin waits to be interviewed (several firms are interested in interviewing him), he realizes that his hair is in the style of 'a reverse Mohawk' (Vadukut 2010, p. 11). Robin quickly takes a cup of water from the water cooler and struggling to tip water onto his hair to 'remould' it, he asks a 'somewhat, skinny girl in a suit' (Vadukut 2010, p. 11) to pour the water over his hair. She obliges although she is clearly taken aback by his request. Robin writes in his diary: 'I thanked her profusely but she walked away without a word. I think I felt a certain spark of chemistry' (Vadukut 2010, p. 12). As Robin Varghese is invited in to be interviewed for a job at J. P. Morgan, his eyes fall on a particular member of the panel – the 'somewhat, skinny girl in a suit' (11) whom he requested help pour water on to his hair a little earlier. Vadukut (2010) writes:

> And at that moment I knew that my immediate future as a young management professional would probably not involve toiling in the venerable corridors of JP Morgan and earning obscenely large salaries in a foreign country. (Vadukut 2010, p. 12)

Varghese's Indianness is explored at various points in the novel. Varghese is careful not to accentuate his Malayali provenance. During a meeting at Dufresne Partners, 'Jenson Joseph – IIM-B – Guruvayoor' asks Varghese what Vineet is doing in the conference room, talking with one of the bosses. He addresses Varghese in Malayalam. Robin writes in his diary of the incident:

> Do not bond with people on the basis of state of language. That is one of my mottoes. Such socializing is an evil that invariably leads to heartburn and complications later.
>
> So I replied, in chaste English as the Queen speaks it herself, that Vineet was probably networking with the suits or knew them from before. Perhaps from Jaipur. Jenson immediately nodded his head in the way that a lot of uncultured Malayalis do. His eyes were shut and he had a stupid grin-like look on his face as he bobbed his head from side to side. (Vadukut 2010, p. 52)

Varghese's refusal to communicate with Jenson Joseph in Malayalam is demonstrative of his desire to be seen as an English-medium, corporate and worldly business process analyst. Furthermore, Varghese sees the act of speaking in Malayalam (and socializing with Malayalis) as stressful (it leads to heartburn) and the play on words 'invariably leads to complications later' (this surgical lexical field creates a serious, life-threatening aspect to the socializing) demonstrates that Varghese is adamantly against any type of interaction in Malayalam with Malayalis.

Varghese further demonstrates his corporate worldliness by referring to the senior managers in the conference room as 'the suits'. This metonymy, not only part of corporate jargon, also distances Varghese from the bosses, in both his position in the corporate food chain and also in terms of his attitudes towards them. Varghese, due to his corporate 'mishaps', is not well regarded by the senior managers and thus his distance from them is further suggested in his use of the term, 'the suits', the metonymy resulting in a depersonalization of the individuals who make up the senior management team.

Varghese's insistence on the use of not only English but also 'chaste English as the Queen speaks it herself' creates a distance between Varghese and Jenson. This language choice, to respond to Jenson in English instead of Malayalam and Varghese's dislike of Jenson's 'uncultured' manner in which he nods his head, presents Varghese as an Indian who wishes to be seen as an equal (stripped of all regional and religious connections) within the (lower ranks of the) corporate world of a business process analyst. Later in the novel, Varghese, having caused significant chaos at an important meeting, resulting, ironically, in the receiving party thinking that Varghese is the leader of the project being presented, is approached by a general manager of a steel plant in Tamil Nadu. Praising Varghese for his leadership on the project, as it proves impossible to convince the general manager that he is not the leader at all, Varghese's diary documents what the general manager said to him:

> "... Besides we are both Malayalis. Why should we have secrets between us?"
>
> His name was V. J. Babykutty and, as clichéd as it sounds, he asked me where I was from in Kerala and tried to see if we were related to each other in any way.
>
> Turns out Babykutty's brother used to work in the Kanjany branch of the South Indian Bank at the same time that Thomas Uncle's son's wife's cousin worked in the post office next door. Both of them, apparently, had once gone on a wildcat labour strike together in 1963 and spent a few hours together in the Kanjany police station. (Vadukut 2010, p. 104)

Unlike Varghese's reluctance to know Jenson Joseph, V. J. Babykutty is much more successful in bonding with Varghese as 'a Malayali'. The connection that is made between Babykutty's family and Varghese's family is preposterous in its tenuous and unconvincing line of connection. The connection is not even a bloodline, but rather a coincidental, accidental meeting of two people who work on the same road. The 'connection', however, is verified by Varghese's father on the phone that night and this endorsement means that the two Malayalis are now associated. Moreover, Babykutty suggests that there should be no secrets between them, rendering their connection to each other deeper, and in a sense 'tribal' as Babykutty accentuates their Malayli provenance. After exchanging mobile numbers, Babykutty sends Varghese a spiritual and motivational SMS, Varghese writes in his diary:

13 August 2006
8.25 a.m.

Quick entry to tell you that Babykutty just forwarded an SMS to me. It is a little poem that asks me to thank Jesus Christ for the gift of this morning. And it ends with the words: "Till tomorrow . . . praise the Lord".
    I think he is going to send me motivational messages every day.
    Fuck. (Vadukut 2010, p. 106)

Varghese is as careful with his religious identity as he is with his regional Malayali identity, in that he does not reveal it to anyone at work. When looking for accommodation in Mumbai, Varghese is approached by Bansal who offers to help him find a place to live. Varghese writes in his diary:

He [Bansal] told me there was a super semi-furnished apartment near the Don Bosco Church that was perfect for me because I was a Christian. I told him in no uncertain terms that I did not want to use my religion to get a place to live. He said that I would get a least a thirty percent discount on the rent from the landlord if I told them I was Christian.
    I told him that I was cool with it. I will get to see the flat tomorrow evening. I will wear my big brown crucifix just to be sure. (Vadukut 2010, p. 61)

Varghese demonstrates his dichotomous relationship both as an Indian in the corporate world and as the Indian that he is, in terms of religion and regional identity, Malayali, Christian.

Vadukut's novel is representative of New India on several levels. The corporate world of the business process analyst that Varghese inhabits is a strong motif of New India as we have seen above in the call centre narratives of Trivedi and Bhagat and Sophie Das in Hasan's *Neti Neti*. Robin 'Einstein' Varghese is a graduate of Ahmedabad Institute as we learn from his diary entry of 5 April, 5 p.m., and that his mother had insisted he should go to Kozhikode (Kerala) and not Ahmedabad 'with all those modern north Indian boys and girls' (Vadukut 2010, p. 31). The 'institutes' referred to here are the Indian Institutes of Technology (IITs – see Glossary) and later, the Indian Institutes of Management (IIMs). The former, the IITs, followed the physicist Homi Bhabha's lead of the Tata Institute of Fundamental Research and the Atomic Energy Commission, mandated to run India's nuclear power plants and the new engineering schools (IITs) were started around the mid 1950s–1960s by Nehru and supported by Bhabha. Both men 'were determined to lessen India's dependence on the West for scientific materials and know-how' (Guha 2011, p. 216). The confluence of the economic opportunities of New India and a generation of IIT and IIM graduates has hugely contributed to the growth and employment scene in post-millennial India and, interestingly, many of the authors of post-millennial fiction in English are themselves, IIT/IIM graduates (Bhagat, Vadukut, Kaul, Uttam, Vaidya, P. S. Basu, Raheja as examples). *The Incredible Adventures of Robin 'Einstein' Varghese* (2010), in this sense, is a marker of modern-day India, its IITs/IIMs, young India and its student body at these institutions. Varghese's life on graduating from Ahmedabad is, therefore, also reminiscent of today's situation within India as many young Indians interview for jobs as business process analysts for multinational firms such as J. P. Morgan, Goldman Sachs and McKinsey & Co. As Varghese waits to be interviewed by Goldman Sachs, he is informed that the company has shortlisted four people already and will not be interviewing further. Varghese writes in his diary:

> I was devastated.
> No BlackBerry. No bonus. No foreign posting. No nothing.
> The world spun around me. My heart dropped to my stomach. Where it stopped beating altogether. Remember that look on that English fellow's face when Aamir Khan hits that last ball in *Lagaan*?
> I felt just like that. (Vadukut 2010, p. 25)

The disappointment expressed here by Varghese lies in the fact that he will miss out on the 'advantages' of a Goldman Sachs job. These advantages are ubiquitous – a BlackBerry phone, a monetary bonus and the opportunity to work abroad in a Goldman Sachs office – and therefore, appealing to anyone wishing to work for the multinational, interviewing for the post anywhere in the world. This pan-business-analyst-identity further de-Indianizes the protagonist Varghese, something he already fosters in his day-to-day working life as we have read in the examples above.

Varghese, like Trivedi's 'Dan' and Bhagat's 'Vroom' is involved in New India's corporate and business analyst scene, but the humour in Vadukut's narrative and the many mishaps of Varghese's employment at Dufrense offers a less-politicized engagement with India's position as a service provider. Curiously though, Vadukut's novel highlights some of the more compromising and ridiculous activities of the business analyst scene, rendering the commitment to globalization and to shared, global business partnerships as somewhat vacuous and insincere.

4.2 MSM

In his comprehensive ethnographic study, *Gay Bombay: Globalization, Love and (Be)longing in Contemporary India*, Parmesh Shahani writes that he is:

> studying gay men in this book and not lesbians, bisexuals, the transgender, *kothis*, *hijras* and the rest of the spectrum of sexual minorities in India. These groups are quite stratified – there is little interaction between them and each of them has an entirely different ethos. (Shahani 2008, p. 30)

Equally, Bhaskaran (2004) writes of the numerous classifications and terms used for the 'spectrum of sexual minorities in India' about which Shahani writes above. Bhaskaran refers to the contemporary usage of the terms: 'men who have sex with men' (MSM) and 'women who have sex with women' (WSW) as well as the term *khush* for WSW, noting that this latter term, alongside the term 'queer' might not be identifiable (politically) for some WSW. Bhaskaran (2004) reminds us that the term MSM 'arose within the sexual health NGO movement of the early 1990s [and] is meant to be a "more culturally appropriate" term for same-sex sexual interaction and desire' (Bhaskaran 2004, p. 98). Shahani (2008), in the extract above, speaks of the sexual minority *kothi* and Bhaskaran (2004) defines *kothis* as 'anatomical men who are effeminate, who generally are defined by and desire the "passive" role of being the one who is penetrated, who do "the women's work", and who identify with women' (Bhaskaran 2004, p. 99). According to Bhaskaran, *kothis*, therefore, do not identify as 'gay' but rather as *kothis*, and are often involved in the commercial sex industry. Interestingly, Bhaskaran writes that *kothi* partners are called *panthis* and are 'anotomical men who understand themselves as real men, and who desire the "active" sexual role of penetrator' (Bhaskaran 2004, p. 99). Furthermore, there are *chhakkas* 'who both penetrate and are penetrated – and are scornfully viewed by some MSMs as inauthentic to their social/sexual roles' (Bhaskaran 2004, p. 99). The character of 'Sanj' or 'Sanjana' in Smita Jain's *Piggies on the Railway* (2010) discussed in Chapter 5 (Section 5.1) might be described as *chhakka*, although Jain does not reveal a lot of detail about the character's sexual activities. The characters of 'Ric and Nic' in Kala's chick lit novel *Almost Single* (2007) – discussed above in Section 3.1 – would be described as MSM, as example.

It is apparent that India's notions of gender and sexuality might be better thought of in terms of sexual *behaviours* rather than more static, inflexible, assigned sexual identities, such as we might find in certain other parts of the world, places where sexual identity terms such as 'gay', 'lesbian', 'bisexual' and 'straight' might be employed. Gopalan (in Bhaskaran 2004) suggests that the term 'gay' and an idea of 'gay identity' in India does not really exist. She suggests that 'identity is a sort of a luxury that doesn't extend beyond the educated upper-classes. The majority of men who have sex with men don't see themselves as gay or even homosexuals' (Bhaskaran 2004, p. 100). One of the two novels discussed below is Joseph's *Saraswati Park* (2010) and this novel includes a character – Narayan – whose sexual activities with the protagonist, Ashish, might exemplify Gopalan's definition above, or in a different framework of sexual identities, Narayan might be described as 'bisexual'. New India, with its increase in media, advertising, and the availability of internet, television and satellite viewing has meant that 'Western' notions of gay identity have permeated contemporary Indian culture and society. Hoshang Merchant, 'a male homosexual, Parsi by religion, Christian by education, Hindu by culture and Sufi by persuasion' (Merchant 1999, p. xvii), is keenly aware of the cultural configurations of homosexuality in both 'The East' (read 'India') and 'The West', having lived in both. Moreover, Merchant identifies the issues with both cultural spheres, the complex issues of 'sexuality' and its many manifestations within an Indian context and the presentation of male homosexuality, in particular through Western cultural configurations. Merchant (1999) holds the 'MTV culture' responsible for false projections of homosexual identities when he writes:

> . . . it [the MTV culture] has projected the West's gay sub-culture in its worst light by highlighting its lunatic fringe as if it were mainstream. Your baker, butcher, banker, bus conductor, neighbour or brother could all be very ordinary and also very gay. (Merchant 1999, p. xiv)

Merchant (1999) suggests that the Eastern (non-Islamic) complexities of male homosexuality are, in some senses, reflective of the polymorphous nature of certain religious ideas:

> The oriental male like the oriental gods is polymorphous perverse. Sexuality in the East has always been a continuum rather than a category. There are a variety of gods in the non-Islamic East and it is nothing but arrogance in this world to say there is only one god or to say there is only one sexual play. (Merchant 1999, p. xvii)

Merchant goes on to highlight relationships from the Hindu epics in which same-sex associations (and activities) are present; Merchant reminds us of the god-child 'Lord Ayyappa', product of the coupling of the male gods Vishnu and Shiva, the 'brother-love' of Laxmana for Rama and the devotion of Hanuman for Rama. Merchant also cites episodes of 'yaraana' (see Glossary) in Bollywood such as the Amitabh-Dharmendra duo of *Sholay* and comments:

> Illiterate street people, the bulk of India's film-going public hoot if Sanjay Dutt should sleep in his girlfriend's lap in *Naam*. They applaud when

the boys are ready to die for each other, hunted down by the Hong Kong drug mafia or the police. These are single-sex love myths alienated urban India lives by. (Merchant 1999, p. xxiii)

For Shahani (2008), Gay Bombay (GB) was born in the late 1990s and the (English) mediascape, among other scapes, was highly significant in playing a part in this forming of GB. News of gay cultures, lifestyles and rights from other parts of the world came to circulate in the Indian media in English (Shahani 2008, p. 276) and with time, Indian English language media broadcast stories and news about LBGT issues, and of this Shahani (2008) writes:

> . . . the coverage, while not always positive, was often supportive, at least in the English language press. The issues covered were diverse (gay activism and conferences, the pink rupee, lesbian suicides, corporate HR policy and LBGT issues. . .); in some cases, the media reflected societal concerns (for example, in framing the emergence of homosexuality in the popular perception as a debate on globalization), in other cases, it played advocate (as in the articles advocating for the abolishment of Section 377). (Shanhani 2008, p. 276)

An influential text in the development of gay writing from India is Hoshang Merchant's edited anthology of gay writing, *Yaraana* (1999), which means 'friendship' (essentially between men), a sense of 'blood-brothers'. It is not uncommon to see young Indian males hold hands or put their arms around each other in public; misreadings of this cultural practice would render most of India's male youth 'gay', when this display of connection, or friendship, is actually termed as 'yaraana' or 'dosti'.

Hindi cinema has also explored this theme of yaraana and one of the earliest films is *Dosti* (1964) by Satyen Bose, which is about friendship between two boys, one of whom is crippled, and the other blind. Together they survive the city of Bombay. Hindi film provides a curious benchmark to how the term 'dosti' or 'dostana' has evolved in its usage. Found in two films by this name *Dostana*, the 1980 Amitabh Bachan and Shatrughan Sinha production and the John Abraham and Abhishek Bachan (son to Amitabh Bachan) production of 2008. In the 1980s *Dostana*, the blood-brother friendship of the two men is not in any way troubled by the fact that Amitabh Bachan's character, Vijay, is a police officer who catches criminals, and Shatrughan Sinha's lawyer character, Ravi, bails out the criminals that Vijay catches. It is the arrival of 'Sheetal', played by Zeenat Aman, which pits the men against each other in rivalry, and the film examines the conflict in this triangle of emotion. The 2008 version of *Dostana*, on the other hand, explores a story of two men who pretend to be gay in order to rent an apartment from an old lady whose current tenant is an attractive woman played by Priyanka Chopra. *Dostana* was filmed entirely in Florida, USA, and interestingly, the film was successful both within and outside India. What is interesting to our discussion here is the ways in which the idea of 'dostana' is presented through the cultural medium of film with the two films spanning 28 years in their respective productions. In the 1980 production of *Dostana*, the idea of male friendship does not include notions of homosexuality whereas the 2008 production plays on the contemporary meanings of 'dostana' or 'dosti' and thus notions of gay identity. The 2008 production, however, eventually falls to the conventional 'heterosexual', boy-meets-girl (or love triangle) plot and the ideas around sexuality are quickly replaced by a more conventional Bollywood love story.

Yaraana, Merchant's important work of the late 1990s, explores the senses of this term and in doing so, compiles a collection of short literary pieces in English as well as in other Indian languages such as Marathi, Hindi and Gujarati. In the introduction to the volume, Merchant engages with some of the social and cultural challenges of 'being a man in love with other men' (back cover) and leaves the literary works that follow his introduction to explore such experiences more poetically. For Merchant (1999):

> India's Hindu culture which is a shame culture rather than a guilt culture, treats homosexual practice with secrecy but not with malice. Many educated Indians confuse "homosexual" with "eunuch". They think homosexuals lack sexual organs or cannot sustain erections. Many passive homosexuals even today are forced to live with eunuchs if not become eunuchs through castration. (Merchant 1999, p. xii)

As detailed above, Merchant makes reference to Hindu epics in his exploration of the 'gay' identity in India. Alter (2011) also writes of sexual activity in the Hindu epics, in particular on the idea of castration and the Shiva lingham, he writes:

> Many myths reflect the dynamic, powerful and complex relationship between chastity, sex erections and desire, but versions of the Pine Forest myth are paradigmatic: Shiva seduces the wives and daughters of rishis, who are unaware of his power and true nature. As a result Shiva is cursed and castrated. Castration produces cosmic chaos, but also awareness of Shiva's true identity. Order is restored when the erect, castrated lingham, the very embodiment of opposition, penetrates the delusions of human consciousness as an object of worship – a symbol of structure itself. (Alter 2011, p. 180)

The lingham, often found in Hindu temples across India, is a symbol of chastity and also of power. In the extract above, we understand that Lord Shiva's power is found in the fact that he is made chaste through castration. According to the story of the events of the Pine Forest, we learn that

Lord Shiva (the lingham) would prove more powerful if he remained chaste (i.e., the seizing of semen within the body) and if he did not follow his desire and obvious ability to seduce the wives and daughters of the rishis in the forest. The narrative expresses the idea that power can be found in the ability to be chaste. Alter (2011), in his book *Moral Masculinities: Sex and Masculinity in Modern India*, talks in some detail about the connections between sexual (im)potency, chastity (*urdhvaretas*) and ithyphallicism and this as a complex nexus of cultural significance which is found across many Indian cultures. Masculinity in terms of power (*shakti*) and health are found in chastity and ithyphallicism and, therefore, the release of semen reduces ones *shakti*. Alter (2011) writes:

> All authors [on the topic of semen and sexual health] regard ejaculation as seriously enervating, the result of which is not simply a reduction in volume but a chemical or psychological transformation of substance. . . . Thus a person who has an orgasm is changed into a less-perfect form of his previous self – a dried-up lemon, or that which is left over when butter is taken out of milk. (Alter 2011, p. 69)

Masculinity, therefore, is embodied in *urdhvaretas* and as we learn from the narrative of Shiva in the Pine Forest, a lack of control results in weakness. Shiva is cursed and castrated for his actions. Alter (2011) reminds us that 'being hijra extends beyond the narrow limits of sexual identity, even though genitalia remain a critical point of reference' (Alter 2011, p. 5).

Vanita (2005) also makes reference to Hindu texts when she discusses the idea of a 'special friendship'. Taking the idea of 'yaraana' or 'dosti' from a female perspective, Vanita reminds us of the Sanskrit term *swayamvara* 'an epithet for a special friend', and this she states: 'indicated the overlap between marriage and friendship' (Vanita 2005, p. 155). This friendship is referred to as *janamantara*, meaning that it is considered a friendship for life, literally, continuing from birth to birth. Vanita points out that *janamantara* is not unlike the idea of marriage since: 'it is based on reciprocity, selfless devotion and sacrifice; as in ideal marriage, the partners live and die together' (Vanita 2005, p. 155). Taken from medieval Sanskrit texts, Vanita tells of Somaprabha and Princess Kalingasena, the attraction Somaprabha feels towards Kalingasena and how she chooses Kalingasena as her *swayamvara sakhi*. Vanita reveals that a number of words for 'love' are used to indicate their feelings – *prema, sneha, priti* (Vanita 2005, p. 155).

A short overview of sexuality in India highlights the various ideas and sexual behaviours present within Indian society. The two novels examined below concern themselves specifically with MSM relationships and not with 'the spectrum of sexual minorities' of which Shahani (2008) writes. The two novels are *The Boyfriend* (2003) by R. Raj Rao and *Saraswati* Park (2010) by Anjali Joseph.

The Boyfriend (2003)

R. Raj Rao's novel *The Boyfriend* (2003) begins at 'Churchgate loos', Mumbai, on a Sunday afternoon. Yudi is always on the look out for potential men and the visit to the 'gay wing' of the Churchgate loos is part of that search. Yudi thinks that he has found his pick-up for the day, unusually, *outside* the toilet block. The guy he is eyeing is scrutinizing the shirts in a shop window. 'If only he *is*, Yudi thought to himself. But the nice ones rarely were' (Rao 2003, p. 6). Unsure at this point, as Yudi is, of the shirt-scrutinizing guy's interest in him (and interest in potential sex), Yudi decides to put into place: step one – he brushes his fingers on to the boy's hand (he is only 19 years old we find out later) and the boy does not pull away, step two – he allows his fingers to rest on the boy's hand, entwining them a little more and, feeling more sure of himself now, Yudi enacts step three – he reaches under the boy's shirt for his crotch (Rao 2003, p. 6). Yudi walks away, into the Churchgate loos. Here, the two men stand side by side at the urinals. Yudi checks out the boy, deciding at best, it could be described as a 'chilli'. With time, the boy looks over at Yudi who proudly displays his 'cucumber'. Once outside the loos, Yudi tells the boy that he has a place nearby. As they leave Churchgate together, Yudi goes to hold the boy's hand, a practice, we learn from Yudi, which is an 'enjoyable preliminary' (Rao 2003, p. 8). Rao (2003) writes:

> Whenever he [Yudi] picked up people, he began with this ritual long before they actually reached his house. Most men, however, disengaged their hands after the first few minutes, saying, "People are watching." To this he would respond by reminding them that they were in India, not America; it was all right for grown men to hold hands as a sign of friendship. (Rao 2003, p. 9)

Yudi regularly picks up men to take home and Rao (2003) writes:

> Whenever Yudi picked up strangers and took them home, he gladly offered them the active role in bed. He had a theory based on years of experience. As long as men were allowed to penetrate, there was no fear of their returning afterwards to demand money or beat you up. (Rao 2003, p. 12)

Indeed, Rao states that 'Yudi didn't mind it if his lovers thought of him as a hijra. It was so much more relaxing if one was freed of the need to perform' (Rao 2003, p. 13). Shahani's (2008) 'spectrum of sexual minorities in India' is invoked here, as Yudi does not identify himself with MSM, rather, we read that Yudi does not mind if men think of him as a 'hijra', curiously, an identity most non-hijras per se, would prefer not to be labelled with. Yudi exerts a confidence in picking up men and also in his ability to be penetrated by them – despite what they may think of him – which seems to come from years of experience in this kind of behaviour. Yudi's impatience with the guy he picks up at Churchgate loos (we learn later that his name is Miland) is evidenced in their first sexual encounter:

> "Nirodh phat gaya, my condom's torn"
> "God!" Yudi exclaimed. "Don't you even know how to use a condom? How old are you? Nineteen, isn't it?" (Rao 2003, p. 13)

Yudi not only dominates Miland in terms of being the more experienced, he also ridicules Miland. Yudi enquires after Miland's surname and finds out that it is 'Mahadik'. 'Maha', in Hindi meaning 'big', and Yudi jokes about Miland's name, saying: 'Maha Dick. Odd surname, though, for someone with such a small one'. To which Miland retorts: 'You're making kachra of my surname' [You are rubbishing my surname] (Rao 2003, p. 16). This tussle between Yudi and Miland is further evidenced in the scene below, where Yudi and Miland travel on the Mumbai trains together:

> They walked to the far end of the platform. A group of kothis hovered outside the gent's toilet. They blushed and giggled as they saw Yudi with the boy, whose hand he deliberately held, to make them jealous.
> "This is another famous cruising spot," Yudi informed the boy. To which his reply was, "I know."
> Yudi wondered just how much he knew. (Rao 2003, p. 18)

Despite Yudi's confidence and years of experience in the Mumbai world of various sexualities, this scene indicates that Yudi, although powerful over Miland, is also keenly aware that there is so much that he *doesn't* know about Miland. As the narrative progresses, we realize that Yudi wants to know about the boy and yet, at the same time, he acts with indifference as well as rudeness and ridicule towards him. Miland, on the other hand, is more keenly aware of the difference between the two in terms of class and caste, as opposed to sexual experience. Miland is from a low caste background, living in a transit camp in Mahim in Mumbai; Yudi, conversely, has enjoyed a privileged upbringing. While out in a bar, Miland tests Yudi's tolerance of caste difference by asking him to eat the food that he is eating. Wafers (*jootha*) have been served with the pitcher of beer they have ordered and Miland promptly picks up each of the wafers, taking a bite out of every one. Miland is surprised to see that Yudi has no problem in eating the wafer that Miland has bitten into; Yudi states:

> "Homos are no different from Bhangis. Both are untouchables. So why should I have a problem eating your jootha?"
> "But you are a Brahman, aren't you?"
> "No, I am a homosexual. Gay by caste. Gay by religion."

"I don't understand what you are saying."

"What I am saying is that homosexuals have no caste or religion. They have only their sexuality." (Rao 2003, p. 81)

This statement takes Miland by surprise so he challenges Yudi by saying that high society, of which he believes Yudi is part, can do as they please, any behaviour is acceptable, whereas for the middle (or lower) class, 'indecent behaviour is a crime' (Rao 2003, p. 82). Yudi laughs at this statement, Rao writes: 'The ice was breaking, and that was a good sign. If Miland was disrespectful, it only meant he was beginning to think of Yudi as his own. They bantered for quite some time, Yudi perceived it as dillagi' (Rao 2003, p. 82).

Yudi, indifferent to Miland's caste, is less inclined to show indifference towards Miland's choice of what he is prepared to do (and not to do) sexually with Yudi. Yudi is once again troubled by not knowing Miland well enough: 'Tell me honestly' he told his boyfriend, 'are you really a homosexual?' (Rao 2003, p. 83) to which Miland, unhelpfully for Yudi, answers: 'Who knows?' (Rao 2003, p. 83). Here we see that Yudi, once again, loses control of the situation. In order to assess Miland's sexuality, Yudi asks Miland if he enjoys having sex with women. Yudi is caught off guard again when Miland tells him that he is not able to say, given that he has never had sex with a woman. It is this fight for control over Miland that motivates Yudi to spend more time with him and eventually, when riots break out in Mumbai, Yudi realizes that the relationship has gone beyond the challenge of knowing and controlling Miland, Yudi is actually in love with Miland.

Miland disappears from Mahim and gets involved with A. K. Modelling Agency where he becomes a prostitute for gay and bisexual men. Attempted rape at the agency forces Miland to escape and he decides to return to his chawl in Mahim where his mother celebrates his return with 'Chicken Biriyani, made with Basmati rice' (Rao 2003, p. 203). Within a week of his return, Miland is told that he is to be married, it is all arranged and he is sent out with the invitations, to be delivered by hand in and around Mahim. His parents also inform him that while he was away, Yudi had visited the chawl looking for him and that he must make contact with him, as Yudi made the parents promise to let him know once Miland had returned. Miland begrudgingly agrees to meet Yudi and when he sees Yudi again, he thinks to himself:

You are the one who has ruined my life. It's because of you that I became a homo. Had it not been for you and your perverse ways, I would never have landed up at a place like that A. K. Modelling Agency and become a prostitute. Shame on you! I wonder whether I'll now be able to lead a normal married life. (Rao 2003, p. 210)

Unlike Miland's feelings about the reunion, Yudi is delighted to see Miland and thus, shocked when he is presented with Miland's wedding card. He sobs as he reads the words: 'Miland with Leela'. In almost role reversal, Miland addresses Yudi with indifference, telling him to 'Stop being so weak-hearted. Take hold of yourself. Everyone gets married, and I too have to get married some day or other. So why not now?' (Rao 2003, p. 211). This scene reinforces the difference in the identities of the two men, demonstrated in the early scenes of their courtship; the difference in class, caste, expectations and financial situations. Yudi remains independent with a mother who 'knew why her son was a bachelor, but it wasn't something she could bring herself to talk about, even in her nightmares' (Rao 2003, p. 193), as opposed to Miland's situation where his homosexual acts are financially motivated and conducted in complete secrecy from the chawl and his community.

Miland goes on to marry and when Miland's wife challenges him to introduce her to one of his friends who isn't a *tapori* (see Glossary), he immediately thinks of Yudi, a high-society reporter who writes articles for the *Times of India*. This irony, the fact that Miland blames Yudi for his 'homosexuality' and yet, reveres him in terms of his societal position is central to the novel's interest in their relationship. This deep irony is also manifest in the manner in which the married Miland earns his 'extra' money, taking the freshly made puranpolis (by his wife) to Yudi's flat and spending the night with him, just as they did in the early days of their courtship. There is however, a key difference in the way that they spend time together nowadays, Miland is paid for his time spent with Yudi. The novel closes after one such visit by Miland, when Yudi exclaims: 'You know, I have come to the conclusion that life is beautiful' (Rao 2003, p. 231).

Saraswati Park (2010)

The character-focus of Anjali Joseph's *Sarawati Park* (2010) is male and although the narrative does include several female characters, the main focus of the story is on Ashish and his uncle Mohan (Mohan mama). Ashish is Mohan's nephew through his sister, Vimla. Ashish's parents are issued a transfer order through his father's job and this takes them out of Mumbai. Ashish is due to resit the academic year at college in Mumbai due to poor attendance of the last session and so Mohan mama and his wife Lakshmi (Ashish's 'mami') who live in a suburb of the city, Saraswati Park, happily agree to have Ashish at their flat for the year while he retakes his exams. Ashish is studying literature and this love of letters is shared by Mohan mama. Mohan works as a 'letter writer' by the GPO, near VT station (see Glossary). This central location means that the many commuters, pigeons and transports of VT are an integral part of Mohan's working day. Joseph (2010) writes of this scape:

A fleet of cockroach-like taxis in black and yellow livery waited at the junction outside the GPO. When the lights changed they all, honking, took the u-turn. A man on a cycle passed; he carried a tangle of enormous red ledgers, each wrapped in plastic, atop his head. The gold on their spines flashed in the sun. (Joseph 2010, p. 8)

Mohan, on his way to catch the train, often stops to buy books from one of the bookstalls near VT. The flat he lives in with Lakshmi is slowly filling up with the books he brings back from these bookstalls of central Mumbai. One day, however, the bookstall sellers are 'moved on', essentially evicted on the grounds of a newly imposed 'anti-hawker' scheme. Mohan runs to the scene of two green municipal trucks with men throwing books into the back of the vehicles. Mohan desperately addresses the bookseller to ask where the books are being taken, he replies: '"Some warehouse or godown, I don't know where. I don't know how we'll ever get them back." The young man stood still, his arms full of thrillers; he looked adrift, as though he had no idea what to do next' (Joseph 2010, p. 11).

Mohan's love of literature is, quietly, a source of comfort and encouragement for Ashish. It encourages him in his studies but it also appeals to the more creative side of Ashish's character. On one occasion, Ashish approaches his uncle about the possibility of 'writing something':

"Mohan mama."
"Hm."
Ashish circled the chair. The light glinted through his uncle's steel-coloured hair and onto his scalp, which showed, oddly pale, at the crown.
"Have you ever thought of writing something?"
"Ha! Apart from letters and money order forms, you mean?" (Joseph 2010, p. 50)

Ashish begins his year of study in a familiar manner; he has been here before. A year behind means that he will be in class with a childhood friend, Mayank, who, through the course of the novel proves to be his most loyal friend. But it is Sunder who Ashish is most keen on locating as he enters his first (repeated) lecture at college. We learn that Ashish's poor attendance record from the previous year is linked to his 'friendship' with Sunder. The two boys' destinies post-college are, however, vastly different. Sunder will enter the successful family hosiery manufacturing company, eventually taking over from his father while Ashish will have to make his own way in the world, meaning that good college results are essential for his career. Ashish is drawn towards Sunder (he finds him 'completely desirable' (Joseph 2010, p. 87) more than Sunder is drawn towards Ashish. The name 'Sunder' translates as 'beautiful' or even 'pretty' and Sunder is described as 'wearing sunglasses and new designer clothing. His shirt hung off his sloping shoulders and stretched at the stomach' (Joseph 2010, p. 88). Sunder's 'pretty' name and his private-self (that which he shares with Ashish) is juxtaposed with his public-self, namely his efforts to be 'all male':

> Ashish filed out with the others into the damp-smelling corridor. He saw Mayank and they were just starting to chat when a familiar voice, deep, loud and unselfconscious, brayed as its owner heaved himself into view from the stairs, "Fuck yaar, these stairs again, I can't believe they don't let us use the lifts. Ashish, what's up? What was first class?"
>
> "Modernism," said Ashish, grinning foolishly.
>
> Sunder thumped him on the shoulder. "You have the notes?"
>
> "Yeah." (Joseph 2010, p. 88)

This public persona of Sunder is contrasted with his 'secret' persona, in particular during moments of sexual intimacy with Ashish. In the extract above, Sunder is bold, 'heaving himself' and his presence into the scene, he is loud and breaks up the conversation between Mayank and Ashish with the word 'fuck', an exclamatory statement followed by his demand for information from Ashish and, moreover, a further demand – the notes to the lecture.

Sunder does not openly talk about his sexuality, in fact he suggests to Ashish that his future will include 'an MBA in America, [and] get married' (Joseph 2010, p. 97), supposedly arranged by his rich parents (and this, we learn later in the novel is what happens). Quietly though, Sunder engages in, albeit ambiguously and/or playfully, an intimate relationship with Ashish. On one occasion, Sunder invites Ashish home to have lunch at his parents' house, which is in Cuffe Parade, an affluent part of Mumbai. Ashish takes the invitation seriously as if it is an invitation to be introduced to Sunder's parents. On arrival at Sunder's home, Sunder's mother sends Ashish to her son's room, he knocks and then walks in to find a nearly naked Sunder: 'Oh hi. Just come in. Shut the door, I'm nearly naked' (Joseph 2010, p. 92). After a few moments, Sunder stands in his 'nearly naked' state directly in front of Ashish:

> "So what do you think?" Sunder enquired in his deep voice.
>
> "Hmmm?" Ashish's voice went squeaky. He would have been turned on if he hadn't been so incredibly nervous; a sort of paralysis focused his mind and his eyes darted to the white-painted bookshelf, off whose edge the electric light glinted, then back to Sunder (*don't* look at his crotch). Finally, Sunder held the two shirts in his hands up again and repeated, this time with a touch of pique, "So whaddya think?" (Joseph 2010, p. 93)

This playfulness, almost teasing, on the part of Sunder is indicative of his attitude towards the intimacy between him and Ashish. The lunch event ends as the boys, having retired to Sunder's room, spend some time 'chatting'. It is at this point that Sunder announces his plan of 'an MBA in America, [and] get married' (Joseph 2010, p. 97). Ashish suggests that he might feel 'too young' to get married after college, to which Sunder replies: 'People in our community always marry early. My dad says it keeps you out of trouble but it's not like it stops you doing what you want' (Joseph 2010, p. 98). The ambiguity around the words 'our community' results in a difficult situation for Ashish to respond to: whose community? who is the referent 'our' here? Moreover, what does Sunder mean when he suggests that marriage does not stop you from doing what you want? Ashish replies, somewhat hesitantly: 'Right' (Joseph 2010, p. 98).

Joseph does not disclose whether the 'fifteen feverish minutes' shared between the two boys that afternoon had taken place before or after this conversation, but we imagine that they had taken place after the boys' 'chat' because Sunder, on returning from the bathroom, looks at Ashish impassively and asks him to leave as he has got to go out with his parents in half an hour's time (Joseph 2010, p. 100).

Ashish and Sunder develop a routine, they see each other at college, go out for coffee after class and go to Sunder's place, especially if his mother is out. Two events, however, change not only the routine, but also the 'relationship' between the two boys. While at college, a classmate calls out to Sunder: 'Oye, Sunder, where are you and your girlfriend off to now?', to which Sunder replies 'Fuck off' (Joseph 2010, p. 111) and, secondly, an event which immediately follows this first incident, while the two boys are in Sunder's room back at the flat – his mother is out – Hitesh, the servant, opens Sunder's bedroom door noiselessly to bring in a tray of drinks and cake. Hitesh finds Ashish with his hands on Sunder's belt. Joseph writes: 'When he [Hitesh] went out, eyes lowered, he closed the door properly; the insolent click was a comment' (Joseph 2010, p. 114). At college the next day, Sunder ignores Ashish, he chooses to sit with the boy who has accused him of having Ashish as his 'girlfriend', and most importantly, Sunder chooses to sit next to a girl. Ashish is left alone, that is until Mayank, sensing his predicament, comes over to talk to him. This loyalty from Mayank follows Ashish quietly through the rest of the novel.

Ashish's life changes from this point on. He spends more time at home in Saraswati Park and on the death of his aunt's brother, Satish, Mohan mama decides they should do something to help Ashish out as he had been so obliging at the condolence meeting for Satish, handing out drinks and talking with people. Mohan ponders over Ashish: 'He was a funny child, not a child at all, really; they should do something for him. Mohan would remind him again to go and see that professor, the one Satish had mentioned, who might give the boy extra tuitions' (Joseph 2010, p. 133). This is how Ashish meets Professor Narayan. Ashish's journeys to the professor's house are detailed in all the motifs of modern-day Mumbai – its 'society' housing blocks, its trains, railway lines, snacks and smells. Narayan welcomes Ashish to his apartment, number 17, Sadanand Society, where Ashish is surprised to find Narayan to be so young: 'There was something nice about his face, he thought disconcertedly' (Joseph 2010, p. 144). Ashish finds out that Satish uncle had been Narayan's teacher and that Narayan would teach Ashish as 'a belated favour to Satish uncle' (Joseph 2010, p. 148).

There is some mystery around Satish uncle's life as we learn only of him as Lakshmi's brother and, furthermore, only of his death. As Mohan mama goes to Satish uncle's flat to clear up his belongings, there is very little to sort out. Satish owned very little in terms of possessions although he had paid for the flat, nicely located in South Mumbai, near the sea. Among medicines and health tonics in a cupboard, Mohan finds an old cigar box in which he finds 'a bundle of letters wrapped in a piece of rose-coloured silk' (Joseph 2010, p. 137). Mohan reads what he can see from the bundle, and some of the letters begin with: 'Dearest S' with the signature 'Vikram' (Joseph 2010, p. 137). Joseph does not reveal much more detail about Satish uncle, although we know from earlier in the novel that he is 'an old bachelor' (Joseph 2010, p. 37) and near the end of the novel we learn that Satish uncle has left his flat to Ashish. The triangle of Satish, Narayan and Ashish as teachers and students is also manifest in the fact that the three men are gay men in Mumbai, all fascinated by literature and its possibilities. The three men also act as signifiers of three different kinds of Mumbai/Bombay as Satish and Narayan have known a 'Bombay' which Ashish knows as 'Mumbai' and the older men's experiences of being homosexual are presented as being quite different from what Ashish is experiencing at college with Sunder. Yet, many of the same questions are present; the life of a 'bachelor', the relationships that are made (and broken) and the acceptance of finding a way into the gay fraternity. Although Joseph is not explicit in this detail, we imagine that Satish mentored Narayan, not only academically but also as a gay man, wanting to find his place in some parts of gay society in the city. Narayan, in turn, by engaging in a relationship with Ashish, does the same. Indeed, Ashish, despite the emotional turmoil he encounters in his relationship with Narayan, is grateful for the experience of knowing Narayan, an older man and the opportunity to live out a 'real' gay relationship. Ashish asks Narayan about his own experience of being gay as a young man (Joseph 2010, p. 208), but the conversation turns more to one of interrogation as Ashish seeks to find out how many partners Narayan has had and if any of them were students like Ashish. Narayan's negative view of 'every relationship that goes on for years' (Joseph 2010, p. 209) disturbs Ashish especially when Narayan chooses Ashish's aunt and uncle as such an example, Ashish insists vehemently: 'They're happy' (Joseph 2010, p. 209).

Through his death, Satish becomes a spectral figure in the narrative but he lives on in both Narayan and Ashish, especially as his will announces that his flat in South Mumbai is to be left to Ashish. This is a particularly poignant detail given that Ashish is not directly linked to Satish in terms of family; Satish is Lakshmi's brother and Lakshmi is Ashish's aunt but this connection is only through his mama (Ashish's mum's brother), Mohan;

an indirect, non-blood link. The detail of the inheritance puts into question whether Satish uncle knew that Ashish is gay. There is only one, short scene where Ashish and Satish are in conversation; it is when Lakshmi invites Satish over for a meal. The four sit around the table when, to Mohan mama's surprise, Ashish begins a conversation with Satish (Mohan regards Ashish as quiet and shy): 'Satish uncle, I was reading in the newspaper about the case of a Hindu Undivided Family where one of the daughters changed sex to become a son, what do you think about it?' (Joseph 2010, p. 39). Despite the fact that Satish was previously a professor of law, the topic 'around the dinner table' is inappropriate and for someone who is normally reserved (Ashish is portrayed thus throughout most of the novel) the topic comes as even more of a surprise to Mohan and Lakshmi. The conversation continues for some time until: 'There was a pause in the conversation. Satish had rounded off his explanation, Ashish made a joke, and both their faces flushed with amusement' (Joseph 2010, p. 40). This brief scene between Ashish and Satish seems to create some kind of bond, but it is not until later in the novel where Satish's spectre-like presence reappears, manifest in the contact with Narayan and the inheritance of the flat in South Mumbai, which endorses Satish's concern for Ashish and his future.

Joseph's novel sits in contrast to Rao's *The Boyfriend* in which at times, graphically captures the sexual encounters of Yudi as a gay man, in various locations of Mumbai. *Sarawati Park* explores in particular, the sexual awakening within Ashish and how, in different ways he copes with this, challenges it and develops with it, most notably in his relationship with Narayan. Joseph does not write of the sexual encounters between Narayan and Ashish in any detail, although we imagine that they are much more 'grown up' than the 'furtive fifteen minutes' which Ashish experiences with Sundar. The emotional aspect of the relationship with Narayan is as important as the sexual, an element of a relationship which was completely absent with Sundar. There are even romantic moments between Ashish and Narayan, most notably in the scene of their first kiss. Ashish and Narayan kiss for the first time after watching the flight of golden eagles at sunset from the roof of Narayan's flat. As they move back inside the flat, Narayan says to Ashish:

> "Your first sighting of golden eagles?"
> Ashish met his eyes and felt inexplicably excited, as well as alarmed. He opened his mouth, and Narayan bent and kissed him. (Joseph 2010, p. 193)

As the visits to Narayan's flat become more frequent, Narayan seems to be troubled by the closeness developing between him and Ashish. Ashish, on the other hand, is happy with this development, his interest in a 'relationship' is clearly evident in his anticipation of the classes with Narayan as well as his planning of a weekend away together after his college classes have finished. Ashish, however, is troubled by the melancholy that he experiences at Narayan's flat; Joseph writes of Ashish, looking out over the railway lines and hearing the sound of the train horn. The mournful, drawn-out horn evokes a sense of melancholy in Ashish and Joseph writes: 'The same melancholy made him uneasy in the flat, as though everything that took place there was in the process of mourning its own demise' (Joseph 2010, p. 215). This 'demise' comes to a point when Narayan refuses to go on the weekend away that Ashish had planned for them:

> "I don't think this is a very good idea," he said.
> "What?" Ashish's stomach began to slide away.
> "Going away – and everything else. I don't think", he repeated slowly, "that we should be involved." (Joseph 2010, p. 218)

This scene sees the end of the relationship, Narayan making a case for the difference in age between them, Ashish's retort that it had never been an issue before and in a near-state of 'tantrums' (Joseph 2010, p. 219), Ashish accuses Narayan of seeing someone else before he walks out, slamming the door behind him.

Some time passes, Ashish sits his exams and learns of his newly inherited wealth. His friend, Madhavi, asks Asish what he plans to do now that the classes are over and now that he has some assets of his own. Ashish explains that a cousin of his has suggested he move to California and follow a course in film animation or screenwriting. Madhavi tells Ashish that he would like the place (California):

> "As in?"
> "As in, you know, it's easier there – to be gay and everything."
> Ashish twisted around. "What?"
> "Oh, come on Ashish."
> He pulled himself up, folded his legs and clutched his knee with one arm. "What makes you say that?"
> "It's obviously, surely. So tell me, what was going on with you and that guy, the tutor? Was something happening?" (Joseph 2010, p. 244)

This scene takes place near the end of the novel and it is the only time where Ashish's seemingly obvious homosexuality (to Madhavi, at least) is spoken. It is an important moment for Ashish as the speaking out of his sexuality, albeit by someone else, breaks a silence within himself as well as within his group of friends. Madhavi even suggests that Ashish's aunt (Lakshmi) must know of his sexuality (Joseph 2010, p. 244). Joseph's portrayal of Ashish throughout the novel is someone who is reserved and quiet, it is only in Ashish's interactions with Sundar and then Narayan where we see Ashish as a talkative, engaging person and where a sense of Ashish as a personality becomes real. This is further developed as Ashish cathartically recounts his 'Narayan story' to Madhavi. She is the only person in the novel who offers a different perspective on Narayan, and specifically, on Ashish's relationship with the teacher. After the break up of his involvement with Narayan, Ashish's confidence in himself, in his sexuality and in the idea of a 'happy relationship' takes a severe knock and it is only Madhavi's comments on the teacher's behaviour which offer Ashish an alternative view of the relationship:

> She tutted. "Lecherous uncles, the worst possible thing."
> Ashish began to laugh. "Narayan's not really a lecherous uncle."
> "No?"
> "No! well –"
> "Yuck, wait till he's older. So undignified, watch my French films, chhi."Ashish giggled, scandalized, but also comforted. (Joseph 2010, p. 245)

Madhavi's use of the term 'uncle' underscores the difference in age between Ashish and the teacher. Moreover, the term 'lecherous uncles' is seemingly used here across both heterosexual and homosexual relationships; she expresses her idea of *any* lecherous uncle (hitting on whoever it might be) as disgusting, by her use of the exclamatory 'chii'. This expression of solidarity with Ashish helps to empower him and it is the prelude to his departure from Mumbai to the greener pastures and opportunities of California. Ashish and his college friend Mayank have a farewell coffee and Mayank asks Ashish if he plans to return to the city. Ashish, unable to say which of the two responses Mayank is waiting to hear, acts out his reply: 'He slapped his right hand to his heart. "My homeland is always with me", he said in Hindi, in a baritone, film-star voice' (Joseph 2010, p. 246).

Although Rao's *The Boyfriend* and Joseph's *Saraswati Park* present two different worlds of homosexual relationships in Mumbai, the former is focused on the sexual acts between the men with the backdrop of a noisy, busy Mumbai, the latter pays more attention to the sexual awakening of the protagonist, set against a more quiet backdrop of the city and the calm, stable enclave of the flat in Sarawati Park; both texts, however, speak to a growing interest in the writing of the Indian 'MSM' experience. Such novels, whether bold in their expression of MSM relations or more subtle in their narration, push the boundaries within the scene of writing in English from India and open up new vistas of expression and configuration around sexuality.

5

Crime writing

This chapter explores the post-millennial scene of crime writing in English. Here, the term 'crime writing' refers to detective fiction such as hardboiled, noir, locked room, mystery fiction or whodunit. Section 5.1 examines Swaminathan's *The Monochrome Madonna* (2010) and Jain's *Piggies on the Railway* (2010). These works include a murder plot that involves a detective to investigate the murder.

Section 5.2 examines Taseer's *The Temple-Goers* (2010), and a novella by Ester David: *The Man with Enormous Wings* (2010). Both works narrate the divisive actions of those who privilege difference over humanity and in both narratives, albeit in different ways, the consequences of these actions – murder and killing – are presented and examined. The backdrop of New India in both these works serves as a poignant, contemporary benchmark for how, in striving for a sense of Indianness today, people are challenged and often driven to commit the most inhumane acts.

Crime writing in English from India is a dominant trend in the development of the post-millennial writing scene, with several crime writing series appearing in the last 10 years in particular. The 'Lalli Mystery' series by Kalpana Swaminathan began with *The Page Three Murders* (2006), followed by *The Gardener's Song* (2007) and, most recently, *The Monochrome Madonna* (2010), although some of her 'Aunt Lalli' detective stories are found in an earlier publication, *Cryptic Death* (1997). *Piggies on the Railway* (2010) heralds the first of a detective series by Smita Jain, the 'Kasthuri Kumar Mystery' series with Kasthuri Kumar (Katie or 'Kumar') as a recently resigned employee of the Indian Police Service (IPS) and now 'private detective'. Madhulika Liddle's mughal murder mystery novel *The Englishman's Cameo* (2009) introduces the seventeenth-century Mughal detective 'Muzaffar Jang' and a series of historical whodunits set in and around Delhi. *The Eighth Guest and Other Muzaffar Jang Mysteries* (2011), the second book of the series was published in 2011, with a novel as its sequel planned for 2012. The historical setting to Liddle's works is reminiscent of Omair Ahmad's novella *The Storyteller's Tale* (2008), although not a murder mystery narrative per se, it too, is set in Delhi in the 1700s; Omair's narrative structure and stylistic attentiveness in particular, locate the novella geographically, historically and within a certain literary tradition.

The strong historical backdrop in Liddle and Ahmad's works is also apparent (albeit in a different manner) in the murder mystery of Ravi Shankar Etteth's *The Tiger By the River* (2002) as the legend of the tiger, the kings of Panayur and ancient Kerala is evoked within this narrative. Etteth's novel *The Village of Widows* (2004), although without the historical backdrop evident in *The Tiger by the River* (2002), is equally a tale of murder and deception, bound up in otherworldliness, resulting in an investigation, led by Deputy Commissioner Anna Khan, into ancient mysteries and peoples. Anna Khan (and Jay Samorin – also a character from *The Tiger by the River*) reappear in Etteth's *The Gold of Their Regrets* (2009) as they investigate a murder linked to a plane crash 60 years earlier in 1945, when a plane carrying thirty million pounds of Nazi gold crashed into the Burmese jungle.

Other murder narratives of post-millennial fiction involve more contemporary settings: *The Srinagar Conspiracy* (2000) is set against the backdrop of the insurgency in Kashmir and the threat to Indian national security; the story involves an imminent visit of the American President to India, Afghanistan-trained militants and Major Vijay Kaul whose job it is to stop the terror. *Close Call In Kashmir* (2010) blends the politics of the India-Kashmir question with the hunt for buried treasure and the illegal trade in antiques. *Shadow Men* (2010) is set in contemporary Shillong and is a murder mystery narrative that draws Raseel into discovering how difference and violence has permeated the very fabric of society in which she lives, this darkness is starkly positioned against the beauty and nature of the hill town in north east India. Tharoor's *Riot* (2001) is also a narrative drawn along lines of difference and a narrative within which a murder takes place. Priscilla Hart, an American doctoral student and volunteer in Zalilgarh, India, dies under mysterious circumstances. She is in love with a married man, V. Lakshman who is also the district magistrate of the town, and the novel charts their affair and eventually, her demise.

Taseer's *Noon* (2011) is another novel that examines the India-Pakistan question, and although primarily set in modern-day India and Pakistan, the novel moves through time, and across ethnic and religious boundaries. Although the narrative does not include a murder per se, there is a theft at the family home, Steeple Hall, putting into question the loyalty of the Hall's employees who are of various ethnic and religious groups. The atmosphere is tense and the threat of further violence is menacing throughout the novel. Taseer's protagonist, Rehan, although Muslim by birth, is raised by his 'Muslim mother' (Udaya) and his stepfather, a Hindu, called Amit Sethia; Rehan describes 'Steeple Hall' as the quintessence of this hybrid family:

> But Steeple Hall, for all its flaws, possessed that rarest of rare attributes. With its jagged skyline of triangles where there had been steeples, its giant Islamic arch of the wrong stone, its many blue and white awnings like those seen by a swimming pool and its Hindu figurines – Amit Sethi's

influence – dotting the lawn, each with a floodlight of its own, it was by any assessment a house that had gone wrong enough to be right. (Taseer 2011, p. 81)

Taseer's first novel *The Temple-Goers* (2010), a murder narrative set in and around New Delhi is also interested in peoples' differences and similarities, in what unites them and what separates them; *The Temple-Goers* (2010) is discussed later in this chapter alongside Ester David's novella *The Man with Enormous Wings* (2010).

In Vikram Chandra's (long) short story 'Kama' (1997), Sartaj is a marginalized police officer, a turbaned Sikh working in the urban setting of Mumbai. The name 'Sartaj' is a recognized Punjabi name, but it is also a Hindi name in the sense that it uses the language of Hindi (not Punjabi) – 'Sar' (head) and 'taj' (crown). It is allegorical of Sartaj's 'self' in Mumbai, moving in both Hindi and Punjabi-speaking (and cultural) circles. The name translates as 'crown of the head' and the sense of this is mirrored in Sartaj's turban wearing. Patel, a wealthy businessman, has been murdered for his Rolex watch; conspicuous by its absence, the white band of skin, revealed by the missing timepiece. Patel is found in a ditch; having rained for three days the body, jammed up against a grill, is covered in mud and water (curiously, this scene is not unlike the one described in Taseer's *The Temple-Goers* (2010), which will be discussed later in this section). A local, Ghorpade by name, is found with the Rolex watch. It appears an open-and-shut case, but Sartaj is not convinced and he delves deeper into the family life of Mr Patel, which eventually reveals the darker side of Colaba district, Mumbai and the politics of Hindu extremism (themes that again, are found in Tasser's *The Temple-Goers*).

Shashi Despande's short story 'Anatomy of a Murder' (2003), like Chandra's 'Kama', is told in an urban setting and involves a murder. It tells of a young man who lives in a chawl, fatherless and struggling financially, he works hard as an assistant in a grocery shop. Marathi is spoken and given the urban setting, the story could take place in any of Mumbai's surrounding towns. The murder is executed in a middle-aged woman's flat. She visits the grocery shop and accidentally knocks over some tins, the young man is rude in his reprimand and her response is apologetic; 'I'm sorry' she says in English. The young man is left with this incident playing over and over again in his mind. The woman returns to the shop and he watches her with a young boy of 14, kindly in her manner and temperament. Time passes and she does not come to the shop, but just as he begins to lose hope of ever meeting her again, he is sent to deliver provisions to a nearby home. She does not recognize him when she opens the door to receive the groceries; he is hurt. She deals with the delivery very matter-of-fact and says to him indifferently 'Close the door after you'. She does not look at him or smile like she had done in the shop. He strangles her in her flat, willing her to smile at him. He slumps down next to the body and remains there until the police arrive and find them both. The story ends with this scene.

Investigative journalism also features as part of some of the new crime writing, such as Swarup's *Six Suspects* (2008); Amit Varma's *My Friend Sancho* (2009), which recounts the tale of the crime reporter Abir Ganguly caught up in a police shoot out that leaves a man dead for which the police are seemingly responsible; and Chatterjee's *The All Bengali Crime Detectives* (2011) as examples.

5.1 Female detectives

'Lalli' mysteries: *The Monochrome Madonna* (2010)

The 'Lalli' mysteries of Kalpana Swaminathan are set in Mumbai, always involve murder and are always cleverly solved by Lalli – and this is usually before anyone else has got close to solving the crimes. Lalli makes her debut in *The Page Three Murders* (2006) as Sita, niece to her Aunt Lalli, loses her boyfriend, her university career and her library in 24 hours because she 'defended a maligned student' (Swaminathan 2006, p. 1). The Lalli mysteries, so far three novels, further extend the growing body of fiction of the 'Bombay novel' in the crime fiction genre, which includes Chandra's work, 'Kama' in *Love and Longing in Bombay* (1997) as well as his epic novel *Sacred Games* (2007) as example.

Although the telling of the Lalli mysteries is always from the point of view of Sita, Aunt Lalli is the detective in the case and we know from the first novel, *The Page Three Murders* (2006), that Lalli spent 30 years in the police. Interestingly though, we know little about Lalli and all Sita reveals about her provenance is: 'Let me tell you right away that she is not a generic aunt. Her auntness is accidental. The accident is my father who recently, and for reasons both private and worrying, reclaimed this extremely peripheral twig of the family tree' (Swaminathan 2006, pp. 2–3).

We do, however, learn that Lalli is:

> . . . sixty-three, five foot six barefoot, a hundred and ten pounds on the bathroom scales. An actor's face, lined, mobile, expressive. Eyes, black and gleaming when quiescent, but with a blaze like a blowtorch on occasion. Hair, as I mentioned earlier, a silvery froth. She moves with a swift economy easily mistaken for grace till you realize it's discipline. *Then* you think stealth, speed, agility. She has square, surprisingly hard hands for a woman who spends most of her time reading. (Swaminathan 2006, p. 3)

It is the opening pages of *The Page Three Murders* (2006) which reveal the most about Lalli, although this is not a great deal of detail and it is this lack of biographical interest and information on Lalli and the fact that she is described as the 'extremely peripheral twig of the family' (Swaminathan

2006, p. 3) which marginalizes Aunt Lalli, leaving space for the character of her niece, Sita. The aunt and the niece live out all the murders of the three books from their flat, number 44, Utkrusha, Adarsh Road, Vile Parle East, Mumbai. The second of the three books to date, *The Gardener's Song* (2007), sees the death of Mr Rao actually take place in Utkrusha, specifically in its lift and all the inhabitants of the L-shaped block of flats are under suspicion. Naturally, everyone turns to Lalli to solve the case, including the police force with whom, as a retired police officer, she is still semi-involved. In *The Gardener's Song* (2007), Sita describes the inhabitants of Utkrusha:

> We're a mongrel lot at Utkrusha, though we prefer to call ourselves cosmopolites. Ours is the only building in Vile Parle East that's emphatically *not* a ghetto, but we do abide by the Parle tradition of dropping the courtesy title. Your name is your only handle. But Karunakar Rao has never within memory been plain Rao. Something about him qualifies for that Mister. (Swaminathan 2007, p. 6)

Mr Rao, the book reveals, is an interfering, meddling inhabitant of Utkrusha and everyone living in the block of flats has some sort of motive for seeing him dead. We learn that his meddling ways have always been part of Utkrusha life, but just before his murder takes place the intensity of his interfering increases. In discussion with Sita, Lalli says:

> "Of late, Mr Rao has been acting out of character," she said.
> "Out of character? He's always been trouble as far as I can remember!"
> "True, but not this way."
> "I don't know what you mean. All I can see is that Mr Rao is making trouble right, left and centre . . ."
> "Exactly. That's all that you can *see*."
> I didn't know what she meant, but it left me with a vague feeling of dread. (Swaminathan 2007, p. 74)

In the third of the Lalli mysteries to date, *The Monochrome Madonna* (2010), Sita is the one to discover the body in the flat of Sitara Shah. Sitara, having phoned Sita with the words: 'I think I'm going to die', is found by Sita, legs hanging out of her loft, woozy and confused; Sita suspects that she's been drugged. The living room reveals a corpse and Sita immediately phones the police. Inspector Shukla arrives. Here, Swaminathan creates a Mumbai-ye Inspector, struggling it appears, to piece together why, and how, Sita – he is told that she is Lalli's niece – is at the scene of the murder.

> "You are a doctor?"
> "No."
> "Best friend, then?"

"No, I know her, but we're not close friends."

"Then why she calls you and not husband?"

"She was too confused and dazed to give me any information. Maybe once the drug has worn off –"

"Drug? She is drug addict?"

I refuted this indignantly, and explained matters. He was far from convinced.

"I have seen nameplate," he said with meaning. "Oh yes, I have seen nameplate. Anything is possible. She is not using husband's name. Why?"

"I don't know."

"Why have you not called him?"

"I don't have his number. I don't know him."

Shukla looked shocked. "You are her best friend, and don't know husband? How is that possible?" (Swaminathan 2010, pp. 13–14)

The use of Indian English to create the character of Inspector Shukla is particularly noticeable given that the other characters in the novel, by comparison, speak less Indian English than the Inspector. In the extract above, Swaminathan reveals a lot about the Inspector's personality, his societal views and opinions, these are made clear through his almost condemnation of Sitara not using her husband's name and through his disapproval of Sita not knowing Sitara's husband when they are 'best friends' – although this is, in fact, an incorrect assertion, as Sita barely knows Sitara. The use of the Indian English, therefore, becomes linked to, almost part of, the moral position of Inspector Shukla and forces a dichotomy of traditional values/Indian English vernacular versus 'modern' values/Sita's 'standard' English usage.

The novel's name, *The Monochrome Madonna*, takes its title from a framed picture hanging on the wall of Sitara's flat, an image central to the narrative on various levels. The following extract describes the moment Sita sees the picture for the first time:

There was a picture on the wall opposite me, a large framed print of Raphael's Sistine Madonna. It was startlingly different from my memory of the painting. This one was monochrome, tinted in tones of burnished sepia and bright gold. . . . In the callous parlance of the day, the Sistine Madonna had been Photoshopped. The figures in the foreground had been edited out. The woman stepping out of the splash of glory, was not, strictly speaking, Madonna at all. She carried no babe. And that wasn't all. Raphael's Madonna hadn't looked so like Sitara. This was *Sitara's* face, tinted in tedious monochrome, staring at me in placid irony. (Swaminathan 2010, p. 6)

The picture of Sitara as the Sistine Madonna is curious for several reasons. The flat is home to Sitara Shah and V. Dasgupta, by these names we might deduce that by birth (if not since) Sitara Shah is most likely to be Muslim, and V. Dasgupta, Hindu. As Sita points out in the expanded version of the extract above (see original text, Swaminathan 2010, p. 6 and also pp. 56–8), the Madonna was often seen at school – in Catholic (missionary) schools in particular – Sita remembers it herself, when she says: 'I know the Sistine Madonna backwards. I spent six years staring at it in school – it had a copy in every classroom' (Swaminathan 2010, p. 6). This too, might be the reason for Vinay Dasgupta's choice of image to 'photoshop' (we learn later in the novel that it is his creation), but since the household is not obviously Christian, it is a curious image to have chosen. As the novel unfolds, we realize that Sitara is far from any image of the Madonna, and as Sita points out in her initial meeting with the picture, Sitara and her husband have no children ('She carried no babe'). When police Inspector Savio asks Vinay about children, Vinay explains that they never wanted for anything more than themselves, for Vinay at least, Sitara was all he needed (Swaminathan 2010, p. 155). In his glorification of Sitara, Vinay photoshops the picture to show Sita in radiant light, sure-footed and stepping out into a world that needs to ready for her. All the other figures in the painting (St Sixtus, St Barbara, the winged cherubs) have been deleted; there is only Sitara in Vinay's picture.

The technology that allows Vinay to produce such an image is of the contemporary. Sitara, sure-footed and in all her glory, stepping out into the world, married, yet, by choice, without a child, might also be read as a motif of the contemporary and of today's Indian society. Vinay reveres his wife publicly by hanging the Madonna picture for all to see, as it hangs opposite the main entrance door, this reverence, almost in servitude to his wife, is at odds with a more traditional domestic scene where intimate gestures between husband and wife are kept private, the role of the wife is more in servitude than the role of the husband towards his wife is, and the married couple, traditionally, would choose to have a family. Inspector Shukla, in the little time he has to learn of Sitara (see extract above; Swaminathan 2010, pp. 13–14) also comments on the 'untraditional' nature of Sitara's union with her husband, Vinay: 'I have seen nameplate,' he said with meaning. 'Oh yes, I have seen nameplate. Anything is possible. She is not using husband's name. Why?' (Swaminathan 2010, pp. 13–14).

Swaminathan is not alone in writing 'murder in Mumbai' and *Piggies on the Railway* (2010) by Smita Jain is one recent novel to join the growing scene of Mumbai crime fiction. As part of the 'Kasthuri Kumar Mystery' series, *Piggies on the Railway* (2010) is both a recent addition to Indian crime fiction writing and to Indian chick lit.

Kasthuri (aka Katie) is a private investigator, trying to make her career in Mumbai after serving in the police force for some years. Although the plot of *Piggies on the Railway* (2010) centres around the kidnapping (and we find out later, the murder) of a famous Bollywood actress, the novel could just as well be described as being in the genre of chick lit, given that much of the narrative draws the reader into the 'personal life' of Katie Kumar, her fashion choices, beautification rituals and men-obsessions as well as her moments of unfortunate 'girly' mishaps.

The plot of 'finding the kidnapper' (and later, murderer) is interspersed with Katie's love affair with Ani who is married to Sweety. In the vein of ironic narrative, Sweety hires a detective to watch Ani in order to catch him with Katie (herself, a personal investigator), but instead of producing photos of Ani and Katie together, Ani is photographed with another girl. In a bid to prove to Katie that Ani is cheating on her too, Sweety contacts Katie to show her what the private investigator has found out. In the following extract, Katie, armed with the photographic evidence from Sweety, asks Ani what is going on:

> Ani stared at the pictures and sank down heavily on the sofa. He seemed to be in shock.
>
> "How . . .?" he started to say.
>
> "Sweety gave then to me. She suspected you were having an affair with me and hired a detective. Imagine her surprise – and mine – when these came up instead."
>
> "I can explain."
>
> "How? That your dick got lost and mysteriously found its way into her vagina?"
>
> He winced but he didn't object. The consequences of his multiple cheating seemed to have dawned on him. (Jain 2010, p. 74)

Unlike Swaminathan, the matter of the 'murder' in Jain's novel is of equal importance to the character of Katie, the private investigator. The narrative does not especially focus on solving the crime, but rather, follows the roller-coaster life of Katie and the developments in her relationships. *Piggies on the Railway*, like Swaminathan's novel *The Monochrome Madonna*, explores contemporary Indian society and more so in Jain's novel, we see the boundaries of the 'female experience' being pushed. Jain is explicit about Katie's sex life at various points in the novel, Katie's affair with Ani is also covered considerably, and her drinking and smoking habits feature throughout. Although India has seen a rise in chick lit in the past 5 years (see Section 3.1), Jain's work is one of the more strident novels to deal explicitly with sex and the identity of the twenty-something Indian woman in India today.

5.2 Difference and death

David's *The Man with Enormous Wings* (2010) is explored here for its focus on murder and death based on difference and how this investigates notions of 'Indianness'. This novella also talks to Chapter 6 of this book as it engages with the fantasy genre. A short discussion on Taseer's *The Temple-Goers* (2010) follows as this novel also highlights the divisive nature of drawing lines along caste and religious difference.

The Man with Enormous Wings (2010)

Esther David's novel *The Man with Enormous Wings* (2010) is dedicated to the city in which she has spent most of her life and which has proved to be the muse for other works of hers such as *The Walled City* (1997). The novella, *The Man with Enormous Wings* (2010), is a series of vignettes, based mostly on the author's (seemingly) own experiences, observations and accounts of life in Ahmedabad, having lived through the riots and known the city intimately pre- and post-violence. David writes on how Ahmedabad is changing in the wake of New India. She laments the destruction of the walls of Ahmedabad as the famous 'Walled City'. She mourns the demolition:

> What are we transforming our grand old city of walla into a stereotyped urban city without character? Why do we want to kill the soul of the city? Once upon a time, the walled city was a fort with twelve darwazas. But today, they have been broken down for railways and roads and only one wall stands as a lone memoir of the old city. We are now a city of roads and have a walled city without walls. (David 2010, p. 45)

Ahmedabad in Gujarat, David recounts, was named in the early 1600s by the Mughal emperor, Jehangir as 'gardabad', city of dust (David 2010, p. 5). The city is testament to the many religions and people who have passed through its streets over the centuries; one renowned religious site in Ahmedabad is Chalte Pir ki Dargah, the grave of Hazrat Gulam Mohmed Syed. David (2010) writes:

> Believers of all religions sit at the entrance, asking for boons, tying threads to the grille, offering chaddars of desi red roses and fragrant green damro leaves as they fix joss sticks in every possible crevice. On Thursdays, the Walking Saint listens to their pleas and bestows boons to devotees. (David 2010, p. 5)

But the 'Walking Saint' or Chalte Pir ki Dargah's tomb, although frequented by all people, does not assume harmony across the communities of Ahmedabad. In *The Man with Enormous Wings*, David explores the events of the 2002 Ahmedabad riots from which ensued bloodshed and the rupture of communities across the city. David likens the fear instigated by the riots to the trembling of the mysterious Shaking Minarets of Ahmedabad (David 2010, p. 12) and for David the kites of the festival of Uttarayan are analogous of the 2002 riots; the *tukkal* (kites) are described as 'expert fighters' and she writes of the *tukkal*, otherwise beautiful in the sky: 'It can hurt. It no longer bonds us together . . .' (David 2010, p. 26).

On Ahmedabad and Gujarat, Amartya Sen (2006) writes:

> The artificial diminution of human beings into singular identities can have decisive effects, making the world potentially much more incendiary. For example, the reductionist characterization of India as a "Hindu civilization" . . . The extremist wing of that [Hindutva] movement even played a critically important part in the fostered violence in Gujarat in 2002, in which most of the victims, ultimately, were Muslims. (Sen 2006, p. 178)

Ideas of Indianness in David's book are revealed through the everyday, in the most innocuous of objects and acts. David, as a Jew in Ahmedabad, is neither Hindu nor Muslim, the very lines along which the communal violence and rioting were drawn. She writes in one of her vignettes about the colour saffron and of secularism. Earlier chapters in this book have already discussed the significance of the colour saffron ('basanti' – Chapter 1 and Chapter 4 Section 4.1) and its connection with a certain identity of Indianness, and in David's writing, she accentuates the connections that people make between the colours worn by the inhabitants of Ahmedabad:

> "People who are secular should be careful about their choice of colours."
>
> "A colour cannot make a statement about who I am. Because colour can also be a camouflage. Look at the chameleon." . . .
>
> "Tell me, what exactly is a secular colour?"
>
> "I do not know." (David 2010, p. 49)

Taken from the title of her novella, David's spectral character 'The Man With Enormous Wings' examines these vignettes of Ahmedabadi life. David's patchwork narrative means that the (often) two or three-page vignettes are stories within themselves, comprehensive and insightful in their completeness. Sometimes, 'The Man' is not manifestly present, although we realize as the narrative develops that the character of 'The Man' is omnipresent. It is at the time of the Godhra, Sabarmati Express carnage, however, that The Man With Enormous Wings appears the most vividly. Coaches S-6 and S-7 of the Sabarmati Express are brought into Ahmedabad full of charred bodies. The emergency cord on the train had been pulled, only for a mob to descend on the train and set the coaches on fire. The predominantly Hindu carriages were carrying mostly women and children on their return from pilgrimage to Ayodhya and they were burnt alive, trapped, locked inside the coaches. The Godhra train burning was pivotal to the unrest within the city; it resulted in an escalation of communal violence as Hindus took revenge for the massacre on the train. The Man With Enormous Wings sits on the carcass of the train, folding his wings around himself: 'He wept, and the charred metal thirstily drank up his tears' (David 2010, p. 74). David includes black line drawings throughout the novella and this particular extract is accompanied by a line drawing of 'The Man', bent low, on his knees in a state of despair.

On another occasion, The Man With Enormous Wings is made more 'real' as he interacts with characters of David's vignettes; he is depicted wearing a shawl and glasses, glasses David accurately illustrates as being very round with a thin frame (David 2010, p. 120). 'The Man' attempts to stop a Hindu mob from entering a chawl in order to protect Kausar, a woman who had nursed 'The Man' when he had been ill. The Man With Enormous Wings 'stood Christ-like at the entrance of the chawl trying to obstruct the crowd' (David 2010, p. 83), but he is unable to stop the mob, they push him aside and trample on him. Kausar, heavily pregnant, is raped and killed, her baby pulled from her belly, pierced with a trident and slit in two. The trident, carried by the mob, a motif of the Hindu god Shiva, is used to wreak destruction and death, an unsavoury twist on the god's identity as the destroyer (Brahma, the creator, Vishnu, the protector, Shiva, the destroyer).

As he surveys the city, The Man With Enormous Wings discovers another victim; the woman named Bilkis has survived brutal sexual violence and she is near death, lying on the ground when 'The Man' finds her. Scared at first that her tormentors have returned, she is quickly put at ease when she sees The Man With Enormous Wings looking down on her compassionately and she knows immediately that she can trust him.

Gently he lowered her and left her at the gate of the collector's house. The guard saw Bilkis, and rushed inside to inform the officer that there was a corpse at the gate. Later, after Bilkis had received medical attention under the protective care of the collector, she recounted the details of the massacre. (David 2010, p. 98)

On other occasions, The Man With Enormous Wings is invisible yet omniscient. As he witnesses Hindu nurses dress a Muslim patient in a sari, adding a bindi to her forehead so that the angry mob entering the hospital will not attack her due to her identity, 'The Man' 'flies' over the hospital and blesses the nurses.

In his most silent and yet, most powerful act against the violence of the riots, 'The Man' turns himself into a tiny fly and sits on the 'monkey-toy' (*see no evil, speak no evil, hear no evil*) on the table of the Inquiry Commission. The act of this transformation from 'The Man' to a fly is reminiscent of the Hindu epics where gods transform into other avatars. The fly is unhappy with the chief's answers to the inquiry, knowing that he is certainly telling lies; 'The Man' witnessed the same chief during the riots offering little protection to the civilians, saying that 'the police could not protect them' (David 2010, p. 117) and so 'The Man'/fly shakes with rage:

> He shook with anger and the impact of his fury made the bungalow tremble. Frightened of the possibility of an earthquake everybody rushed to the door when they saw a strange creature with enormous wings flying out of the window. The monkey-toy fell to the floor. (David 2010, p. 117)

This might of 'The Man', even as a tiny insect, his ability to shake the earth and cause panic is also reminiscent of scenes from the Hindu epics. Curiously, 'The Man's' powers extend beyond the physical in this scene, as during the inquiry, the deputy's eyes meet with the fly's eyes but instead of seeing a fly on the 'monkey-toy', the deputy sees The Man With Enormous Wings, and David (2010) writes: 'Their eyes had met for a split second and the deputy knew he would speak the truth' (2010: 117). In speaking the truth, the deputy – to the horror of the police officers around him – reveals the truth behind the rioting. The scene closes as the deputy hands over the affidavit in which he had documented the riots, upon which everyone looks in horror. David concludes: 'The old man with the enormous wings had had his victory' (David 2010, p. 118).

The novella closes as The Man With Enormous Wings lands on the ground in a heap, his wings broken and singed. He lands between the two warring communities of Ahmedabad; between the Hindus and the Muslims. Confused as to who or what this creature might be, the communities decide together to lock up the winged man in a cage. The people unite in both their curiosity and their fear of this unknown being and this focus distracts them from their own differences. They are united in their *common* fear of the unknown and the different. This narrative is also played out in the film *Delhi 6*, discussed in Section 6.1. Similarly, the divided community of 'Delhi 6' is united in its greater cause of finding (and destroying) the monkey-man which has appeared menacingly in their neighbourhood, attacking people indiscriminately. David's novella closes as The Man With Enormous Wings flies off into the sky, behind him, he leaves a statue and one man addresses another, asking: 'Did he say he was Mohundas Karamchand Gandhi?' (David 2010, p. 122).

The Temple-Goers (2010)

Taseer's novel *The Temple-Goers* is set, for the most part, in and around Delhi. It tells the tale of a young writer called Aatish who, on moving to Delhi, finds a local gym he wishes to join, called 'Junglee'. It is here at 'Junglee' that Aatish meets Aakash Sharma, a trainer at the gym and they become friends. Aatish moves in the elite circles of Delhi life, educated, with a girlfriend, Sanyogita who's aunt, Chamunda, is Aatish's mother's best friend. Chamunda is heavily into the political scene. On the other hand, Aakash is Hindu, Brahmin, living and sleeping four to a room in the challenging district of Sectorpur, Delhi. He isn't particularly educated but he has ambition. At the beginning of the novel, Aakash does not have a girlfriend but as he starts to spend less time with Aatish, Aatish senses that Aakash has met someone. Aakash, a high caste Hindu meets, and then marries Megha a lower caste Hindu than himself, an Aggarwal (of the business caste) whose father owns several factories and is an *arabpati* (see Glossary), meaning that Megha comes from a very rich family. Interestingly this means that Megha's financial status is much higher than that of Aakash, if not her religious status. The novel deals with big themes; life partners, sexuality, money, politics, religion and Aakash pulls Aatish into most of these, knowingly or unknowingly, throughout the narrative. The book draws to a close with the murder of Megha. After her appearance at Aakash's high Brahmin celebration or *jagran* (an all-night wake of devotional singing, story telling and prayers), which is described by Uttam, Aatish's driver, as ' . . . rubbish, just a way for the Brahmin's to make money' (Taseer 2010, p. 184), Megha disappears shortly afterwards.

Unbeknown to most people at the *jagran*, Megha has been married to Aakash for some months and the family members who know of this, are bitter towards the alliance. The *jagran* comes to a climax just before dawn as the storyteller narrates the fable of the King's murder of his son – he severs his body into 'small, small' pieces with a sword. Within hours of the close of the *jagran*, Megha's body is found cut up into 'small, small' pieces in four black bin bags in a hyacinth-choked canal in Sectorpur (a scene not unlike the one described in Chandra's 'Kama'). All eyes are on Aakash and he is immediately arrested, but is later released due to lack of evidence. He makes a life for himself in politics through Chamunda and Aatish sees him frequently on the television; a stark reminder that even in the days of 'Junglee', Aatish had recognized that Aakash had 'ambition'.

The Temple-Goers does not involve a detective or investigator as such, but as Megha's murder is announced on the news, the police are naturally involved. We read that the Delhi police (although Sectorpur is really outside their jurisdiction) go undercover on the case. Sparky Punj, Aakash's lawyer (and former 'Junglee' patron) reveals that he's heard the police talk of the murder:

Nepali job. Hundred and one per cent a Nep job. You've seen some of the crime they're responsible for. I tell you, these guys are fucking crazy. It takes nothing for them to flip. Ninety-nine per cent of this crime, at least in Delhi, is done by Neps. And they just slip back across the border when things get too hot. (Taseer 2010, p. 255)

Thus, the violator of this heinous murder is suggested to be an anonymous 'other', from a neighbouring land (Nepal) and thus the reader never really knows 'the truth'. This suggestion, of the anonymous 'other' is also echoed in Sawian's *Shadow Men* (2010), another recent publication in the crime writing scene in English in India.

6

Fantasy and epic narrative

This chapter looks at the genre of speculative fiction, focusing on fantasy fiction of New India, which includes urban fantasy (Section 6.1) and a growing body of fiction that draws on Hindu epic narratives (Section 6.2). Section 6.2 debates whether this particular body of fiction should actually be categorized as 'fantasy', highlighting the role of reception, and how the classification of 'historical fiction' might actually serve as a more accurate term. This chapter is therefore divided into two sections: 'New [Fantastical] India' (Section 6.1) and Bharati Fantasy or Historical Fiction? (Section 6.2).

Since this chapter examines speculative fiction and specifically the fantasy genre, it is important to explain how the genre term 'fantasy' under this umbrella term of 'speculative fiction' is understood here. One of the more well-known genres of speculative fiction is SF, and SF novels, like fantasy novels are becoming more popular in emerging Indian fiction in English, see, for example, the SF novels of Joshi's *The Last Jet Engine Laugh* (2001), Chatterjee's *Signal Red* (2005) and Chabria's *Generation 14* (2008) as examples.

In line with some of the departures in fiction, Bollywood film post-millennium is also interested in innovations in SF and fantasy narratives. With increasing digital and technical abilities, Bollywood produced its first major SF film with one of Bollywood's most popular actors, Sharukh Khan in 2011. The film, entitled *Ra. One*, directed by Anubhav Sinha was a box office smash hit in India and despite the popular casting and boy-meets-girl Bollywood motif, it was the visual effects and its release in 3D which helped to secure the film's success. The superhero, played by Sharukh Khan, is named 'G.One' and the antagonist (played by Arjun Rampal) is named 'Ra. One'. These names produce, through their Indian English pronunciation, the Hindi words: 'jeevan' and 'raavan'. The labiodental sound /v/ that is found in both words, reproduced here as the phoneme /v/, although in reality, a voiceless phoneme, together with the Indian English pronunciation of the phoneme represented here as /n/, but again, in reality, a velar, nasal phoneme, transforms these two names semantically, into 'life' and 'evil', respectively. These two characters are borne out of a very contemporary India of video/online gaming and the troubles begin when the computer-animated characters use the new technology to escape the virtual world, entering the real world. Other post-millennial SFF Bollywood films include *Koi Mil Gaya* (2003) and *Kriish* (2006).

Roberts (2010) makes the careful distinction between SF and other genres found under the umbrella term of 'speculative fiction'. He talks of the 'grounding of SF in the material rather than the supernatural' (Roberts 2010, p. 5) and although he recognizes the need for the 'science' in SF, Roberts concludes that the materialism isn't always scientific. Of most importance here, is the distinction Roberts makes between SF and other forms of literature such as 'the fantastic' when he writes: '. . . the premise of an SF novel requires material, physical rationalization, rather than a supernatural or arbitrary one. This grounding of SF in the material rather than the supernatural becomes one of its key features' (Roberts 2010, p. 5). He goes on to state:

> It seems [that] this "point of difference", the thing or things that differentiate the world portrayed in science fiction from the world we recognise around us, is the crucial separator between SF and other forms of imaginative of fantastic literature. (Roberts 2010, p. 6)

Narratives in the fantasy genre, therefore, often write the supernatural, write of fictional worlds and of superheroes. Unlike SF, fantasy does not have to 'technically' (or scientifically) make sense, how things logistically happen are very rarely explained, rationalized or explicated. Mendlesohn (2008), in also comparing fantasy to SF, states that fantasy 'relies on a moral universe: it is less an argument with the universe than a sermon on the way things should be, a belief that the universe should yield to moral precepts' (Mendlesohn 2008, p. 5) and importantly, that 'Fantasyland is constructed, in part, through the insistence on a received truth' (Mendlesohn 2008, p. 7). For Clute and Grant (1999): 'A fantasy text is a self-coherent narrative. When set in this world, it tells a story which is impossible in the world as we perceive it. When set in an otherworld, that otherworld will be impossible, though stories set there will be possible in its terms' (Clute and Grant 1999, p. 338). Section 6.1 examines texts that can be categorized as fantasy, as opposed to SF, and this includes an analysis of Samit Basu's *Turbulence* (2010) and Usha K. R.'s *Monkey-man* (2010).

Section 6.2 explores two novels, *Chanakya's Chant* (2010) by Ashwin Sanghi and *Bali and the Ocean of Milk* (2011) by Nilanjan P. Choudhury and challenges the idea that these novels might be categorized as 'fantasy' (as defined here). These novels draw heavily on ancient stories and Hindu epics and, therefore, Section 6.2 will argue that to understand these works as 'fantasy' is to misread this body of fiction which might be better categorized as 'historical fiction'.

6.1 New [Fantastical] India

Post-millennial fiction in English in the fantasy genre is framed by the names of Basu, Amish and Banker in particular. Basu's 'Game World Trilogy': *The Simoqin Prophecies* (2004), *The Manticore's Secret* (2005) and *The Unwaba Revelations* (2007) as well as his 2010 novel *Turbulence* can all be described as fantasy works. The urban fantasy novel of Usha K. R.'s *Monkey-man* (2010) is also of the fantasy genre as we are never told how the 'Monkey-man' comes into being, we don't know if he/it eats, sleeps or talks, but the novel examines the consequences of the elusive 'Monkey-man' and the impacts on society. Urban fantasy novels share a lot of similarity with the genre of fantasy although their settings are more contemporary (in terms of their 'futuristic' motifs) and are always urban. Usha K. R's *Monkey-man* (2010) also carries motifs of the 'slipstream' genre and slipstream according to Ashley (2008):

> uses the tropes and ideas of science fiction, fantasy and horror but it is not bound by their rules and will make those elements only a minor feature of the story rather than its raison d'être. Likewise a plot and set-up may appear conventionally literary but fall outside the staid boundaries of mainstream. (Ashely 2008, p. ii)

David's novella, *The Man with Enormous Wings* (2010), discussed in Section 5.2 also demonstrates some of the motifs of the genre of slipstream. Like Usha K. R.'s *Monkey-man* (2010), David's narrative is set in modern-day, post-millennial India and Ashley (2008) writes of the slipstream genre that for him 'here in the noughties . . . [Slipstream] is a vital genre and is the only meaningful literary response to the challenges of the new millennium' (Ashley 2008, p. ii).

Turbulence (2010)

When asked in 2005 his thoughts on the Indian SFF scene, Basu responded: '. . . Indians are culturally geared towards a fondness for fantasy or science fiction' (Basu 2005), explained he says, by the cultural backdrop of the Indian epics and folk tales old and new. Basu is known for his work in the fantasy genre through his 'Game World Trilogy', published in 2004, 2005 and 2007, respectively, where characters and plots are of the kind of mythology that makes *The Ramayana*. His 2010 publication *Turbulence*, although also written in the fantasy genre, is, however, quite different from the worlds of the 'Trilogy'.

The storyline of *Turbulence* is set in contemporary India. The narrative reveals that World War III has not yet taken place, Vir, the superhero who has 'flying' powers is born in 1984 and is somewhere in his late-twenties, the Mumbai motifs are current-day and Sachin Tendulkar is still in cricket, albeit at the end of his career. It is, of course, not the contemporary India that we know and the band of superheroes, holed up in an unknown location in Mumbai, are striving to save the world from dark forces. The superheroes have one thing in common; they were all on the same flight from London to New Delhi. The people who survived the flight and left as superheroes, are few and their newly acquired 'powers' are stuff of dreams, literally. Vir had dreamt that he could fly, Uzma dreamt that she was the most successful actress ever and that everyone loved her unconditionally, and Tia dreamt that she could be in more than one place at one time, in order to flee the confines of a difficult marriage (and the difficult in-laws) and yet be with her three-year-old son constantly. Tia is able to become many Tias instantly. Narayan dreamt that he was a great inventor and is known in his superhero form as 'The Scientist'. In his sleep, he invents creations such as 'Xontrium Ego Suspension' and the 'Tachyon Dislocator'. Aman is the protagonist of the novel, who eventually combats the evil forces of Jai and the underworld as Aman has the ability to control and manipulate the worldwide web.

Turbulence opens as Vir stands in the storm clouds over Pakistan, ready to execute a mission:

> Vir can fly. He stands tall, legs slightly apart, a wingless angel swaying in the wind, rivulets of icy water running down his body. A young man of great presence, of power and dignity only very slightly diminished by a passing migratory bird's recent use of his shoulder as a pit-stop. (Basu 2010, p. 2)

The motifs of the superhero are formulated here in this introductory scene: Vir is tall and strong, he stands with his legs slightly apart – as seen in the hallmark stance of 'Superman' – and, like other superheroes, Vir has dignity. Vir's character, however, harbours a slight arrogance, a character trait that is alluded to here in this extract. As the other superheroes are introduced, it is apparent that it is only Vir who displays any kind of superiority about his superpowers. Basu quells Vir's egotism with the introduction of the passing bird's 'pit-stop', as a reminder that although he is a superhero, he is not totally immune from life's small misfortunes.

Vir has second thoughts about the mission he has been ordered to carry out and this is the reason why he is standing in the storm clouds over Pakistan. A call on his mobile from the Squadron Leader forces him to make a decision:

> Vir heaves a deep breath and looks down at the factory again. The mission is simple enough. He flexes his muscles, preparing to let go, to drop like a meteorite.
>
> The phone beeps. Vir takes the call.
>
> "Vir Singh?"

"Sir."

"Can I interest you in buying a new credit card?"

"*What?*"

"Kidding. Listen. Abort your mission. Fly home."

"Who is this?" It's not the voice of anyone Vir knows.

Young, male, Indian from the accent. Vir hears '70s rock music playing faintly in the background.

"So, what's the plan, Vir? Bust into the nuke factory, kill a few people, fly out with some uranium? Does that sound smart to you?"

"How did you get this number?"

"On a toilet cubicle wall with Call For Good Time written beside it. What are you, stupid? You're about to make the biggest mistake of your life. Your father was sent to a needless death in an obsolete MiG-21. And now you're about to throw your own life away, and start a war in the process. Abort!" (Basu 2010, pp. 3–4)

In contrast to the formal and militarized instructions that Vir is used to receiving on his mobile phone, a male Indian voice talks to Vir in a chatty almost jocular fashion about the mission he is about to complete. This conversation could be Vir's conscience playing out the mission since we know that Vir is concerned about the potential consequences of what he is about to do. However, the conversation is too direct for this to be the case, the use of the direct speech and probing questions moves the conversation away from the possibility of this exchange being an inner monologue. Moreover, Vir doesn't recognize the voice on the other end of the phone and he doesn't much care (we read later) for the sarcasm bound up in the questions: 'Does that sound smart to you?' and 'What are you, stupid?'.

As the novel moves on, the band of superheroes eventually find each other and live together in a house in Mumbai. Here, they plan how they will overcome the evil forces of 'Jai' and, given their strength as a group of people with different super powers, how each character will fulfil their potential. Basu weaves in (morphed) realities of contemporary Indian society such as the television station DNNTV (Basu 2010, pp. 40, 84), the Kalki party, its politics and its 'blue' baby in the Ram Lila ground (Basu 2010, p. 84), the television show *Indian Idol* (Basu 2010, p. 157), terrorism and natural disaster (Basu 2010, p. 175), the Indian Air Force (Basu 2010, p. 182), underworld gangsters such as Dawood (Basu 2010, p. 191) and the Mumbai attacks (Basu 2010 p. 209).

The narrative of *Turbulence* (2010) shares some of its features with the Indian literary traditions referenced in Chapter 1 of this book, such as Dandin's *Kavyadarsa*. The storyline is epic in the sense that it is an otherworldly good versus evil plot and is reminiscent of '. . . war and the Hero's victories' (Devy 2010, p. 27). Through the character of Vir in particular, the narrative is 'embellished with descriptions of cities, oceans, hills, the seasons, the moonrise, the sunrise' (Devy 2010, p. 27) as Vir is able to fly around the world, not unlike Hanuman, the Monkey God of the Ramayana, who flies between India and Lanka to help save Sita.

Turbulence (2010) also includes a storyline 'of enjoyment (love), of separation (of lovers)' (Devy 2010, p. 27) as Aman and Uzma fall in love, are separated in the fight against Jai but are reunited at the end of the battle. The story closes as Aman leaves Mumbai to 'wander around the world beating bad people up and giving away their money' (Basu 2010, p. 335), and although he asks Uzma to join him, she decides to wait for his return. The scene ends as Uzma wistfully watches Aman leave, while Aman, forcing himself not to look back at Uzma, persuading himself to continue walking down the path, prepares himself for his next mission. This scene is not unlike scenes in *The Ramayana*. Rama is exiled to the forest and facing separation from his wife Sita, on the point of departure Sita pleads with Rama to take her with him to the forest. The separation of the lovers is also played out when Ravana captures Sita, and Rama fights the dark forces in order to be reunited with his wife. (See also the post-millennium film *Raavan* (2010) in Hindi, *Raavanan* (2010) in Tamil for a contemporary take on the narrative.)

Monkey-man (2010)

Emerging India is a clear motif in Usha K. R.'s *Monkey-man*. The novel is set in January 2000, in contemporary Bangalore; the city that has morphed from 'pensioner's paradise' to IT hub of India. Radhakrishnan (2011) writes of the city:

> Bangalore is the beating heart of India's IT industry, the most visible city in a short but growing list of Indian IT cities that includes Mumbai, Hyderabad, Chennai, Pune, and Gurgaon. . . . In Bangalore, more than practically any other Indian city, the positive effects of the IT industry seem pervasive, whether in the crowded mall or the mushrooming tech parks, in the innumerable engineering colleges or the new high-end international airport. (Radhakrishnan 2011, p. 26)

The contemporary setting of urban India is the basis for this urban fantasy narrative, most of which is given over to the examination of four principal characters: Shrinivas Moorthy, reader in History at the National Trust First Grade College; Miss Neela Mary Gopalrao, a thirty-something executive assistant at the Centre for Socio Economic Studies (CSES); Miss Pushpa Rani, a call centre employee; and Mr Balaji Brahmendra or 'Bali Brums' to his fans, a hugely popular radio jockey of the city's brand new FM channel 'Voices From Heaven', to whom Neela listens (and emails) daily. It is the elusive 'Monkey-man', from which the book takes its title, which links these four characters. They are all brought together in the closing scene (apart from Pushpa Rani due to her father's ill health) as Bali Brums interviews Shrinivas Morthy and Miss Gopalrao on-air as the first people to have seen the 'monkey-man' in and around Ammanagudi Street.

The book's narrative hangs on the sightings of the 'monkey-man', although curiously, the sightings of the monkey-man and the discussions of the sightings are a small component of this novel overall, since Usha K. R. devotes most of her narrative to the detail of the characters and their lives. Through her markedly various characters, Usha K. R. explores an India of then and now. Shrinivas laments the passing of the flour mill where his wife used to send the rice to be ground and mourns the arrival of 'the new super market' (Usha K. R. 2010, p. 13) and yet, Pushpa Rani is upwardly mobile in the 'new' Bangalore; successfully moving her family to a better flat. Usha K. R (2010) writes of Miss Pushpa Rani's struggle to secure a decent job and wage:

> She refused an offer of marriage from her mother's brother, and another offer from a well-off cousin to go to Bombay to mind his house and children whilst he and his wife went to work. Instead, she set her face resolutely towards Bangalore, whose lights were fast approaching Sundarapalya. (Usha K. R. 2010, p. 90)

Her struggle is worth the effort and Pushpa Rani enters the Bangalore workforce through a job in an office as a daily-wage typist. From here, she climbs further as she sets her eyes on a call centre job, learning that 'a little bit of money and mentoring could change your life completely' (Usha K. R. 2010, p. 90). The opportunities that Pushpa Rani seizes in the new Bangalore not only offer comfort and financial independence for herself, but also a better quality of life for her family, as she moves them (including her ailing father) out of Sundarapalya and onto Ammanagudi Street, a pleasant district of Bangalore. Pushpa Rani's call centre job has endowed her with the strength to be independent and support her family on many levels:

> Now, when she put on her headphones, smiled into the mouthpiece as she had been taught ("when you smile it reflects in your voice and in your heart") and said, "Thank you for calling. How may I help you?" in an accent free of the influence of her mother tongue, she knew that she was straddling the world, reaching across oceans and continents to another person in a place she recognized only as a pink splotch on a map, to help him, to make a difference in his life. (Usha K. R. 2010, p. 91)

Despite the novel detailing the characters' lives and the trajectories that they follow, the monkey-man looms large throughout Usha K. R.'s narrative. We know from the prologue that he 'exists' and the novel proceeds on the expectation and, furthermore, on the anxiety of his next appearance.

Although a work of fiction, Usha K. R.'s novel is reminiscent of Delhi's *kala bandar* (the 'black monkey') of 2001, when there were numerous reports of monkey-man attacks in and around the city. Such was the scare and infamy of the 'monkey-man', Bollywood produced a movie called *Delhi 6* in 2009, which was loosely based on these happenings (directed by Rayesh Omprakash Mehra). Mixed in with the regular Bollywood motifs of boy-meets-girl plot, there is the narrative of mass hysteria and societal frenzy due to the monkey-man sightings. The narrative of *Delhi 6* suggests that the monkey-man resides in the people of the 'Delhi 6' community, a force that is omnipresent and pervasive. It is only when the divided community of 'Delhi 6' unite against the monkey-man that their ethnic and religious differences are sidelined, united then in their common humanity against the bigger evil, that of the monkey-man. This ethereal force of the monkey-man is present in both *Delhi 6* and (near the end of) Usha K. R.'s novel too. It is the Cassia tree roots pushing up Ammanagudi Street that are responsible for tripping up Neela and then Pushpa Rani, followed shortly afterwards by Shrinivas's near-crash on his scooter; each contact with the Cassia tree root is closely followed by an encounter with the monkey-man. Pushpa Rani trips up in the darkened street, on looking up, she meets the eyes of a creature and she knows it is the monkey-man. She rushes home to find, as she suspected, her ailing father, near death after a fall.

Indeed, all the incidents which take place in conjunction with the sighting of the monkey-man whether it is the earlier sightings by Shrinivas as he moves his scooter out of the parking lot, or when his wife is supposedly scratched by the monkey-man on the balcony as she discovers the death of the kittens (Usha K. R. 2010, p. 240) or in the closing incidents of Pushpa Rani and the 'cassia roots' (Usha K. R. 2010, p. 238); the 'monkey-man' brings only misfortune, death or sadness. As we read above, 'monkey-man' when in Hindi reads: *kala bandar* (black monkey) and this nomenclature only heightens the foreboding sense of calamity, given the 'darkness' or 'blackness' (*kala*) that he embodies.

As mentioned above, a key feature of the genre of 'urban fantasy' (and also of 'slipstream') is its location in the contemporary and in the urban. Today's Bangalore is very real in Usha K. R.'s novel and this is what renders the narrative menacing; its call centres, its 'Centre For Economic Studies' and its Radio DJ, all read as if they are plucked out of the contemporary urban Bangalore scene of the 2000s. The supernatural force of the 'monkey-man' is also very real once the cultural links to the *kala bandar* are made and in turn, curiously, this renders Usha K. R.'s narrative 'real' yet, simultaneously, 'fantasy'. When read against the cultural significance of the *kala bandar* and the 2009 film *Delhi 6*, Usha K. R.'s novel raises questions about the nature and pace of change in one of India's most progressive and fiscally successful cities. Usha K. R. moves between old and new Bangalore, those who have known Bangalore for many years (such as Shrinivas Moorthy) and those who are new or younger to the city (such as Miss Pushpa Rani), and as the novel closes with the characters' lives changing and developing in many directions, we are reminded of the constancy of Ammanagudi Street, which remains more or less the same, as the various people come and go.

6.2 Bharati fantasy or historical fiction?

This section of Chapter 6 examines a growing body of post-millennial writing which might be categorized as being written in the fantasy genre – according to Roberts' definition above – and yet, drawing significantly on Hindu epics and narratives such as *The Mahabharata*, *The Ramayana* and the teachings of the Vedas and the Upanishads, this body of fiction might also be read as historical fiction and thus not as fantasy.

Interestingly, the narratives of this new fiction are set in different eras, some contemporary (*Gods of War*), some historical narratives (*The Onus of Karma*) or in more ancient eras, in line with the Hindu epics (see Amish Tripathi's 'Shiva Trilogy' as an example). For some novels, such as Dhar's *Vimana* (2011), the historical setting of the book blends ancient times with contemporary thought, weaving modern-day political and cultural references into the narrative, albeit manifestly into another much older era. Choudhury's *Bali and the Ocean of Milk* (2011) is an example of such a novel and is discussed in detail below. *Chanakya's Chant* (2010), also discussed below, literally blends the ancient world of 340 BC with the modern day, alternating chapter by chapter the two different periods, these two eras of over two millennia apart, are linked through the lives of the two protagonists, through politics and the struggle for a united country.

This body of fiction includes writers such as Amish Tripathi and the 'Shiva Trilogy', and to date, two of the three novels in this trilogy have been published: *The Immortals of Meluha* (2010) and *The Secret of the Nagas* (2011). Ashok Banker, who is known for his 'epic Indian fiction', *The Ramayana* as well as *Krishna Coriolis: Slayer of Kamsa* (2010) and *Gods of War* (2009) also features in this body of new writing. Krishna's *The Onus of Karma* (2010) is both an adventure novel and a historical novel revisiting eighteenth-century Madras. Both the British and Haider Ali want the divine wheel, the Sri chakra, and as a protector of the chakra, Ramaswami is caught in many battles to protect and save it. The plot thickens as Haider Ali is responsible for the rape of Ramaswami's mother, a rape witnessed by Ramaswami's father, an event that saw both parents murdered. Ramaswami or 'Rama' as he is known, is informed by his neighbour Sivaraman, of their murder: 'It was Haider Ali. He was after the Sri chakra. I'm sorry Rama, but you must leave. The British are everywhere. If they find you here, they will go after you and the village all over again' (Krishna 2010, p. 115), but it is Mohan who tells Rama the complete truth, including the information about the rape of his mother. Mohan is a childhood friend and Rama can trust him. It is this bond that results in Mohan leaving the village with Rama to go after Haider Ali, and so the two leave the village for Madras. Although the novel is greatly historical – the East India Company, Haider Ali and Tipu Sultan – the Sri chakra renders the narrative myth-like and at times fantastical.

As the analysis of *Chanakya's Chant* (2010) by Ashwin Sanghi and *Bali and the Ocean of Milk* (2011) by Nilanjan P. Choudhury will go on to demonstrate below, this body of new writing challenges the idea that it should be categorized as 'fantasy' and thus takes issue with Clute and Grant's (1999) idea of: 'when set in an otherworld, that otherworld will be impossible, though stories set there will be possible in its terms'. This section suggests that this body of new writing should be categorized as historical fiction and *not* as fantasy fiction, and that the complexity of this categorization lies primarily in the reception of the fiction. The analyses of the novels below demonstrate that an Indian readership (theoretically) find the 'otherworld' of ancient Bharat *possible* (it is, after all, part of this readership's historical and cultural heritage) whereas a Western readership (theoretically) find the 'otherworld' *impossible* as per the Clute and Grant definition above, rendering therefore, this fiction as 'fantasy'.

However, *if* this fiction is to be considered as fantasy, then it is manifestly of Mendlesohn's (2008) 'immersive fantasy' according to her taxonomy of: 'portal-quest', 'immersive', 'intrusion', 'liminal' fantasies. For Mendlesohn (2008) 'The immersive fantasy is a fantasy set in a world built so that it functions on all levels as a complete world' (Mendlesohn 2008, p. 59) and, moreoever, that 'immersive fantasy' does not need the dividing line between real and non-real (as other types of fantasy do – such as portal-quest, intrusion and liminal). The following analysis of *Chanakya's Chant* (2010) and *Bali and the Ocean of Milk* (2011) demonstrates these characterizations of 'immersive fantasy' according to Mendlesohn, but this idea will be challenged along the lines of an argument of 'reception', making a case for how this fiction might be more appropriately categorized as historical fiction.

The authors of this new body of fiction write within a recognizable Western construct of the fantasy genre (see Roberts (2010), Mendlesohn (2008) and Clute and Grant (1999) for their definitions of this above) and yet, these novels are discernibly Indian, in the sense that they draw on Hindu epic narrative as well as myths and folktales of various Indian cultures and traditions. Many of the authors of this body of new fiction create a sense of otherworldliness in their narratives but the extent to which the otherworldliness might be perceived as being such, is dependent on the reader's own knowledge of Hindu epics and history. A reader with little or no knowledge of the history, religion and people of Bharat will most likely read these new novels as significantly 'otherworldly'. Less so, might a readership where Hindu mythology, history, religion and Sanskrit terms will be more readily part of their cultural heritage. As we know from Roberts' definition of fantasy above, the characters, plot and narrative style is always fantastical in the sense that it is 'not real', but describing this new body of writing as 'fantasy' holds its own issues of definition and taxonomy, given that for some readerships (read: within India) the narratives of these novels *are* real.

Given this complex position on genre classification, we will now look at how 'historical fiction' might be defined and how this, as a genre classification, might be better employed to describe and classify this new body of writing over the genre term 'fantasy', in particular, in relation to the reception of this fiction within India and more broadly within Indian readerships globally.

Historical fiction

According to de Groot (2010) 'historical fiction is written by a variety of authors, within an evolving set of sub-genres, for a multiplicity of audiences' (de Groot 2010, p. 2) and he writes that: 'the figures we meet in historical fiction are identifiable to us on the one hand due to the conceit of the novel form, in that they speak the same language, and their concerns are often similar to ours, but their situation and their surroundings are immensely different' (de Groot 2010, p. 3).

This characterization of historical fiction speaks *generally* to this new body of writing from India which draws on Hindu epics and ideas of Bharat, but this characterization of historical fiction is *particularly* demonstrated in Sanghi's *Chanakya's Chant* (2010). The novel blends the ancient world of 340 BC with the modern day, alternating chapter by chapter the two different periods that are historically, over two millennia apart. The two eras are linked through the lives of the two protagonists – Chanakya and Gangasagar – through a common theme of politics and the struggle for a united country. Chanakya is a (authentic) famous political strategist from the Gupta period and is therefore, an 'identifiable' cultural icon for a readership within India. What is particularly interesting about *Chanakya's Chant* is the alternating chapter structure between ancient Bharat and contemporary India, which results in both familiarity and estrangement. On the one hand, the novel conforms to de Groot's definition of the familiar and the 'different' being created through the genre of historical fiction, but the contemporary interludes of the alternating chapters reworks this equation. As a result of the familiar (that is, contemporary India) being foregrounded through the alternating chapters, a more concrete link between past and present is created. The use of the parallel characters (Chanakya and Gangasagar) in particular, forges this link. For de Groot (2010), 'History is other, and the present familiar' (de Groot 2001, p. 3) and *Chanakya's Chant* and Dhar's *Vimana* in particular, explore this idea.

de Groot (2010) reminds us that:

> An historical novel is always a slightly more inflected form than most other types of fiction, the reader of such a work slightly more self-aware of the artificiality of the writing and strangeness of engaging

with imaginary work which strives to explain something that is other than one's contemporary knowledge and experience: the past. (de Groot 2010, p. 4)

This position talks to some of the questions of reception presented above and is not unlike the position taken by Mendlesohn (2008) on reception, when she writes: 'I believe that the fantastic is an area of literature that is heavily dependent on the dialectic between author and reader for the construction of a sense of wonder, that is a fiction of consensual construction of belief' (Mendlesohn 2008, p. xiii).

Both genres then, require of the reader, a willingness to enter into worlds that are strange and imaginary – to various degrees and in different ways. According to de Groot, historical fiction 'entails an engagement on the part of the reader (possibly unconsciously) with a set of tropes, settings and ideas that are particular, alien and strange' (de Groot 2010, p. 4), an engagement that is reproduced in the reading of fantasy. What lies at the crux of this suggestion – and therefore shapes our idea of reception of these new fictions – is the degree to which the unknown and the strange present themselves.

In the analyses of the two novels below, *Chanakya's Chant* and *Bali and the Ocean of Milk*, the idea that although both genres require readers to accept the 'strange' or the 'unfamiliar', it is the readership and cultural reception of these novels which position the works within their genre classifications. That is not to say that all Hindus read this new body of fiction in the belief that all Hindu epics are *real* accounts, this is a particular and personal belief within the Hindu community(ies) inside and outside of India. Thus, the reception of this body of writing is various; one end of the spectrum reveals a reader of little or no knowledge of Hindu mythology, for whom the characters and plot lines (shape-shifting, longevity of hundreds of years as examples) are most clearly of the fantasy genre, while the other end of the spectrum reveals a reader who knows the Hindu epics and *believes* in them – in terms of spirituality – and therefore reads this new body of fiction *outside* of the fantasy genre, as historical fiction per se. The suggestion at its most fundamental therefore, is that one reader's fantasy novel is another reader's historical fiction and vice versa. To read this body of fiction as historical fiction requires a shared historical and socio-cultural heritage with the worlds presented in the text and a belief (to a degree) in the epics from which much of these narratives are drawn, indeed, without this shared knowledge base, this body of new fiction presents itself more as fantasy narrative than historical fiction.

To better articulate this idea, we might reverse the circumstances, suggesting that an Indian readership of British historical fiction might read such fiction as fantasy on the basis that the historical and socio-cultural heritage presented in the text is 'unfamiliar' (see: Gregory's *The Virgin's Lover* or Mantels' *Wolf Hall* as examples). This argument is less convincing.

The reception of Indian historical fiction (at least, the particular body of fiction which is being discussed here) in the West is inclined to be thought of as fantasy according to how this genre has been defined and characterized in the Western academy to date. The characters of the type of Indian historical fiction discussed here are often ones that have the ability to fly, the ability to shape shift, hold extraordinary powers of strength or ability and are sometimes hybrid animal-humans. It is these particular elements of the Indian historical fiction presented here which means the reception of such fiction in the West predisposes itself to the fantasy genre and why, in reversing the circumstances as suggested above, does not result in Indian receptions of British historical fiction being of a similar experience. There is also an important argument in suggesting that the impact of colonization and the canon of British literature in India lessen the 'unfamiliarity' of such texts and Chapter 1 of this book offers some insight into this ongoing, although waning, literary relationship.

In brief, the continuum of 'difference' and therefore the demand on the readership to imagine the worlds presented in these narratives, determines how this fiction is received and categorized in terms of its genre. The analysis of the two novels below demonstrate how both positions of reception are *conceivable* and thus I will move between an analysis based on the historical fiction genre and an analysis based on the fantasy genre.

Before we move to the analysis of *Chanakya's Chant*, it is important to reiterate an interest of this book that is, how the new writing talks to notions of New India. Brosius (2010), during her fieldwork in the mid-2000s, found that the link between old and new middle-classness in New India could be found in both parties' claim of the epic Hindu texts, such as the Vedas. Brosius (2010) writes:

There is, for instance, a recurring claim towards the common source and value-creating force of "the Vedas" among members of the Hindu middle classes, in order to claim noble ancestry to a Golden (Hindu) Age, even by people of low caste lineage. By means of such a "theming" strategy, members of the old and new middle classes transform themselves into custodians of national values and cultural heritage as well as torchbearers of modernity. (Brosius 2010, p. 18)

The question, in terms of new fiction, is whether the fiction enables such theming, and the connecting of the old and new middle classes in their shared Hindu heritage and indeed, if the authors are part of this theming too. The authors of this fiction are, indeed, curiously positioned on this spectrum; they write from a knowledge base of the Hindu epics and this might well be regardless of their personal, spiritual position. As a writer, they then 'craft' fictional elements around the parts of the narrative that are drawn from the Hindus epics. In this way, the author writes fantasy fiction for some readers or simply historical fiction for others (for whom the Hindu epics are not fantasy) and, moreover, for those who might take issue with an author extending Hindu epic narrative into fictional (untrue) accounts around the lives of the gods and people of ancient India.

This complex nexus of identity, literary expression and Hinduism talks to some of the issues outlined in Chapter 1 of this book; in particular, the idea of 'Indianness' as one rooted in a nation which is predominantly Hindu. Bery (2005) writes of Corbridge and Harriss's notion of Hindu nationalism as being an organic and homogeneous whole, a Hindu nation that is threatened by non-Hindus. Of interest to this section is Bery's (2005) writing on nationalism:

> . . . like the modernizing one, is primarily a product of the nineteenth century, it projects itself backward into ancient India as its source. The ideology of Hindutva which inspires Hindu nationalism is founded, in Chetan Bhatt's words, on the notions of "territory, blood, culture and religion." (Bery 2005, pp. 118–19)

The invocation of the past, of ancient India in particular, is an important element of the writing presented in this section, along with the geography and the territory of Bharat, and the gods of Hinduism, although Krishna's *The Onus of Karma* (2010) is an exception in this body of fiction in that its narrative is not solely based on Hindu culture and religion, rather it presents the 'threats' (see Corbridge and Harriss's citation above) of the British and the Muslims as they battle over the sri chakra.

Chapter 1 described how some of the ancient Indian and Sanskrit literary aesthetics are present in post-millennial fiction in English and this particular body of writing discussed in this section is naturally an example of this, given the historical and cultural backgrounds evident in its narratives. It is consistent to find acknowledgement of *The Natyasastra* and Dandin's *Kavyadarsa* in many of the works in this body of fiction, albeit to varying degrees. As the two novels of Sanghi and Choudhury explored below will demonstrate, elements of Indian and Sanskrit literary ascetics talk to Devy's definition – see Chapter 1 for Devy's characterizations of these aesthetics.

Chanakya's Chant (2010) by Ashwin Sanghi and *Bali and the Ocean of Milk* (2011) by Nilanjan P. Choudhury are explored in terms of how they talk to the fantasy genre, historical fiction and also how they talk to ideas of New India, including debates around Indianness.

Chanakya's Chant (2010)

Chanakya's Chant (2010) by Ashwin Sanghi brings together the epic, the ancient and the modern. The narrative moves between the ancient world of 340 BC and the present day and this is structured through alternative chapters of the past and the present, the narrative beginning in 340 BC and ending in present day. In parallel with the two eras are two protagonists: Chanakya and Gangasagar. The two men face similar perils in politics and war, deeply involved in power and political 'strategy'. Chanakya's character is based on a man by the same name, of the Gupta period of Indian history, who was a political strategist to the king. The novel, therefore, blends historical fact and fiction, alongside Hindu epic and mythology and it is 'the chant', created by Chanakya's only love, Suvasin, which binds the two protagonists across the ages.

The present-day character is Gangasagar, Professor of History, who survives a plane crash and in the forest in which he finds himself post-crash, he unearths a tablet of stone upon which is inscribed:

Adi Shakti, Namo Namah; Sarab Shakti, Namo Namah; Prithum Bhagvati, Namo Namah; Kundalini Mata Shakti; Mata Shakti, Namo Namah (Sanghi 2010: ix)

[Primal shakti, I bow to thee; all-encompassing shakti, I bow to thee; that through which God creates, I bow to thee; creative power of the kundalini; mother of all, to thee I bow. (Sanghi 2010, p. 34)

Gangasagar takes the tablet of stone to his old school master who duly translates the chant and, in addition, discovers inscriptions on the reverse of the tablet, detailing the manner in which the chant must be recited; 400 chants everyday for over 4,000 days. The chant reveres female power (shakti) and Gangasagar devotes his daily prayers and the rest of his life to the chant, channelling his energy and prayers to Chandini Gupta, a poor child growing up in Kanpur. Chandini, under the guidance and (unbeknown to her) the 'chant' prayers of 'Uncle Ganga' becomes a successful politician, culminating in her position as the prime minister years later. As she is sworn in as prime minister, a bullet from a Stinger.22 Magnum hits her left shoulder and she is knocked unconscious as the blood spreads across her blouse. But the wound is not fatal and she will survive. Gangasagar knows this, so as the scene unfolds on the television in his hospital room, he chants for the last time: *Adi Shakti, Namo Namah; Sarab Shakti . . .* He dies with the Sanskrit words of the chant on his lips, knowing that the chant he has recited for so many years is now embodied in Chandini Gupta.

The genre of fantasy often appeals to the spiritual, the supernatural (sometimes the superstitious) in its creation of the narrative and this is manifest in some of Sanghi's characters and plot lines. One of the characters in the novel is the *vishakanya* and of the creation of this 'poisoned maiden' Sanghi (2010) writes:

. . . Chanakya has personally supervised the creation of an entire army of such maidens. His secret service would identify young and nubile girls whose horoscopes foretold of widowhood. These beautiful damsels would be sequestered at an early age and fed a variety of poisons in graduated doses, making them immune to their ruinous effects. By the time each of Chanakya's vishakanyas reached puberty, they were utterly toxic. A simple kiss with an infinitesimal exchange of saliva was lethal enough to kill the strongest bull of a man. (Sanghi 2010, pp. 3–4)

Sanghi reasons how the creation of the vishakanyas comes about as he explains the Vedic astrology behind their existence, Sanghi (2010) writes:

The ancient seers of Magadha had observed that birth under specific positions of the moon made certain women extremely unlucky for the longevity of their partners. Girls born on Tuesdays during the seventh lunar day of Vishaka possessed unfortunately potent horoscopes that guaranteed that any man they cohabited with would die. (Sanghi 2010, p. 383)

Here, Sanghi offers an explanation as to how some women are born to be 'poisoned maidens' (vishakanyas) and, in doing so, disputes any idea that the vishakanyas are borne out of superstition. It is 'the ancient seers of Magadha' who have studied the phenomenon and therefore *know* that certain women are predestined to become widows. We see in other elements of Sanghi's narrative, the thin line that exists between 'truth', in the sense of 'reality' (or 'coincidence') and ideas of astrology, predestiny and superstition. These two worlds exist side-by-side in this novel not simply through the juxtaposition of the two historical periods, arranged in their alternating chapter structure, but rather, embedded more deeply *across* the time periods in both the actions of the ancient people of Bharat – namely, Chanakya – and also in the actions of Gangasagar, a man of twenty-first century India.

The notion of predestiny versus coincidence is very much explored in the post-crash scene where Gangasagar finds the black granite tablet on which the chant is inscribed. He discovers the stone *accidentally* at the site of the plane crash, the crash that Gangasagar has just managed to survive. Although Sanghi explains how Gangasagar comes to find the tablet of stone, the coincidence of the plane crash (he would not have boarded the plane if he had thought it was unfit for travel) and the fact that the plane crashes, not only on the site of where the stone lies (dated 340 BC) but also that the impact of the plane is strong enough to unearth the stone, supports the design of the fantasy genre. The idea of coincidence, fate and superstition runs throughout *Chanakya's Chant* as we see in the extract above, but these elements are manifest in different ways. In the scene of the plane crash, Sanghi creates a vague space of understanding between 'possible' reality and fantasy as we wonder how predestined Gangasagar really is to unearth such a tablet of stone.

The chant itself offers a kind of fantasy and magic too. The chant's instructions make clear that unless the chant is observed 400 times a day, for over 4,000 days, the chant will not result in actualizing a woman leader, of the kind of powers and strategy that Chanakya held. The result of Chandini

Gupta as the nation's prime minister might be understood as emanating directly from Gangasagar's observance of the chant, or rather, it might be coincidental that Chandini Gupta becomes prime minister, she is, after all, groomed and educated by 'Uncle Ganga' to those ends; the power of the chant, it might be argued, is irrelevant.

Sanghi also uses the character of the dwarf in his novel to invoke ideas of the fantastical. On one occasion in the story, a team of dwarves help to rescue Chanakya from a prison cell:

> He was startled to see an entire band of dwarves pulling the rope that held him. Their leader stepped forward and explained: "Do not be alarmed, acharya. Katyayanji asked us to help. He needed us gnomes to access the ancient escape duct leading from the prison. . . ." "Dwarves have always had a very important function in Magadha, acharya. We've been guarders of the royal *kosh* – the treasury." (Sanghi 2010, pp. 84–5)

Although it might be argued that the inclusion of the dwarves talks to notions of fantasy fiction, there is question as to what degree of fantasy this plot might be. Sanghi rationalizes the dwarves' involvement as 'keepers' of the royal treasury due to their ability to enter covert places such as secret ducts and this is demonstrated in the extract above as well as in the larger section of the narrative from which this extract is taken. As we read in the narrative's rationalization of the vishakanyas, a logical and commonsensical idea behind the inclusion of the dwarves in the narrative is also presented.

Given that the ideas of astrology, predestiny and superstition run across the two eras of this novel, debate on the role and value of such philosophy in modern New India is evident, albeit quietly displayed throughout the narrative. Sanghi weaves in references to some of the modern-day cultural and societal issues of the noughties, but instead of presenting this in the 'present-day' chapters, Sanghi presents these issues through the chapters set in 340 BC. This technique of joining the mutual concerns of two societies set apart by over two millennia results in the powerful message of the universal challenges of politics and society in general. Sanghi's narrative technique demonstrates how the issues of the Bharat people are still alive today; people and culture are still struggling with many of the same issues, two millennia later. The link to the possibility of change is embodied in the object which 'travels' from one era to the other, the black granite tablet with the inscription of the chant on it, and furthermore, in the person who is so dedicated to make change happen for the better, Gangasagar, that he is prepared to recite the chant 400 times a day for over 4,000 days. Debates on society, Indianness, farmer suicides and war are just some examples of the topics that Sanghi links across the two millennia:

> It's unfortunate that the concept of *Bharat* – the common abode and cultural heritage of us Indo-Aryans – has been subjugated by petty rulers

and kingdoms. Our scriptures, traditions, culture, prayers, and deities are common. Why is it, then, that we refer to our homes as Magadha, Gandhar, Kashi, Kosala, Mallayrajya or Panchala? Why don't we say that we're citizens of Bharat? It's these fundamental divisiveness that will bring about our downfall in the future. (Sanghi 2010, p. 43)

How many more farmers have to commit suicide because the tax inspectors of Dhanananda loot their grain? How many more soldiers must die in battle because their armour has been compromised to make wine goblets for the king's pleasure? (Sanghi 2010, p. 7)

"Correction. In order to become a master, a ruler must *profess to be a servant* of the people."

. . .

"Acharya, is war the only solution to political differences?"
"Wise pupil, politics is war without bloodshed and war is simply politics with bloodshed." (Sanghi 2010, p. 45)

In *Chankaya's Chant*, Ashwin Sanghi crafts a complex narrative around the idea of 'history repeating itself' and this is timely, given some of the changes (both opportunities and challenges) that India is encountering in the twenty-first century, as *Bharat* evolves, once again, at pace.

Bali and the Ocean of Milk (2011)

The narrative of Nilanjan P. Choudhury's *Bali and the Ocean of Milk* (2011) follows the lives of two arch-enemies, Bali and Indrah, and how, both in need of the elixir of life, *amrita*, work together to obtain it. The only way to release the elixir of life is to work together to churn the Ocean of Milk from where the amrita will be released. Bali, an asura, is the ruler of Tripura and Indrah is ruler of the devas. The plot line is drawn along the lines of the epic tales of the gods (Indrah) fighting against the asuras (Bali), a good versus evil battleground in which the gods, through epic feats, sometimes resulting in epic disaster, fight for their worlds. Bali, despite being an asura, is regarded as a benevolent asura and the novel demonstrates his goodness despite his heritage.

Bali, having recently survived an attempt on his life, knows only too well that other attempts will be made; the amrita would mean that he would be sure to survive any such attempts on his life so the proposal to churn the Ocean of Milk is a promising one for Bali. Indrah, on the other hand, is suffering from a lack of strength, vitality and, most importantly, powers, since he committed, unknowingly, 'Brahminicide' (he killed a Brahmin by his own sword). The result of the Brahminicide is the dissolution of his powers. With the amrita, Indrah would be rejuvenated, his powers would be restored and, moreover, he would live eternally, that is, until the end of the Kali Yuga.

The two enemies decide to work together to secure the amrita and plan to churn the Ocean of Milk as two teams. Each team provides six members and by this, Choudhury names the project 'Oceans Twelve' after the number of those needed for the job. True to the epic story, the snake and the tortoise are used to churn the ocean. Choudhury (2011) writes:

> "Easy, easy now . . . not so hard . . . owwww! That hurt real bad!" The giant snake hissed.
>
> "Stop grumbling, will you?" the tortoise gurgled from below the waves. "You volunteered for this job!"
>
> "Sure, because you told me that we would be able to extract the nectar in a jiffy," the snake replied. "These damned guys have been pulling away at me for two bloody days now and we haven't seen the backside of a jelly fish. I'm sore and hurting all over, my bottom feels like it's been scraped with sandpaper. I am sick and tired of this tug-of-war!" (Choudhury 2011, p. 143)

Choudhury's banter between the snake and the tortoise adds an element of the modern-day to the narrative. The project's name 'Oceans Twelve' makes a contemporary reference to the Hollywood film of the same name starring George Clooney and Brad Pitt and the snake's Americanized exclamation of 'That hurt real bad!' further underscores a sense of the modern.

The churning of the ocean results in disaster of epic proportion. As both the devas and the asuras fight to drink the amrita, a second jar of mixture is released from the ocean and before they can stop it, the top is released and the *halahal* powder is set free. The *halahal* powder, the opposite of the life-giving amrita, destroys the world, ravaging it with fire and smoke. Indrah escapes the anarchy on his chariot while Bali is left to survive, saving Prithvi, the earth goddess on his way. He calls out to Lord Jai to save the world and just as everything seems to be lost forever, Jai opens his mouth in an enormous yawn that draws in all the fire and smoke, saving the world from eternal catastrophe.

Jai saves the world and Bali's revenge results in the capture of Indrah and puts him away in a specially sealed cave to rot forever, only to return some time later to the cave to release Indrah in order for them to unite against a worse threat, that of Suketu, a radical priest from the cult of Mahakali who is following strict asura customs, systematically killing Brahmins, and running Tripura under the MCP – the Moral Cleansing Programme. The novel closes as Bali and Indrah unite to kill Suketu, a battle that sees the benevolent asura king Bali killed by Suketu, and Suketu killed by Avani (Bali's queen) with the help of Jai. Indrah of the devas lives on, leaving Avani to rule over Tripura as he decides to return home to Amravati.

One of the recurring motifs in Choudhury's novel is the shape-shifter or the *mayavi* and the novel opens with one such mayavi:

> It was about the size of a man's thumb but as it glided swiftly across the grounds it began to grow larger. By the time it had reached the wide stone staircase that led into the palace, it was almost half-a-hand long and thick as a fist. Black diamond-shaped scales were now visible along the length of its body. (Choudhury 2011, p. 7)

It is this mayavi that goes on to attack king Bali, leaving him close to death. In order to find out who is responsible for the king's near-death, the king's personnel return to the room where he was found bitten by a snake. Bhrigu finds a lump of mud in the room, on to which he pours a potion, he explains:

> All magical creatures, including Mayavis, revert to their birth form when they die – in this case a lump of clay. Traditionally, Mayavis are created from the clay of moon dust. The creator sows his own seed into the clay and gives it life. Don't ask how. It's a complicated process, but in the end, the clay can transform itself into different forms and functions, which is how a Mayavi possesses shape shifting powers. (Choudhury 2011, p. 72)

Bhrigu cannot explain how the process of creating the mayavi actually happens and this, in itself, might be understood as a marker of the genre of fantasy (see Roberts (2010) above). Bhrigu simply describes it as being 'too complicated' for explanation. The ability to shape shift can be understood differently from the 'traditional' fantasy meaning, as some Hindu gods are known in their various avatars. In this sense, these gods are also able to shape shift, that is to appear as one and then to appear as another. Vishnu is mostly associated with avatars in Hindu scriptures, although Shiva and Ganesha are also described as appearing in avatars. Although there is a link in terms of the ability to transform from one to another, the predominant difference between the two ideas, and this is explored in Choudhury's novel, is that the mayavi's ability to shape shift is primarily to attack or kill and, in this sense, the shape shifting is for evil or negatives ends. The avatars of Lord Vishnu, as an example, are not for such ends, on the contrary, given that Vishnu is essentially 'the protector'. With this in mind, we might understand Choudhury's creation of the mayavis actually of the fantasy genre according to Roberts' definition, despite their etymology of Hinduism and the cultural anchoring of the idea of shape shifting in the Hindu scriptures and texts through the notion of avatars. As we have discussed above, for a readership with little or no knowledge of Hinduism and its practices, the idea of shape shifting would most likely appear as being of the fantasy genre and have no connection with the idea of Hindu avatars. This blending of Hindu culture, practice and/or religion with 'fictional' sequences interwoven, is one of the most interesting developments within this body of fiction.

Choudhury's novel, despite its seemingly ancient historical context, weaves in tropes of the contemporary. Indrah pulls out a 'high-pitched wailing' conch shell from his robes which vibrating, repeats in an irritating monotone 'You have a message, you have a message' (Choudhury 2011, p. 90). Indrah presses his forefinger onto the shell and a roll of parchment falls out of the conch and onto his lap; this is his message. In an intimate scene between Urvashi and Indrah, Urvashi goes to the dressing chamber to fetch her 'love cuffs':

"What are those?" Indrah asked.

"Love cuffs," Urvashi crooned, dangling them over his nose, "Lined with fur. They're the rage on Earth." (Choudhury 2011, p. 201)

As Indrah and Bali prepare to churn the Ocean, Privithi, the earth goddess, is brought into the narrative as she has grave concerns about the damage the churning of the ocean will have on the ecosystem. Privithi is depicted as an ancient version of a modern-day 'eco-warrior' when Choudhury (2011) writes:

She wore a plain cotton sari, the colour of young banana leaves. Her large dark eyes, usually wide open in dismay or delight, were lined thick with kohl. An oversized red bindi adorned her forehead and a tiny silver ring flashed in her nose. She wore a tribal necklace made of wooden beads and matching earrings that rattled when she bobbed up and down during the course of her impassioned speeches. (Choudhury 2011, p. 78)

The attention to Privithi's choice of plain clothes and her choice of 'tribal' jewellery as well as her 'impassioned speeches' play to a certain stereotype of modern-day environmental activists, in India as well as elsewhere, the return to 'mother-earth', which in the case of Privithi, is embodied in herself as the 'earth goddess'. Privithi is dismayed at the thought of churning the ocean, stating her opposition strongly and reminding Bali and Indrah of how much the marine ecosystem will be destroyed by this act. She shouts: 'Fellow gods, this is madness. Our greed is blinding us. The violence we inflict in nature will come back and destroy us' (Choudhury 2011, p. 83). Similar concerns are voiced within India today as the nation's economic boom of the noughties raises questions of 'greening' India, the installation of LPG autorickshaws in the metropolises, litter campaigns and beautification programmes for urban centres. New India also looks to protect its *adivasi* or 'tribals' (the term used within India), their land and heritage. Arundhati Roy, author of *The God of Small Things* (1997) has since concentrated her writing on environmental issues, including the Narmada Dam project and India's nuclear weapons activities. Roy is a figurehead of the anti-globalization/alter-globalization movement and comparisons might be drawn between this activity and the character of Privithi in Choudhury's novel, who voices the eco-concerns and consequences of the actions of the 'powerful' (in this case, the gods, Indrah and Bali) on the earth.

The more sinister narrative that runs throughout Choudhury's novel is around the question of Indianness. The notions of Indianness are embodied in the idea of Indrah, the 'good' god, against Bali the 'asura' set up within the epic tales of Hinduism. What we learn from this story is that Bali, despite being an asura, is a benevolent god and cares to do good, not evil. It is the wicked Suketu, the priest leading the Brotherhood, who is responsible for the systematic killing of the Brahmins and who establishes the Moral Cleansing Programme within Tripura (Choudhury 2011, p. 270). Bali is beguiled by Suketu, namely because Suketu helped to save Bali's life and it is due to this relationship with Suketu that Bali is drawn into the evil-doings of the Brotherhood. With time, Bali realizes that many Brahmins are being killed and so Bali unites with Indrah to stop the brutal cultural cleansing programme.

Through this narrative plot, contemporary questions of Indianness are raised in parallel, exploring the ills of extremism within ideas of nationalism. India today is made up of not only many different Hindus but also other religions and practices and given that Choudhury's novel essentially probes the idea of difference and discrimination, it is a timely and valid debate. The Ahmedabad riots, the storming of the Golden Temple, the Hindutva movement, the Bombay riots, Shiv Sena, the Mumbai attacks of 26/11, the 2012 SMS threat of North Eastern workers in Bangalore, and much more might all be read through Choudhury's novel and although the plot takes many twists and turns as the characters are loyal and disloyal at once, characters are untrustworthy – manifest above all in the shape shifting – and no one is really sure who is fighting for which side, the novel concludes that harmony *can* be achieved. The novel underscores the cost of war built on difference and discrimination but equally, it offers hope as Tripura, ruled by Queen Avani (widow of Bali), is helped by Indrah to restore reconciliation and peace before he leaves to return to his own land.

This examination of *Chanakya's Chant* and *Bali and the Ocean of Milk* reveals that the narratives blend Hindu culture, practice and/or religion with 'fictional' sequences that are often akin to the fantasy genre. What this section suggests is that to read this body of fiction as simply fantasy is to ignore the significance of this writing and the strong cultural and philosophical roots from which it draws so extensively.

7

Graphic novels

Duncan and Smith (2009) define the 'graphic novel' as 'longer than the typical comic book and most feature self-contained, rather than continuing stories' (Duncan and Smith, 2009, p. 4). Comic books might be contrasted, therefore, with the idea of a graphic novel. Comic books are not a new phenomenon in India as they were particularly prominent in 1970s and 1980s India through the Amar Chitra Katha series of comic books; the series came to be known by the acronym, 'ACKs'. Introduced in 1967, Amar Chitra Katha comic books concerned themselves with Indian epics and the Puranas such as 'Hanuman', 'Krishna' and 'Tales from the Upanishads', classics from Indian literature such as 'Anada Math', 'Malavika' and 'Urvashi', fables and humour such as the 'Jakata Tales' and 'Panchatantra Tales', as well as stories of Indian 'brave hearts' such as 'Akbar', 'Jallianwala Bagh' and 'Tipu Sultan' and finally, visionaries such as 'Jawaharlal Nehru', Mother Teresa' and 'Rabindranath Tagore'. ACK 'special issues' include: 'Dasha Avata', 'Gandhi', 'Jesus Christ' and 'Valmiki's Ramayana'. It is clear from these examples that the Amar Chitra Katha series of comic books celebrate Indian heritage and look to inform young readers, in particular, on Indian history, culture and religion. The ACKs are still available today as paper comic books, and they are also available online and through 'dial-a-comic' within India. The market for comic books within India is therefore an established one; however, Banerjee's graphic novel *The Harappa Files* (2011) in Section 7.1 and *Kashmir Pending* (2007) in Section 7.2 achieve something quite different from the ACKs and their celebration of Indian culture and history.

The advent of the graphic novel came about in the 1960s when authors were looking for new forms for the novel. The term 'graphic story' was used in the 1960s and 1970s, but it was the term 'graphic novel' that found prominence. It was during the 1980s when three influential graphic novels were published that the term came be to recognized more widely; *Maus*, *Batman: The Dark Knight Returns* and *Watchmen*. Duncan and Smith (2009) tell us that sales of graphic novels are currently on the rise, they write: 'In 2007 sales rose more than 19 percent from the previous year alone, with more than 3,300 titles released that year' (Duncan and Smith 2009, p. 81). Reasons for this rise in the interest and sales of the graphic novel might be attributed to the fact that *Maus* won the recognition of the Pulitzer Prize committee in 1992 and that libraries have stocked this work as well as other graphic novels more readily ever since. Equally, the rise in Japanese comics (Manga) in US and European markets has also impacted the sales and distribution of the graphic novel.

India has witnessed a number of graphic novel productions in the timeframe outlined above. The first recognized Indian graphic novel is *The River of Stories* (1994) by Orijit Sen. Produced by Sen in partnership with a Delhi-based environmental action group, Kalpavriksh, *The River of Stories* narrates a tale of environmental disaster and the adivasi (or 'tribals' – see Glossary). *The River of Stories* begins with a dream in which Vishnu (read: Lord Vishnu, protector – see Glossary) is watching the Minister of Sport and Youth Affairs give a Republic Day speech, the content of which aggravates Vishnu. Through the television, the minister hears Vishnu's complaints and addresses him directly, suggesting that the future of globalized India lies in development and progress. Vishnu, a recent graduate of sociology reminds the minister of those people who are hungry, jobless and illerate. The minister replies:

> It's all a matter of national priorities, friend. If we wait for every adivasi to leave the jungle and adopt a civilised way of life . . . we shall be left far behind in the global race. In any case, it's only a question of time! You say they need food and water? We'll give them potatoe chips and Pepsi cola . . . [aur bolo! in hindi script – "tell me, what more?"]. (Sen 1994, pp. 5–6)

The River of Stories explores the difficult nexus of adivasi living, development and politics and most pertinently, the advent of the planned dam that will destroy the livelihood of the adivasi. *The River of Stories* depicts the narrative through line drawings, often intricately drawn (see pp. 48–9 as an example). Such a hand-drawn map shows the site of the advasi, community points of interest, monuments and shrines sit alongside clearly marked topographical markers of forests and mountains. The detail and investment in the map grounds the advasi peoples in the landscape historically and culturally, claiming the land, as it were, for themselves. Supplanted over this detailed map is a narrative panel, showing a news reporter from 'TV News', holding his camera and microphone as he asks the adivasi: 'Can you tell our viewers why you are marching to the dam site?' To which they reply: 'Because our minds are made up. If the *sarkari* won't stop this dam, they'll have to do it on our dead bodies!' (Sen 1994, p. 48).

The graphic novel includes an article piece from *Voice* entitled: 'Rewasagar Dam: monument of progress or wall of despair', which appears to be an authentic text, produced around the time of the controversy. Overall, the graphic novel is made up of a series of complex narrative panels, back-fill drawings, upon which the narrative panels sit, there are some pages of free text and drawings – page 12 includes advasi-style drawings in order to depict how the universe, its animals and humans were created, as an example – as well as pages of larger pictures with little or no text.

The narrative ends as it starts, with a dream. Sitting peacefully under the mahua tree, an advasi is interrupted by the arrival of the same sports and youth affairs minister we meet in the 'prologue dream'. The minister arrives in his helicopter and asks what the advasi is doing. The advasi replies that he isn't doing anything, to which the minister suggests he get up and join the national mainstream and earn some money. With money, the minister advises, the advasi could buy up land, grow more food and make profit. The advasi replies:

> "What do I do with all that profit?"
>
> "Why you could go into business! Employ others to do all the work . . . while YOU sat back and just enjoyed life!"
>
> "Oh I see! – But THAT, my friend . . . is just what I was doing anyway, till you came along on that noisy bird of yours!" (Sen 1994, p. 48)

The form of the graphic novel is befitting of this narrative on several levels. The ability to tell the story through the graphic narrative panels as well as through the line, back-fill drawings and maps allows the advasi 'storytelling' structures to permeate the narrative. The use of music, diagrams and oral storytelling are incorporated into the graphic novel using the pictorial, and the choice of a non-linear sequentiality also supports the oral storytelling form, this, in particular, would be compromised in a traditional 'novel' narrative structure, for example. The peripheral nature of the graphic novel in the market, as highlighted in the work of Duncan and Smith (2009), also reflects the alternative position that *The River of Stories* takes on development, progress and the advasi people. Unlike the 'national mainstream' that the minister urges the advasi man to be part of, this graphic novel embodies the overall sense of alterity and peripheral existence in its choice of form and structure, consciously fashioning it away from the mainstream.

It was not until nearly 10 years after the publication of *The River of Stories* (1994) that the market of and for graphic novels within India grew significantly. A rise in the production of the graphic novel in India can be seen post-millennium, and the 2000s have enjoyed a number of graphic novels by the most renowned graphic novel author, Sarnath Banerjee. Banerjee has also illustrated other authors' books; for example, see the frontispiece in Gokhale's *Priya In Incredible Indyaa*, (2011) and Gokhale's reprint of *Paro: Dreams of Passion* with Penguin from 2011. Sarnath Banerjee's own works include: *Corridor* (2004) a graphic novel that explores New Delhi, specifically the area around Connaught Place, and *The Barn Owl's Wondrous Capers* (2007), which moves through Calcutta, Paris and London, from the eighteenth century to the turn of the millennium and, most recently, Banerjee's *The Harappa Files* (2011), which is explored in this chapter. Other graphic novels published in this period include *Kashmir Pending* (2007) by Ahmed and Singh (discussed here in section 7.2), *The Hotel at the End of the World* (2009) by Parismita Singh, Appupen's *Moonward* (2009) and Vishwajyoti Ghosh's *Delhi Calm* (2010). 2012 sees the publication of an anthology of comics edited by some of these graphic novelists called *Pao* as well as a graphic novel entitled *Rabbit Rap: a 21st century fable* written and illustrated by Musharraf Ali Farooqi and Michelle Farooqi.

7.1 'Post-liberalized India'

The Harappa Files (2011)

The Harappa Files engages significantly and at times, controversially, with issues of New India. As Banerjee writes, 'post-liberalized India' (Banerjee, 2011, p. 15) poses new challenges and dilemmas and throughout *The Harappa Files*, Banerjee explores these challenges that relate in particular to class, economic prosperity and governance. In the opening pages of the novel, Banerjee offers some background to how the *The Harappa Files* has come about: 'In the following two years, Banerjee created a series of graphic commentaries that addressed the cracks of post-liberalized India, a fast capitalizing society that suffers from bipolar disorder' (Banerjee 2011, p. 15).

The Harappa Files acts as a generational and cultural museum for an India that is changing at pace. Throughout the graphic novel, Banerjee presents 'artefacts' from the India of the 1970s and 1980s and his observations of these artefacts are riddled with, now adult understandings, of these items' affiliations to class, caste, and religion. The act of remembering, of memory and recollection is a dominant strand throughout *The Harappa Files* and this act of remembering an India of 'then' helps to interrogate an India of 'now'.

As one such example of recollection, Banerjee remembers 'the telephone sanitizer', Gobindo, who worked at his father's office. Gobindo from West Bengal, a Midnapuri, is ridiculed for his eating habits, namely, that his daily meal is a mountain of rice with a little 'watery dal' on the top. Banerjee writes: 'When two Midnapuris sit down to eat, facing each other, two pyramids of rice block their vision. Only in the middle of lunch can they discover the identity of the person sitting across from them' (Banerjee 2011, p. 165). Banerjee offers anecdotally, a memory from his childhood: 'Gobindo sometimes ate at our house, in the kitchen, always facing the wall, as if he were doing something criminal' (Banerjee 2011, p. 166). This adult reflection on a childhood memory is a familiar feature of *The Harappa Files*. The memories are usually of the everyday, insignificant in their happening, gathering significance with Banerjee's adult recollections and the framing of these memories with New India and new ideas of middle-classness.

As Banerjee states in the opening pages (Banerjee 2011, p. 15), he scrutinizes the 'cracks of post-liberalized India' and his discussion on class is a reoccurring preoccupation throughout the book. Often, discussion of class is linked to food – the types of food and frequency of eating food in particular, as presented above in the 'Gobindo' extract. Another example of the food–class nexus, is found on page 31 of *The Harappa Files* where there is an image of a 'dabba', it reads: 'India is not a fear society, we need to see shit happen before we start flapping our arms. The only way the elite will take notice is if their hot lunch gets cold' (Banerjee 2011, p. 31).

August 2011 witnessed a 13-day fast by Anna Hazare at the Ramlila grounds in New Delhi. Anna Hazare's choice to fast was to influence the contentious 'Lokpal' bill, a bill designed to combat corruption in India, specifically at government level. Anna Hazare's fast garnered much support across India and after a week of Hazare's fasting, the 'dabbawallahs' of Mumbai joined him in his demonstration by going on strike, resulting in non-delivery of thousands of 'dabbas' to the middle classes all over Mumbai. Banerjee's observation on the mechanics of India's class system and that demonstration might only be recognized once food is compromised, is timely. In the case of New India and its economic growth, issues of food consumption, marketing and production are inextricably linked, and Banerjee interrogates some of these difficulties at various points in *The Harappa Files*.

Banerjee's preoccupation with class in *The Harappa Files* is also seen in his recollection of 'smell' during his childhood and how 'smell' for him at least, was linked to class. Banerjee writes: 'Jagat Bahadur smelled of Lifebuoy soap, as did the gardener, driver, cook and the entire canteen staff in my father's office. It was the smell of the working class' (Banerjee 2011, p. 82). This piece of text is accompanied by an image of a man lifting a traditional exercise mace, a *gadda* and a radio sits beside, advertising Lifebuoy:

> Tandroosti ka raksha karta hai, Lifebuoy, Lifebuoy hai, jaha tandroosti waha Lifebuoy. (Banerjee 2011, p. 82)
>
> [Lifebuoy! Lifebuoy! protects your health, where there is Lifebuoy, there is good health]

Banerjee writes: 'On the other hand, middle-class men like my father used Liril and played badminton on Sundays' (Banerjee 2011, p. 83). Banerjee juxtaposes the two classes, the working class and the middle class, through both smell (of soap) and exercise type. The image of the working-class man is strong as he lifts weights and the carbolic smell of the Lifebuoy soap affirms his presence, indeed, the smell of the Lifebuoy soap is stronger than the soap used by the middle-class man, whose exercise type is badminton, an energetic but not heavy form of exercise (compared to the *gadda*).

7.2 Conflict

Kashmir Pending (2007)

The graphic novel *Kashmir Pending* is published in full colour with the narrative panels printed on a matt black background for the majority of the

95 pages. The darkness of the pages echoes the darkness of the narrative, one set in the valley of Kashmir amidst violence, imprisonment and death. Based on a true account, the narrative is written by Naseer Ahmed and the artwork by Saurabh Singh. *Kashmir Pending* is published by Phantomville, based in New Delhi; one of the editors being Sarnath Banerjee.

The prologue begins in silence. A series of long, stretched panels shows a young man on a boat on a lake. The boat looks like those found on Lake Dal in Sringar, a 'shikara' and from this shikara a young man throws a stone across the water in the direction of some other boats, boats that are patrolling the lake, boats containing armed security forces. As the stone falls near one of the boats, the young man jumps out of his shikara on to the lakeside while one of the security force team raises his gun and breaks the silence and a speech bubble reads: 'Kid's going to run into trouble one day' (Ahmed and Singh 2007, p. 4).

The story of the protagonist, Mushtaq Miyan, is told mostly from inside a jail in Srinagar and this constitutes the majority of the graphic novel. Mustaq narrates his tale to a fellow inmate, Ali who is 22 years old, about how he first spent time inside a jail; a stint of 22 days due to his involvement in a street riot. On his release, Mustaq was hailed as a hero in his neighbourhood and from thereon, he became more involved in political life. A leader named Qasim inspired Mustaq to think about supporting 'free Kashmir' he tells Ali and his meeting with Qasim, he reveals, changed his life forever. A protest march in Lal Chowk leads to more bloodshed and to the death of a local shopkeeper; many people gather for prayers around the dead man's body. Mushtaq tells Ali: 'This overwhelming response to his death strengthened my resolve and hardened my belief' (Ahmed and Singh 2007, p. 39). Mushtaq decides to enlist and makes 'free Kashmir' his mission in life. In a camp in Masara, Mushatq and his friend Aziz are trained to fight: 'We were being prepared to face the enemy. The weapons had changed. No more stones and crude bombs, we were now armed with automatics' (Ahmed and Singh 2007, p. 46). The two men decide to crossover into Afghanistan as they are tired with the in-fighting at the Masara camp. The two men stay at the training camp in Afghanistan for three months before deciding to return to Srinagar but they need help in crossing the border. A guide is found to help them make the passage safely but Mushtaq is disgusted that the guide takes Rps 2000 from them all in order to ensure their safe passage: 'The pettiness of the guide astounded me. After all, he is man from the valley, this is his fight as much as mine. Did he not have any sympathies for the cause?' (Ahmed and Singh 2007, p. 54).

Mushtaq continues to tell his story to Ali and he explains how once back in Sringar, he and Aziz begin their plans for a revolution but another faction of the free army also trying to liberate Kashmir, the 'K force', stops the advancement of their plans. The 'K force', financially strong from the extortion (of civilian protection schemes) they are involved in, are a well-organized and powerful group. Aziz is killed at their hands; a bullet, seemingly fired from one of their weapons kills him in a shoot-out between the free forces and the security forces. The death of Aziz changes Mushtaq forever he tells Ali, as he holds himself responsible for the death of his dear friend, Aziz. Then, one day at a roadblock, Mushtaq decides to hand over the bag of grenades he is carrying with him and gives himself up. He tells Ali that he did this instead of killing yet more innocent people who were gathered along the roadside amidst the security forces; he laments that the grenades would surely have taken their lives too. Mushtaq ruminates: 'In the land of violent decisions a gesture of peace is an absurd move. It is looked at with suspicion and disbelief' (Ahmed and Singh 2007, p. 80). In the epilogue, Mushtaq, having been released from prison a year earlier, tells of his new life as a restaurant owner. On Ali's release from prison, Mushtaq goes to meet him but he knows from Ali's eyes that this meeting is only to say goodbye:

> Young men like Ali are too charged to see through the manipulation. They dedicate their lives to the cause handed to them by these leaders. These men won't flinch from strapping dynamite to their bodies and blowing themselves up in the middle of the marketplace. (Ahmed and Singh 2007, p. 84)

The silence of the prologue is reinvoked in these closing scenes of the epilogue, as the panels show close-up images of the security forces' boots, guns and helmets and then Ali, wrapped in a shawl, entering the marketplace, shadows falling across his face, his eyes set, focused, determined.

As the epilogue's silence reminisces the prologue's similar silence, we remember the young man in the shikara on Lake Dal and know that it was Mushtaq. The drama of the scene which is about to play out is heightened by the knowledge that Mushtaq was fighting with mere stones but for Ali, with a suicide bomb strapped to his chest. And so, Ali, all these years later, in the same silence, approaches the security forces with the same intention of destruction as Mushtaq had, throwing his stones from his boat on the still waters of Dal Lake. Mushtaq laments: 'I wish I could have done something to save him' (Ahmed and Singh 2007, p. 91), although Mushtaq knows inside his heart that he couldn't have saved Ali from what he did.

The final panel of the graphic novel shows Mustaq in his restaurant, a glass of tea on the table in front of him, only half of his body is visible through the (sun) light falling on his face. The scene is immensely dark, only the light from outside the building creeps in through a space between the roof and the top of the wall. The scene is lonely and yet, in comparison to the Mushtaq of the shikara on Dal Lake, more peaceful and with a chink of hope embodied in the light that falls on his face.

The form of the graphic novel for *Kashmir Pending* underscores the permeating force of violence and death in conflict. The drawings depict the violence *graphically* in the sense of the actual form of the line drawings, as well as the 'content' of the horror of life in Sringar and in the training camps. The cycles of violence and death that are repeated in this narrative are also demonstrated in the non-linear structure of the graphic novel panels. The pictorial representation of anger and violence is represented variously; a close-up image of a young angry face (Ahmed and Singh 2007, p. 18), brutal beatings (Ahmed and Singh 2007, p. 29), gun-shot wounds where the blood sprays across the scene (Ahmed and Singh 2007, p. 27), images of men taking aim with their gun – images which are zoomed in for detail and a sense of presence (Ahmed and Singh 2007, p. 26), hands clasped tight at prison bars (Ahmed and Singh 2007, p. 42), security forces wielding lathis (Ahmed and Singh 2007, p. 19), arson (Ahmed and Singh 2007, p. 92), stone and grenade throwing (Ahmed and Singh 2007, pp. 76–7), as examples. These various images of violence and anger result in a strong theme that runs throughout the narrative and this is juxtaposed with the silence and comparative calm that exist in both the prologue and the epilogue. The cyclical motif of the narrative is greatly exemplified in Mushtaq's own experience too and the prologue/epilogue structure reinforces the sense of his own (and Ali's) journey.

Mushtaq's Kashmir experience might be contrasted to that of Aziz or Ali, both men dying because of their wish to free Kashmir, but Mushtaq has, for some reason, fate or otherwise, lived to tell the tale. Mushtaq's story, therefore, feeds into the notion of 'Kashmir Pending'. He knows what it is to engage with 'the struggle' and unlike others, he has survived and it is this survival which means that he also knows what it is to opt out of 'the struggle'. Mushtaq tells how he eventually gives himself up, spends time in prison and on his release, he chooses to begin a new life as a restaurant owner. During this new life, however, the violence continues on around him, men still fight to free Kashmir, people continue to kill for the cause and people continue to die for the cause and in this sense, the situation in Kashmir is cyclical. Moreover, for as long as such a situation continues, Kashmir is in limbo, it is, as the title suggests: 'pending'.

Conclusions: New/Old stories in Old/New ways?

Reading New India has been concerned with a body of post-millennial fiction in English from India and how the themes of young India, middle-classness and questions of caste and religious identity in particular, are manifest in this new writing. An over-arching interest has been in how these themes speak to, and of, notions of New India. In addition, the volume has been particularly interested in how the new writing draws on (in various ways) ancient Indian literary traditions and Hindu epic narratives as well as the role of Indian English(es) in the fiction.

This book has presented both a detailed survey of the broad and various body of post-millennial fiction in English from India as well as detailed, close readings of a careful selection from this body of fiction. An observation of this book has been the benchmarking of Indian 'postcolonial literary texts' (see Section 1.2) against the post-millennial fiction, with the suggestion that a large proportion of post-millennial fiction in English from India is not recognizable by the tropes and guises of Indian postcolonial texts. This 'benchmarking' draws on the work of Gilbert (2001, p. 1) and of Boehmer (2005, p. 3) and their definitions and characterizations of the postcolonial and of postcolonial literature (see Dawson Varughese (2012) for further discussion of this).

Reading New India suggests that there are themes from this body of new fiction, found *across* the novels, which speak to, and of, New India. In addition to themes, there are also a number of growing genres and forms of writing which have been explored here in Chapters 2 to 7, namely, urban narratives, chick lit, crick lit, call centre and corporate narratives, sexuality (presented here as MSM), crime writing, fantasy, historical fiction and graphic novels. Some of these genres, such as crime writing, have a longer history of writing in English from India, whereas crick lit and call centre narratives have a much more recent advent in the scene of writing in English.

This concluding chapter will consider these various 'themes' across the fiction that has been explored in this book before closing in consideration of the future of fiction writing in English from India.

Television, film and media

Television features variously across the novels explored in this volume. The role of television in cricket and the IPL in Chauhan's *The Zoya Factor* (2008) as well as in Sundar's *The Premier Murder League* (2010) are an important part of the authors' depictions of both the game, and the 'event' that cricket has become, particularly since the inauguration of IPL.

Merchant (1999) also speaks of television when he writes of the MTV culture and its impact on notions of 'youth' as well as the false projections of homosexual identities (1999, p. xiv) and the character of Rumi in Chauhan's *Battle For Bittora* (2010) in particular, speaks to Merchant's concerns over Western notions of gay identity on Indian youth. This is evidenced in Rumi's behaviours, particularly in his interactions with Jinni where they discuss (and argue) over the sexual orientation of their favourite superheroes and for Jinni at least, in Rumi's continual wearing of the black armbands 'in remembrance of the victims of 26/11' (Chauhan 2010, p. 9).

The characters of 'Ric and Nic' in Kala's novel *Almost Single* also speak to notions of Merchant's (1999) Western gay identity: Ric is Aisha's 'party hag' (Kala 2007, p. 101) and the gay couple arrange a lavish break-fast for the girls after their Karva Chauth fast. Aisha, the protagonist of Kala's novel says of Ric and Nic, 'with the sensitivity that is the reserve of gay men, [they] have brought a hamper with the ultimate Moët and Chandon, Boursin cheese, shepherd's pie, garlic bread, a tossed salad and brownies, not to mention linen serviettes and real silverware. Not exactly religious fare, but then, we aren't great on religion either (Kala 2007, p. 119).

This kind of activity might be considered part of Merchant's (1999) description of the impact of MTV culture, stating that it 'has projected the West's gay sub-culture in its worst light by highlighting its lunatic fringe as if it were mainstream. Your baker, butcher, banker, bus conductor, neighbour or brother could all be very ordinary and also very gay' (Merchant 1999, p. xiv).

Other Western-influenced television programmes include reality TV shows such as *Indian Idol* (mentioned in Basu 2010) and *Master Chef India*, programmes that, like the events of IPL and the advertising in between the televised games, are riven with Bollywood celebrities and film personalities.

The rise of television and satellite in India has resulted in Bollywood films being screened on television and although cinema (or 'theatre') going is still very popular in India, satellite in particular, from the mid-1990s onwards has created a new 'home' lifestyle for many Indians. With the rise in television and satellite has come a plethora of news and media channels. Mention of media and news channels is made in several of the new fiction novels, including Sundar's (2010) description of the hungry media polls, gauging public opinion on the latest cricket scandal, where 'experts' are called on to the news channels to endlessly debate the latest debacle. Contemporary news channels engage with all kinds of social media (emails, Twitter, Facebook, as examples) in addition to online link-ups across India, meaning that certain groups of India's population express their opinions and reactions to breaking news stories almost immediately. This was certainly the case, to give a literary-orientated example, of the Jaipur Literature Festival of 2012, when threats against Salman Rushdie's life were made which stopped Rushdie attending and speaking at the event. A range of people's opinions, positions and politics on Rushdie was shared via the news channels' social media engagement, the public's 'tweets' often rolling across the bottom of the television screen as they became available. Basu (2010) in his novel *Turbulence* makes reference to contemporary news channels through a fictional television station he names, 'DNNTV' (Basu 2010, p. 84). He writes: '. . . this is a landmark moment in the history of the world. This report will be broadcast worldwide, and it is brought to you by us' (Basu 2010, p. 84). Echoing current practices in media today Basu (2010) writes:

> While other media channels have missed this breaking story, choosing only to focus on the first match of the new Indian Giga-League Gully Cricket Tournament . . . we at DNNTV are here with you because we have confidential sources on the inside, and soon, exclusive footage that will show you what happened inside this hospital today. (Basu 2010, p. 40)

Post millennium, media channels have also engaged with social issues in particular positive ways, for example, the notorious murder case of Jessica Lal. Public SMS messaging polls demonstrated the public outrage at the procrastination and the seemingly corrupt processes around the Lal murder case. The media created platforms for people to express their opinions, which in turn, mobilized agents involved in the case, pressuring them for a just and fair outcome. There was also a public display of support for the case through a candlelight vigil at India Gate in New Delhi and this was also facilitated through SMS messaging. This public event was influenced by the film *Rang De Basanti* (2006), which as part of its own storyline, holds a candlelight vigil at India Gate. This re-enactment of the vigil helped raise public awareness over justice and corruption – the Bollywood film 'No one Killed Jessica' was based on these events and was released in 2011.

Middle-classness – class, caste, religion

The body of post-millennial fiction explored in this book engages frequently with questions of middle-classness. Several of the novels include a character who considers herself/himself as 'middle class'. In Hasan's *Neti Neti: Not This, Not This* (2009), Mr Bhatt is portrayed as a 'proper' citizen and his devout Hinduism is part of this proper and middle-class identity. At various points in the narrative, Mr Bhatt attempts to put Sophie 'on the right path', discouraging her from mixing with the friendship group she has and encouraging her to engage with more spiritual activities.

In a similar vein, Kala's novel *Almost Single* (2007) has a character who carefully observes religious practices and makes it her business to assess whether the young women residents in her block are conducting, what she considers at least, a 'proper' lifestyle. Kala (2007) writes that 'Mrs Mukherjee has a very fixed notion of "bhadralok" and Misha just doesn't cut it. It has become her life's ambition now to get Misha evicted' (Kala 2007, p. 81). Mrs Mukherjee's sense of 'middle-classness' is not how Misha and Aisha understand the idea of 'middle-classness'. Aisha considers herself to be of the same class as Mrs Mukherjee, Aisha has a respectable job and earns a very good salary and, therefore, considers herself, like Misha as middle class. Misha comes from a well-to-do family in Bhatinda and works as an insurance advisor, a job that was secured by her Papaji (her father). She works because she wants to and not because she has to, as Misha is financially independent. Mrs Mukherjee's notions of middle-classness, female behaviour and conduct are not in line with how Aisha and Misha understand these notions and it is only when the girls take part in the Karva Chauth fast, that Mrs Mukherjee's opinion of the girls improves.

Like Mrs Mukherjee in Kala'a *Almost Single*, Mrs Puri in Adiga's *Last Man In Tower* is also interested in the lives of her fellow residents, in particular in the life and 'lifestyle' (class) of her neighbour, Ms Meenakshi who works various hours of the day and night as a journalist. Moreover, it is the lifestyle of Ms Meenakshi, her boyfriend-visitor and the item that the cat found in Ms Meenakshi's rubbish – a condom – that concern Mrs Puri the most. Mrs Puri describes Ms Meenakshi's lifestyle as 'the modern shame-free way of living' (Adiga 2011, p. 22) and Mrs Puri's lines of difference are drawn along those of modernity (versus tradition) of an unmarried, single woman (versus a married woman) and a working woman – a journalist – (versus a family-orientated woman). These differences are located in a New India in comparison to the India and the experience of a woman in a different India, one that Mrs Puri has known – all of which talks to Radhakrishnan's (2011) and Varma's (2007) notions of the 'new' middle class(es).

Questions of class (and caste) are also present in Rao's narrative on homosexuality through the characters Yudi and Miland. Miland who is from Mahim and lives in a chawl is particularly interested in understanding how 'class' works within the gay community. Miland tests Yudi (knowing that Yudi is a Brahmin) by eating a little of his own food then asks Yudi to eat the rest. To Miland's surprise, Yudi is prepared to eat the food:

"But you are a Brahman, aren't you?"

"No, I am a homosexual. Gay by caste. Gay by religion."

"I don't understand what you are saying."

"What I am saying is that homosexuals have no caste or religion. They have only their sexuality." (Rao 2003, p. 81)

Chauhan's novel *Battle for Bittora* also flouts the rules of caste (and religion). The two protagonists, Jinni and Zain, are political opposites as well as being opposites in their religious affiliations – Jinni is Hindu and Zain is Muslim. The factor that betters their polemic situation is that they are both upper middle class. Jinni is Brahmin Hindu and from a wealthy family and Zain is Muslim, from a Nawab heritage. The common ground between these two characters is eventually found in their class background, which overrides the issues of not simply 'caste' (as we read above in Rao's characters of Yudi and Miland) but also of religion. Jinni's grandmother, curiously, cannot see beyond the religious differences and at various points in the narrative, she draws on Muslim stereotyping in order to tell Jinni what she thinks of the situation:

> See doesn't realize that all musalmaan men think this way about Hindu women – that we are all nympho. See thinks all this is a game, with rules and *times-please* and good manners. Arey bhai, this is politics! It ij free-style fighting! No holes barred! (Chauhan 2010, p. 269)

Vadukut's novel *The Incredible Adventures of Robert 'Einstein' Varghese* also underscores the idea of class as a vehicle for social mobility – irrespective of caste and/or religion. The protagonist, Varghese, identifies himself as an employee of the business analyst world and, at various points in the story, works hard at not being identified through his regional and religious identities. Trivedi's 'Dan' in *Call Me Dan* is also not inclined to identify himself in terms of his religious and caste backgrounds despite the fact that his parents' identities are configured in this manner. 'Dan' or 'Gautam' as he is known at home, is identified more by the India that he is living and experiencing and Trivedi (2010) writes about Gautam in New India thus:

> [Gautam has] choices no generation before his has had, not just in what he can buy, but in how he can earn it. . . . Gautam had lost two jobs before he was thirty, testament not to turbulence, but perhaps to the fact that there are jobs to lose. (Trivedi 2010, p. 147)

Like Varghese then, Dan is also identified through his job and how successful he is at making his life (and money) in an India that offers the opportunity to do so.

We might also see how Banerjee's graphic novel engages with questions of class. *The Harappa Files* captures New India in 'a series of graphic commentaries that addresses[d] the cracks of post-liberalized India, a fast capitalizing society that suffers from bipolar disorder' (Banerjee 2011, p. 15). In Section 7.1, I described *The Harappa Files* as a generational and cultural museum for an India that is changing at pace and in creating this 'museum' Banerjee moves between the 'old' India and the 'post-liberalized India' he talks of, the India that is suffering from 'bipolar disorder'.

Finally, the growth in fiction analysed in Section 6.2 (Bharati fantasy or historical fiction?) also explores issues of class, mainly through religion. The interest and growth in this fiction might be attributed to a desire to 'return' to Bharat; a reaction against the many forces of change that have affected Indian society in the last 10 years or more. As most of the fiction in this book demonstrates, India has experienced global, and predominantly Western influences on its society in this short timeframe – whether this has been through television and media, technology or consumerism. These changes, some might argue, have diluted the essence of being Indian. A return to 'Bharat' therefore, through this particular body of post-millennial fiction, revives Indianness through the very geographies, topographies and epic narratives of these fictions. On the other hand, the sense of 'Bharat' evident in these fictions is deeply situated in a Hindu India, an India of Hindu cultural and religious practices, and therefore, has ramifications on how we might understand and receive this fiction given today's Indian readership.

Another important motif of the post-millennial fiction explored in this volume is the 'urban'. Chapter 2 focuses on narratives that are set in urbanscapes. Many of the other fictions discussed in the other chapters are also set against urban backdrops: *Almost Single, Call Me Dan, One Night @ The Call Centre, The Boyfriend, Saraswati Park*, the Lalli Mysteries and Jain's *Piggies on the Railway* as well as *The Temple-Goers, The Man with Enormous Wings, Turbulence, Monkey-Man* and *The Harappa Files*. The cities of New Delhi, Mumbai, Bangalore and Ahmedabad are the locations for these narratives and it is noteworthy to see how few of the new writings' narratives, to date, take place in non-urban centres.

Old and new: The future of 'Reading India'

This chapter, entitled: 'New/Old Stories in Old/New Ways?' is phrased as a question rather than a statement. The reason why this idea of 'New/Old Stories in Old/New Ways' is posed as a question is because Indian fiction in English is enjoying a period of relatively high yield; nevertheless, with global economics affecting India more significantly of late, it is questionable whether some production, and moreover, consumption, of this fiction will remain at the level it currently enjoys.

A second reason as to why this chapter title is posed as a question is because the 'newness' of the post-millennial fiction in English from India does mean that the observation of trends in the fiction requires more time to see *exactly* how the genres themes and forms outlined here in this book, actually play out and develop over time. Although this book has shown apparent departures in post-millennial fiction in English from India, there are questions around these new forms and departures: has chick lit already enjoyed its heyday? Will call centre narratives wane if India's service industry changes in response to global economic pressures? As India strengthens its role as part of the BRICS nations, will new narratives of the corporate world appear? Is this current conservative body of crick lit set to expand as the IPL 'event-marketing' goes from strength to strength? And will Bharat-orientated fiction explode as a return to 'Bharat' counteracts the increasing global and 'Western' influences on India?

The questions around genre and form are not the only questions that should be asked in relation to this new body of writing; indeed, the issue of 'English' is also one that might be poised for change. The focus of *Reading New India* has been on post-millennial fiction in English from India – it has been out of the scope and focus of this book to look at other Indian language fiction in detail – but it is important to note that publishing in other Indian languages has also proved plentiful, post-millennium. Hindi, Bengali, Tamil and Malayali literature as examples, have also enjoyed the economic growth of publishing houses, resulting in a growth of fiction lists in these languages. Interestingly, the departures in genre and form found in the English-medium post-millennial fiction have not necessarily been echoed in other Indian language fiction, further supporting the enduring idea of the eclectic and various India. Furthermore, the future of publishing in Indian fiction could well not be found in these Indian language fictions, but rather in fiction 'in translation', as Indian language fiction is translated from one 'regional' language to another. And English no doubt, alongside Hindi and Bengali, will be one of these 'translation' configurations.

The global economy and its effect on New India, the newness of this body of fiction and the future of English within India all put into question how fiction in English from India will develop further. The impact of the Indian diaspora on this body of fiction might also be considered as a factor that will shape future publishing trends. This book has not engaged with Indian diasporic writing and this has been due to the scope and interest of this book's thesis. This volume has been interested in how domestic socio-cultural issues and politics have impacted the new writing from within India; however, as India continues to develop its economic policies as well as its policies and position on Indian identity for people of Indian origin, many new narratives of the New India experience, domestically and otherwise, will surely appear.

In all, the transitory nature of this body of post-millennial writing in English from India, not only within the body of writing itself and the trends that it has demonstrated to date, but also in a much broader sense, in its position alongside (other language) fiction competitors in India, means that a strong, definitive statement on the future of Indian fiction in English is very difficult to generate. Since the millennium, social and cultural change has come quickly and the span of 12 years – the fiction discussed here is published between 2000 and 2012 – is, in comparison to the longer view of literary trends, a short time period.

In summary then we might say that the body of post-millennial fiction in English examined in this book has shown how 'new' stories are told in 'old' ways – Basu's novel *Turbulence* explored in Section 6.1 where the near-future setting of Mumbai and the superheroes with world-changing powers locate the text as 'new' but the characters and their epic plot, the otherworldliness of the good versus evil plot and the characters' individual 'super powers' which might be interpreted as being akin to some of the Hindu gods' abilities and powers, locate the fiction in older literary Indian aesthetics.

The graphic novels explored in Chapter 7 are also examples of how 'new' stories are being told in 'old' ways. The heritage of India's Amar Chitra Katha comics, introduced in 1967 means that the form of the comic or graphic novel is not necessarily 'new' to the Indian market, but the themes of these graphic novels are very much so.

The fiction examined in *Reading New India* also clearly demonstrates that 'new' stories are also being told in 'new' ways and Section 3.2 'crick lit' and Chapter 4 (Young India), are examples of this. Crick Lit is a new genre of fiction within Indian writing in English and given the recent developments in cricket in India, the fiction is writing 'new' narratives in 'new' ways. The same might also be said for the fiction explored in Section 4.1 in particular, 'new' fictions of the corporate and call centre worlds are told in 'new' ways, such as Vadukut's series of Word document 'diary entries', burned onto CDs, found in a pizza box in a flat in New Delhi.

This body of post-millennial fiction has also demonstrated how 'old' stories are also being told in 'new' ways. The most obvious example of how 'old' (ancient) stories are being told in 'new' ways is evident in the texts explored in Section 6.2 ('Bharati Fantasy or Historical Fiction?'). This type of fiction draws heavily on early ideas of narrative and on ancient, Hindu Bharat, but the fiction retells these narratives in new ways that include developing the fictional elements of this historical fiction and changing the time period(s) in which the narratives are set.

The significant element of this configuration of 'old' and 'new', 'stories' and 'ways' is significant because of its absence. There is a lack of 'old' stories being told in 'old' ways in the body of post-millennial fiction in English from India, and most noticeably in the selection of fiction investigated here in this volume. By 'old' stories, I refer to Indian postcolonial fiction, benchmarked in Chapter 1 through the definitions of the postcolonial by Gilbert (2001) and Boehmer (2005). This volume has aimed to demonstrate that a significant amount of post-millennial fiction in English from India is less recognizable by the tropes and guises of postcolonial texts and that in parallel with many of the political, economic and socio-cultural developments of the last 10 years in India, India's fiction in English is engaged with telling 'new' stories, often, but not always, in 'new' ways. These new fictions in English talk directly of, and to New India and at the heart of these fictions is the exploration and examination of 'Indianness' in India today.

REFERENCES

Adiga, A. (2011), *Last Man in Tower*. London: Atlantic Books.

Ahmed, N. and Singh, S. (2007), *Kashmir Pending*. New Delhi: Phantomville.

Alter, J. S. (2011), *Moral Materialism: Sex and Masculinity in Modern India*. New Delhi: Penguin India.

Anand, M. R. (1940), *Untouchable*. London: Penguin.

—(2006), *Selected Short Stories*. New Delhi: Penguin India.

Anonymous (2010), *The Gamechangers*. New Delhi: HarperCollins.

Ashley, A. (ed.) (2008), *Subtle Edens*. Norwich: Elastic Press.

Banerjee, S. (2011), *The Harappa Files*. New Delhi: HarperCollins.

Basu, S. (2005), www.users.rcn.com/singhvan/SamitBasu.html [accessed Jan 2011].

—(2010), *Turbulence*. Gurgaon: Hachette India.

Bery, A. (2005), 'Reflexive worlds: The Indias of A. K. Ramanujan', in P. Morey and A. Tickell (eds), *Alternative Indias: Writing, Nation and Communalism*. Amsterdam, NY: Rodopi, pp. 115–38.

Bhagat, C. (2008), *One Night @ The Call Centre*. New Delhi: Rupa & Co.

Bhalla, A. (2006), *Shashi Deshpande*. Devon: Northcote House Publishers.

Bhaskaran, S. (2004), *Made In India: Decolonizations, Queer Sexualities, Trans/national Projects*. New York: Palgrave Macmillan.

Boehmer, E. (2005), *Colonial and Postcolonial Literature*. Oxford: Oxford University Press.

—(2009), *Empire Writing: An Anthology of Colonial Literature 1870–1918*. Oxford: Oxford University Press.

Bose, M. (2006), *The Magic of Indian Cricket: Cricket and Society in India*. London: Routledge.

Brosius, C. (2010), *India's Middle Class: New Forms of Urban Leisure, Consumption and Prosperity*. New Delhi: Routledge.

Chauhan, A. (2008), *The Zoya Factor*. New Delhi: HarperCollins.

—(2010), *Battle For Bittora*. New Delhi: HarperCollins.

Choudhury, N. P. (2011), *Bali and The Ocean of Milk*. New Delhi: HarperCollins.

Clute, J. and Grant, J. (1999), *The Encyclopedia of Fantasy*. London: Orbit.

Das, G. (2002), *India Unbound: From Independence to the Global Information Age*. New Delhi: Penguin India.

David, E. (2010), *The Man With Enormous Wings*. New Delhi: Penguin India.

Dawson Varughese, E. (2012), *Beyond the Postcolonial: World Englishes Literature*. Basingstoke: Palgrave.

De Groot, J. (2010), *The Historical Novel*. London, New York: Routledge.

Desai, A. (1982/2001), *Where Shall We Go This Summer?*. Delhi: Orient Paperbacks.

Devy, G. N. (2010), *Indian Literary Criticism: Theory and Interpretation*.
    New Delhi: Orient Blackswan Private Limited.
Duncan, R. and Smith, M. J. (2009), *The Power of Comics: History, Form and
    Culture*. New York, London: Continuum.
Filmer, P. (1998), 'Analysing literary texts', in C. Seale (ed.), *Researching Society
    and Culture*. London: SAGE, pp. 275–342.
Gilbert, H. (2001), *Postcolonial Plays*. London, New York: Routledge.
Gregoriou, C. (2009), *English Literary Stylistics*. New York, Basingstoke: Palgrave
    Macmillan.
Guha, R. (2011), *India After Gandhi: The History of the World's Largest
    Democracy*. London: Picador India.
Hasan, A. (2009), *Neti Neti: Not This, Not This*. New Delhi: IndiaInk.
Jain, S. (2010), *Piggies on the Railway*. Chennai: Westland Ltd.
Jalan, B. (2012), *Emerging India: Economics, Politics and Reforms*. New Delhi:
    Penguin/Viking.
Jeffries, L. and McIntyre, D. (2010), *Stylistics*. Cambridge: Cambridge University
    Press.
Joseph, A. (2010), *Saraswati Park*. London: Fourth Estate.
Kala, A. (2007), *Almost Single*. New Delhi: HarperCollins.
Khilnani, S. (1999), *The Idea of India*. New Delhi: Penguin India.
Lau, L. (2006), 'Emotional and domestic territories: The positionality of women as
    reflected in the landscape of the home in contemporary South Asian women's
    writings'. *Modern Asian Studies*, 40, (4), 1097–1116.
Laurenson, D. T. and Swingewood, A. (1971), *The Sociology of Literature*. London:
    MacGibbon & Kee.
Mendlesohn, F. (2008), *Rhetorics of Fantasy*. Middletown, CT: Wesleyan University
    Press.
Merchant, H. (ed.) (1999), *Yaraana*. New Delhi: Penguin India.
Mishra, V. (2009), 'Spectres of setimentality: The Bollywood film'. *Textual Practice*,
    23, (30), 439–62.
Mondal, A. A. (2005), 'The limits of secularism and the construction of composite
    national identity in India', in P. Morey and A. Tickell (eds), *Alternative Indias:
    Writing, Nation and Communalism*. Amsterdam, NY: Rodopi, pp. 1–24.
Nair, J. (2005), *The Promise of the Metropolis: Bangalore's Twentieth Century*.
    New Delhi: Oxford University Press.
Pathak, R. S. (2003), *Indian English Literature: Marginalized Voices*. Delhi:
    Creative Books.
Prasad, A. M. (2005), *Indian Writing in English: Critical Appraisals*. Delhi: Sarup
    & Sons.
Radhakrishnan, R. (2011), *Appropriately Indian: Gender and Culture in a New
    Transnational Class*. Durham, London: Duke University Press.
Rao, R. R. (2003), *The Boyfriend*. New Delhi: Penguin India.
Roberts, A. (2010), *Science Fiction*. London, New York: Routledge.
Sadana, R. (2009), 'Two tales of a city: The place of English and the limits of
    postcolonial critique'. *Interventions*, 11, (1), 1–15.
Sanghi, A. (2010), *Chanakya's Chant*. Chennai: Westland.
Sen, A. (2006), *Identity and Violence: The Illusion of Destiny*. London: Penguin.
Sen, O. (1994), *The River of Stories*. New Delhi: Kalpavriksh.

Shahani, P. (2008), *Gay Bombay: Globalization, Love and (Be)longing in Contemporary India*. New Delhi: SAGE.

Singh, K. (1956/1981), *Train to Pakistan*. New York: Grove Press.

—(2002), *Truth, Love and a Little Malice*. New Delhi: Penguin India.

Sundar, G. (2010), *The Premier Murder League*. New Delhi: Penguin India.

Swaminathan, K. (2006), *The Page Three Murders*. New Delhi: IndiaInk.

—(2007), *The Gardener's Song*. New Delhi: IndiaInk.

—(2010), *The Monochrome Madonna*. New Delhi: Penguin India.

Swaminathan, S. (2007), 'From the margins', in I. Pande (ed.), *India 60: Towards a New Paradigm*. New Delhi: HarperCollins, pp. 56–64.

Talib. I. S. (2002), *The Language of Postcolonial Literatures: An Introduction*. London: Routledge.

Taseer, A. (2010), *The Temple-Goers*. London: Penguin.

—(2011), *Noon*. London: Fourth Estate.

Tickell, A. (2005), 'The discovery of Aryavarta: Hindu nationalism and early Indian fiction in English', in P. Morey and A. Tickell (eds), *Alternative Indias: Writing, Nation and Communalism*. Amsterdam, NY: Rodopi, pp. 25–52.

Trivedi, A. (2010), *Call Me Dan*. New Delhi: Penguin India.

Usha, K. R. (2010), *Monkey-man*. New Delhi: Penguin India.

Vadukut, S. (2010), *The Incredible Adventures of Robin 'Einstein' Varghese*. New Delhi: Penguin India.

Vanita, R. (2005), *Love's Rite: Same-sex Marriage in India and the West*. New Delhi: Penguin India.

Varma, P. K. (2007), *The Great Indian Middle Class*. New Delhi: Penguin India.

Verdonk, P. (2002), *Stylistics*. Oxford: Oxford University Press.

FURTHER READING

'Crossing the bounds of traditional story-telling'. *The Times of India*, 26 January 2011.

'Summer of Pulp'. *Financial Express* 30 May 2010.

'The New Phenomenon called young adult fiction!'. *Press Trust of India*, 8 September 2010.

'Graphic Description'. *The Hindu*, 7 October 2010.

'On The Right Page'. *The Hindu*, 23 October 2010.

'Identity Matters'. *The Hindu*, 28 October 2010.

'All set for The Hindu Best Fiction Award'. *The Hindu*, 31 October 2010.

'All write, now'. *The Hindu*, 11 December 2010.

'New Horizons, New Challenges'. *The Hindu*, 1 April 2009.

'Subversions Rock'. *The Hindu*, 12 December 2009.

'Lord of Whims'. *India Today*, 22 September 2003.

'Essays in Criticism'. *The Hindu*, 6 April 2003.

GLOSSARY

Aarti: (Hindu) prayer

Achkan: long jacket, worn by men, northern Indian

Adivasi or **adi-vasi:** known in India as 'tribals', otherwise, 'aboriginal peoples'. Within India, adi-vasi hold certain constitutional rights and privileges in order to protect their heritage and cultural practices.

Aggarwal: business caste

Airtel: one of India's mobile phone networks

Arabpati: billionaire

Asura: demon

Ayodhya: Lord Ram's place of birth

BJP: Bharatiya Janata Party

BPO: Business Process(ing) Outsourcing (such as call centres)

Bali: one of the asura kings but benevolent

Banian: usually white, a (sleeveless) vest-like cotton undergarment for men

Beta/beti: child (son/daughter)

Bhadralok: a Bengali expression meaning a well-mannered person of a middle-class background

Bhagat Singh: pre-independence freedom fighter, Punjabi

Bharat: eldest brother of Lord Ram, adopted name of India

Brahma: Lord Brahma, the creator of the universe

Bucks: slang term for rupees, '70 bucks' – '70 rupees'

Chhakka: 'fag' in British English (slang). According to Bhaskaran 'who both penetrate and are penetrated – and are scornfully viewed by some MSMs as inauthentic to their social/sexual roles' (Bhaskaran 2004: 99).

Chawl: slum

Chii: an exclamatory sound used to indicate disgust at someone or something

Churchgate: terminal station on the Western train line in Mumbai

Colaba district: a district in South Mumbai

Crore: ten million

Dabba: usually steel, a container or series of food containers that stack on one another, held together with a steel handle. Rice is kept in one container, 'curry' in another container and so on. (cf: dabba-wallas of Mumbai).

Darwaza: door

Dawood Ibrahim: don of an underworld, organized crime syndicate

Desi: 'of the land', Indian, belonging to India

Devas: Gods

Devi: term of respect for a lady, also Hindu Goddess

Dhol: drum played with sticks

Didi: term of endearment meaning 'sister' but also used in non-sibling relations. A polite term of address to unmarried, young women.

Dillagi: flirting

Dosti/dostana: see **yaraana** below

Emergency: known as 'The Emergency' is the period from June 1975 to March 1977 when the President of India, under advice from Prime Minister Indira Gandhi, declared a state of Emergency. This involved the suspension of elections and some civil liberties. This period is often cited as the most controversial and troubled period in recent Indian history.

Goonda giri: a type of hooliganism, street-based involving petty crime and harassment, often involves types of money extortion and gangs

Hanuman: Hindu god who helped Sita from Lanka

Havan: ritual fire used for purification purposes (of mind and spirit)

Hijra: Eunuch (castrated male) or transvestite

Hinglish: combination of Hin(di) and (En)glish, also known as 'Indlish' (Indian English)

IIM: Indian Institute of Management

IIT: Indian Institute of Technology

IPL: Indian Premier League (cricket)

Indrah: Leader and King of Hindu gods

Jagran: an all-night wake of devotional singing, story telling and prayers

Juhu: beach area in West Mumbai, frequented by celebrities, top restaurants and bars

Kala Bandar: the black monkey

Kali Yuga: present era of Hindu mythology, known as 'age of vice'. Fourth and final era of man according to Hinduism.

Karva Chauth: a one-day fast kept by women (usually Hindu and some Sikhs) for the longevity of their husbands

Kothi: hermaphrodite or according to Bhaskaran: 'anatomical men who are effeminate, who generally are defined by and desire the "passive" role of being the one who is penetrated, who do "the women's work", and who identify with women' (Bhaskaran 2004: 99).

Lakh: a hundred thousand

Lathi/lathi charge: long, wooden pole used to maintain order (similar to a truncheon but different in shape), a lathi charge is where security forces (police) use the lathi to chase and drive protesters away from a scene

Laxman: brother of Lord Rama

Lehenga: an outfit (often worn for weddings) that is made up of a long, full skirt and fitted top, with dupatta (long scarf-like piece of material, can be used to cover the head or shoulders)

'Life partner' or **'jivansati':** soul mate or the person who is destined for you – often the focus of Bollywood films; to find your 'life partner'

Lingham (Shiva lingham): erect phallus, object of worship in Hinduism

Lokpal Bill: a bill designed to combat corruption in India, specifically at government level. Anna Hazare's famous fast took place in August 2011 to push the bill forward.

Lord Ayyappa: product of the coupling of the male gods Vishnu and Shiva resides in Sabarimala, Kerala

MSM: 'men who have sex with men' (msm)

Mac: slang term for a Goan Christian

Mahabharata: second revered epic of Hindu belief and mythology

Malayalam: language of Malayali Keralites, Kerala, South India

Mama: 'uncle' from the mother's side, that is, mother's brother

Mithai: Indian sweets (or sweetmeats)

NDTV 24 × 7: English-medium news channel

NDTV India: Hindi-medium news channel

NRI: Non-resident Indian (usually in living America, UK, Canada, Singapore, etc.)

Na?: tag question, used frequently in Indian Englishes (isn't it?)

Natya Shastra: aesthetic of the performing arts

Nawab: North Indian term (Muslim) for prince or someone (man) of royal blood

Paan: an assortment of sweet and savoury elements (depending on personal taste), combined in a folded betel-nut leaf, usually presented in a triangle shape. Chewed after meals and considered as having properties to aid digestion and freshen breath.

Pandit: Hindu priest

Puranpolis: flat, sweet bread made with lentil/chick pea flour and jaggery

Qualis: Toyota Qualis, 6 or 8-seater vehicle

Rakesh Roshan: director of *Koi Mil Gaya*, *Kriish* as an example, also famous Bollywood actor, father of Bollywood movie star, Hrithik Roshan

Rakeysh Omprakash Mehra: director of the films *Delhi 6* and *Rang de Basanti*

Rama: Lord Rama, avatar of Lord Vishnu and the hero of the first Hindu epic, Ramayana

Ramayana: epic story of Lord Rama's triumph over evil

Rang De Basanti: film directed by Rakeysh Omprakash Mehra in 2006

Sangh Parivar: a family of associations that represent the Hindu national movement

Satsang: Hindu spiritual event where meditations, scripture readings and discussion takes place

Shaadi website: a website where people can search for suitable, potential life partners for marriage (not a dating website per se, the emphasis is on meeting someone with marriage in mind). The most popular of these websites is: www.shaadi.com.

Shakti: power or strength

Shiv Sena: an organization founded in the 1960s by Bal Thackeray, it began as a pro-Marathi organization, although more recently it fosters a pan-India outreach. The organization supports a Hindu nationalist agenda. Shiv Sena is well known for its insistence on Mumbai for Maharashtrans and on the Marathi community being given preference over migrants from other Indian states.

Shiva: Lord Shiva, the destroyer also known as Mahesh

Swami: Hindu holy man or guru

Tapori: street-guy, rogue (operates independently unlike 'goonda'; see above: **goonda giri**)

Twenty20 (T20) cricket: a game that is made up of 20 overs from each playing side

Urdhvaretas: chastity or retention of sexual fluid

Veda: most ancient Hindu scriptures or 'sacred knowledge'

Vedanta: Hindu philosophy based on the *Upanishads* (which serve as an epilogue to the Veda). Vedanta is also a trend in Indian philosophy advocating the identity of the individual self with a transindividual super-self.

Vishnu: Lord Vishnu, the protector (who has ten avatars – Ram, Krishna as examples)

VT station: Victoria Terminus train station in Mumbai for the Central line

WSW: 'women who have sex with women'

Yaraana (or 'dosti/dostana'): friendship between men/males

26/11: the Mumbai attacks or 'bombings'

*Rupee to pound sterling rate: 78 Rps = £1 (at the time of writing, 2012)

CHRONOLOGICAL TIMELINE

1947: India's independence from British rule

1947: India's first prime minister, Jawaharlal Nehru – Indian National Congress Party

1965: Nehru dies

1966–1967: Indira Gandhi as prime minister

1975–1977: State of Emergency

1977–1979: Desai voted in which saw the end of the Emergency and Congress ousted.

1980: Sanjay Gandhi dies in a plane crash

1980–1984: Indira Gandhi as prime minister

1984: Indira Gandhi is fatally shot by her bodyguards

1984–1989: Rajiv Gandhi as prime minister (married to Sonia Gandhi)

1990–1991: C. S. Singh as prime minister – Bharatiya Janata Party (BJP)

1991–1996: P. V. N. Rao as prime minister – Congress

1991: India opened up the economy, new reforms

1992: Ayodhya violence

1992–1993: 'Bombay Riots' in December 1992 and January 1993 following the violence at Ayodhya

1996: Prime Minister Vajpayee – BJP

1996–1997: Prime Minister Gowda

1997–1998: Prime Minister Gujral

1998–2004: Prime Minister Vajpayee – BJP

2001: New Delhi's *kala bandar* (the black monkey)

2002: Ahmedabad communal riots between Hindus and Muslims

2004: 'India Shining' campaign by the BJP

2004–current (2012): Manmohan Singh as prime minister – Indian National Congress

2010: Commonwealth Games held in New Delhi

2011: Anna Hazare fasts at the Ramlila grounds in New Delhi (Lokpal Bill)

AUTHOR BIOGRAPHIES

Adiga, A. (b.1974) Aravind Adiga was born in Madras (now call Chennai) to Dr K. Madhava Adiga and Usha Adiga, kannadigas, both of whom hailed from Mangalore. Adiga grew up in Mangalore in the south of India and studied at Canara High School, then at St Aloysius High School, where he completed his SSLC in 1990. After emigrating to Sydney, Australia, with his family, he studied at James Ruse Agricultural High School. He studied English literature at Columbia College, Columbia University in New York, and graduated as salutatorian in 1997. He also studied at Magdalen College, Oxford.

As a former India correspondent for *TIME* magazine, his articles have also appeared in publications including the *Financial Times*, *Independent* and the *Sunday Times*. While corresponding for *TIME*, he remained a South Asia correspondent for 3 years before going freelance. During his freelance period, he wrote *The White Tiger* (2008). Aravind Adiga's debut novel, *The White Tiger*, won the 2008 Booker Prize. He is the fourth Indian-born author to win the prize. The novel studies the contrast between India's rise as a modern global economy and the lead character, Balram, who comes from crushing rural poverty. Adiga's second book, *Between the Assassinations*, was released in India in November 2008 and in the US and UK in mid-2009. The book features 12 interlinked short stories. The stories take place in the fictitious town of Kittur in Southwest India. It was originally modelled on Adiga's hometown of Mangalore, but was substantially changed to make room for more diverse plots and characters. The stories revolve around different classes, castes and religions in India. In each story, another set of characters is introduced, but places and names appear again in other stories. His latest novel, *Last Man in Tower* published in 2011, tells the story of a struggle for a slice of shining Mumbai real estate. He currently lives in Mumbai, India.

Anand, M. R. (b.1905–2004) Mulk Raj Anand was born in Peshawar and educated at the universities of Punjab and London and later Cambridge University, graduating with a Ph.D. in 1929. Anand's literary career was launched by family tragedy, instigated by the rigidity of the caste system. One of the pioneers of Indo-Anglophone fiction, Anand was one of the first India-based writers in English to gain an international readership notable for his depiction of the lives of the poorer castes in traditional Indian society. He was one of the first Indian novelists to write in English, using Hindi and Punjabi phrases, to enrich the language.

Anand's first novel was *Untouchable* (1935), a chilling exposé of the day-to-day life of a member of India's untouchable caste. It is the story of a single day in the life of Bakha, a toilet cleaner, who accidentally bumps into a member of a higher caste. His second novel *Coolie* (1936), the story of a 15-year-old child labourer who dies of tuberculosis, was seen as a powerful critique of India's caste system and the British colonization of India.

Anand returned to India in 1946, making Bombay his home and centre of activity. He founded and edited the fine arts magazine *Marg*, and has been the recipient of the Sahitya Akademi Award, several honorary doctorates and other distinctions. His work includes poetry and essays on a wide range of subjects, as well as autobiographies and novels. Prominent among his novels are *The Village* (1939), *Across the Black Waters* (1939) and *The Sword and the Sickle* (1942), all written in England, and *Coolie* (1936) and *The Private Life of an Indian Prince* (1953), perhaps the most important of his works written in India. He died in Pune on 28 September 2004 at the age of 98.

Arnold, E. (b.1832–1904) Edwin Arnold was born at Gravesend, Kent, the second son of a Sussex magistrate, Robert Coles Arnold. Arnold was educated at King's School, Rochester; King's College London; and University College, Oxford, where he won the Newdigate prize for poetry in 1852. He became a schoolmaster at King Edward's School, Birmingham, and in 1856, he went to India as principal of the Government Sanskrit College at Poona, a post which he held for seven years, including a period during the mutiny of 1857, when he was able to render services for which he was publicly thanked by Lord Elphinstone in the Bombay council. A loyal supporter of the Conservative Party, Arnold was granted a knighthood by the Marquess of Salisbury in 1888. Later that year, he resigned as editor of the *Daily Telegraph* and became the paper's travelling commissioner. Arnold's most notable work was *The Light of Asia* (1979) subtitled 'The Great Renunciation'. In the form of a narrative poem, the book endeavours to describe the life and time of Prince Gautama Buddha, who after attaining enlightenment became The Buddha, The Awakened One. The book presents his life, character and philosophy in a series of verses. It is a free adaptation of the Lalitavistara. A few decades before the book's publication, very little was known outside Asia about the Buddha and Buddhism, the religion which he founded, and which had existed for about 25 centuries. Arnold's book was one of the first successful attempts to popularize Buddhism for a Western readership. The book has been highly acclaimed from the time it was first published, and has been the subject of several reviews. It has been translated into several languages, including Hindi. It was an immediate success, going through numerous editions in England and America, though its permanent place in literature is quite uncertain. It is an Indian epic, dealing with the life and teaching of the Buddha.

Other works by Arnold include *The Light of the World* (1891), *The Indian Song of Songs* (1875), *Pearls of the Faith* (1883), *The Song Celestial* (1885), *With Sadi in the Garden* (1888), *Tiphar's Wife* (1892) and *Adzuma or, The Japanese Wife* (1893).

Aurobindo, S. (b.1872–1950) (Sri) Aurobindo Ghosh was born in Calcutta, India. His father, Dr Krishna Dhan Ghose, was district surgeon of Rangapur, Bengal. His mother, Swarnalata Devi, was the daughter of Brahmo religious and social reformer, Rajnarayan Basu. *Aravinda* means "lotus" in Sanskrit. Aurobindo spelt his name *Aravinda* while in England, as *Aravind* or *Arvind* while in Baroda, and as *Aurobindo* when he moved to Bengal. Aurobindo spent his first 5 years at Rangapur, where his father had been posted since October 1871. Dr Ghose, who had previously lived in Britain and studied medicine at King's College, Aberdeen, was determined that his children should have an English education and upbringing free of any Indian influences. Thus, in 1877, he sent the young Aurobindo and two elder siblings – Manmohan Ghose and Benoybhusan Ghose – to the Loreto Convent School in Darjeeling.

Aurobindo spent two years at Loreto Convent. In 1879, Aurobindo and his two elder brothers were taken to Manchester, England, for a European education. The brothers were placed in the care of a Rev and Mrs Drewett. Rev Drewett was an Anglican clergyman whom Dr Ghose knew through his British friends at Rangapur. The Drewetts tutored the Ghose brothers privately. The Drewetts had been asked to keep the tuitions completely secular and to make no mention of India or its culture. While in England, Aurobindo studied at St Paul's School, London, and at King's College, Cambridge. Returning to India in 1893, he worked for the next 13 years in the Princely State of Baroda in the service of the Maharaja and as a professor in Baroda College. During this period, he also joined a revolutionary society and took a leading role in secret preparations for an uprising against the British Government in India. Aurobindo became an Indian nationalist, freedom fighter, philosopher, yogi, guru and poet. He joined the Indian movement for freedom from British rule and for a duration became one of its most important leaders, before developing his own vision of human progress and spiritual evolution. He was also one of the famous radical leaders of India during the Indian National Movement. The central theme of Aurobindo's vision was the evolution of human life into life divine. In 1906, soon after the partition of Bengal, Aurobindo quit his post in Baroda and went to Calcutta, where he soon became one of the leaders of the Nationalist movement. He was the first political leader in India to openly put forward, in his newspaper *Bande Mataram*, the idea of complete independence for the country. Prosecuted twice for sedition and once for conspiracy, he was released each time for lack of evidence. Aurobindo synthesized Eastern and Western philosophy, religion, literature and psychology in writings. Aurobindo was the first Indian to create a major literary corpus in English.

His works include philosophy; poetry; translations of and commentaries on the Vedas, Upanishads and the Gita; plays; literary, social, political and historical criticism; devotional works; spiritual journals and three volumes of letters. His principal philosophical writings are *The Life Divine* and *The Synthesis of Yoga*, while his principal poetic work is 'Savitri: A Legend and a Symbol' (1954).

Banerjee, S. (b.1972) Sarnath Banerjee was born in Calcutta. He studied image and communication at Goldsmiths College, University of London. Banerjee is an Indian graphic novelist, artist and film-maker and has also provided illustrations for novels by other authors. He designed the cover for Upamanyu Chatterjee's novel, *Weight Loss* (2006). Banerjee is the co-founder of the comics publishing house Phantomville, along with Anindya Roy. He currently lives and works in Delhi, India.

His first novel, *Corridor* (2004), published by Penguin Books, India, was widely marketed as India's first graphic novel. However, *River of Stories* (1994), a graphic novel by Orijit Sen, actually holds this honour. *Corridor*, written and illustrated by Sarnath Banerjee, is set in contemporary Delhi. The novel is about a shop owner by the name of Jehangir Rangoonwalla and his interaction with other residents of Delhi who visit his shop. Banerjee's second novel, *The Barn Owl's Wondrous Capers*, was published in 2007. The novel reinvents the legend of The Wandering Jew as a Jewish merchant called Abravanel Ben Obadiah Ben Aharon Kabariti who once lived in eighteenth-century Kolkata (Calcutta) and who recorded the scandalous affairs of its British administrators in a book called 'The Barn Owl's Wondrous Capers'. Although it has several subplots, the novel is basically about the narrator's quest to find the 'Barn Owl's Wondrous Capers', which his grandfather Pablo Chatterjee found at an old Jewish trinket shop in Montmartre, Paris, in the 1950s. Pablo's wife gave away the book, as well as her husband's other belongings, upon his death; the narrator tries to recover the book, which was one of his childhood favourites. His latest novel, *The Harappa Files*, was published in 2011.

Banker, A. (b.1964) Ashok Kumar Banker was born on 7 February 1964 in Mumbai, India. Banker worked as a successful freelance journalist and columnist for several years, breaking front-page news for publications such as the *Times of India*, Mumbai, and cover stories for *Outlook* magazine, New Delhi. He has written professionally since his early teens, and has worked as a door-to-door surveyor for market research firms, a print journalist, columnist, scriptwriter for television series and documentaries, and in advertising. Banker is a contemporary Indian novelist; his work is the focus of several academic studies for its cross-cultural themes and realistic portrayals of Indian urban issues. He was earlier also known as a reviewer and commentator on contemporary Indian literature, and as a candid essayist with a particular focus on media hypocrisy in India, and the Western racial bias against South Asian writers. Banker has published in several genres, ranging from contemporary fiction about urban life in India to multi-volume mythological epics, as well as cross-genre works. Three of his novels contain autobiographical elements and are closely related to one another. His first novel (though the fifth published) *Vertigo* (1993) is about a man struggling to make a successful career and home life in Bombay. *Byculla Boy* (1994) takes its name from the Byculla suburb of Bombay. 'Beautiful Ugly' and the complementary documentary of the same title are a tribute to his mother, portraying the tragic events of her life. Other published works include *Amazing Adventure at Chotta Sheher* (1992), *The Iron Bra* (1993), *Murder & Champagne* (1993), *Ten Dead Admen* (1993), *The Missing Parents Mystery* (1994), *The Pocket Essential Bollywood* (2001), *Gods of War* (2009), *Prince of Ayodhya* (2003), *Siege of Mithila* (2003), *Demons of Chitrakut* (2004), *Armies of Hanuman* (2005), *Bridge of Rama* (2005), *King of Ayodhya* (2006), *Slayer of Kamsa* (2010) and *Vengeance of Ravana* (2011).

Basu, S. (b.1979) Samit Basu grew up in Calcutta, where he studied at Don Bosco School, and later Presidency College, Kolkata, where he obtained a degree in Economics. He dropped out of the Indian Institute of Management, Ahmedabad, and then went on to complete a course in broadcasting and documentary film-making at the University of Westminster, London. Apart from his novel writing, Basu is a columnist, screenwriter, documentary film-maker and freelance journalist writing on travel, film, books and pop culture. *The Simoqin Prophecies* was written when Basu was 22 and published when he was 23, making him one of India's youngest authors at the time. *The Simoqin Prophecies*, written in English, has been published in Swedish by Ordbilder, and German (from Piper Verlag). The subsequent volumes in the trilogy, *The Manticore's Secret* and *The Unwaba Revelations*, were released in 2005 and 2007, respectively. The GameWorld trilogy has been widely well reviewed and all three books have reached Indian bestseller lists but have not made a significant impact on international markets. Basu has contributed to *The Harper Collins Anthology of New Indian Writing* (2004). Basu has also written short stories for children, which appear in the *Puffin Book of Bedtime Stories* (2005), the *Puffin Book of Funny Stories* (2005), 'Seven Science Fiction Stories' (2006), 'Superhero!' (2007), 'Bewitched' (2008) and several other anthologies.

Bhagat, C. (b.1974) Bhagat was born in New Delhi to a middle-class Punjabi family. His father was in the army and his mother was a government employee in the agricultural department. Bhagat's education was mostly in Delhi. He attended the Army Public School (1978–91), Dhaula Kuan, New Delhi, and then studied Mechanical Engineering at the Indian Institute of

Technology (IIT) Delhi (1991–94). He graduated from the Indian Institute of Management (IIM) Ahmedabad (1995–97), where he was named "The Best Outgoing Student". After graduation, he worked as an investment banker in Hong Kong. He had been working in Hong Kong for 11 years before moving to Mumbai to pursue his passion for writing. His works include *Five Point Someone* (2004), which is about three boys in IIT who can't cope with the system. Their poor grade point average brands them as the under performers of IIT society – and tests everything else they hold important – friends, love, dreams and responsibilities. The novel *One Night @ The Call Centre* (2008) revolves around a group of six call center employees working in Connexions call center in Gurgaon, Haryana. It takes place during the span of one night, in which all of the leading characters confront some aspect of themselves or their lives they would like to change. The story takes a dramatic and decisive turn when the characters get a phone call from God. *The 3 Mistakes of My Life* (2008), based on fictional events, is set in the years 2000–05, when a young boy in Ahmedabad named Govind dreams of starting a business. To accommodate his friends Ishaan and Omi's passion, they open a cricket shop. However, each has a different motive: Govind's goal is to make money; Ishaan desires to nurture Ali, a gifted batsman; Omi just wants to be with his friends. Govind is the narrator and the central character of the novel, and the story revolves around the three mistakes caused by him and the religious politics. *2 States: The Story of My Marriage* is partly autobiographical, the story is about Krish and Ananya who hail from two different states of India, are deeply in love and want to get married. *Revolution 2020: Love, Corruption, Ambition* (2011) is a story of a love triangle, corrupt systems and a journey of self-discovery.

Chetan Bhagat won the Society Young Achiever's award in 2004 and the Publisher's Recognition award in 2005.

Chandra, V. (b.1961) Vikram Chandra was born in New Delhi. He completed most of his secondary education at Mayo College, a boarding school in Ajmer, Rajasthan. After a short stay at St Xavier's College in Mumbai, Vikram came to the United States as an undergraduate student.

Chandra's first novel, *Red Earth and Pouring Rain* (1995), was inspired by the autobiography of James Skinner, a legendary nineteenth-century Anglo-Indian soldier; it won both the Commonwealth Writers Prize for Best First Book and the David Higham Prize for Fiction. The novel is named after a poem from the *Kuruntokai*, an anthology of Classical Tamil love poems. *Love and Longing in Bombay*, a collection of short stories, was published in 1997. This collection of stories won the Commonwealth Writers Prize for Best Book (Eurasia region), was short-listed for the Guardian Fiction Prize, and was well received by international press and media. *Sacred Games*, Vikram Chandra's most recent novel, was published in 2008. Set in a sprawling Mumbai, it features Sartaj Singh, a policeman who first appeared in *Love and Longing in Bombay*.

Chaudhuri, N. C. (b.1897–1999) was born in 1897 in Kishoreganj, which today is part of Bangladesh but at that time was part of Bengal, a region of British India. He was educated in Kishorganj and Kolkata (then known as Calcutta). For his FA (school leaving) course, he attended the Ripon College in Calcutta along with the famous Bengali writer Bibhutibhushan Bandopadhyay. Following this, he attended the prestigious Scottish Church College, Calcutta, where he studied history as his undergraduate major. He graduated with honours in history and topped the University of Calcutta merit list. At Scottish Church College, he attended the seminars of renowned historian Professor Kalidas Nag. After graduation, he enrolled for the MA level course at the University of Calcutta. However, he did not attend all of his final exams of the MA programme, and therefore did not earn his MA degree.

Nirad C. Chaudhuri began his career as clerk in the accounting department of the Indian Army and also started writing stories for popular magazines. His first article on Bengali poet, Bharat Chandra, was published in *Modern Review*, a popular English magazine of those times. After this, he entered the field of journalism and began editing various magazines. Nirad C. Chaudhuri also temporarily introduced two highly esteemed Bengali magazines, *Samasamayik* and *Notun Patrika*. Finally, in 1938, Nirad got a job as the secretary to the great Indian political leader, Sarat Chandra Bose. Due to this, he got ample opportunity to meet various renowned leaders of India like Mahatma Gandhi, Jawaharlal Nehru and others. In 1932, Nirad C. Chaudhuri married Amiya Dhar who was herself a very prolific writer. Later on, Nirad C. Chaudhuri was elected as a political speaker for the Calcutta branch of the All India Radio.

His most famous work, *The Autobiography of an Unknown Indian*, published in 1951, put him on the shortlist of great Anglo-Indian writers. The dedication, which was actually a mock-imperial rhetoric, infuriated many Indians, particularly the political and bureaucratic establishment. Other notable works include *A Passage to England* (1959), *The Continent of Circe* (1965), *The Intellectual in India* (1967), *To Live or Not to Live* (1971), *Scholar Extraordinary, The Life of Professor the Right Honourable Friedrich Max Muller, P. C.* (1974), *Culture in the Vanity Bag* (1976), *Clive of India* (1975), *Hinduism: A Religion to Live by* (1979), *Thy Hand, Great Anarch!* (1987) and *Three Horsemen of the New Apocalypse* (1997).

Chauhan, A. (b.1970) Anuja Chauhan is an Indian author and advertiser. Born in the small town of Meerut, in the north Indian state of Uttar Pradesh, Chauhan spent most of her childhood in various cantonment towns in North India, as her father served in the Indian Army. He took premature retirement at the rank of Lieutenant Colonel, migrating to Australia thereafter. She did her schooling at the Army Public School, New Delhi, Sophia Girls Convent, Meerut Cantonment and Delhi Public School, Mathura Road, New Delhi. She has a Bachelors degree in economics from Miranda House, Delhi University, and a postgraduate diploma in mass communication from the Royal Melbourne Institute of Technology.

As a writer, she is best known for her best-selling, contemporary rom-com novels. *The Zoya Factor* (2008) is set in the glamorous, high-pressure world of Indian cricket. It is about a Rajput girl named Zoya Singh Solanki who meets the Indian cricket team through her job as an executive in an advertising agency and ends up becoming a lucky charm for the team for the 2010 Cricket World Cup. Her second novel, *Battle For Bittora* (2010), is set in the heat and dust of a Lok Sabha (lower house of Parliament) election. Neither of her novels has been published outside India.

Choudhury, C. (b. —) Chandrahas Choudhury is a book critic and author. His story 'Dnyaneshwar Kulkarni Changes His Name' was featured in the anthology *First Proof 2* and he is a regular contributor to the *Observer*, the *Sunday Telegraph*, *Mint* and *Pratilipi*. His first novel, *Arzee the Dwarf*, was published in 2009 and is a story of a process of illusion, loss and discovery, none of which are entirely stable states in the book. Choudhary is also the editor of the anthology of Indian fiction, *India: A Traveler's Literary Companion* (Whereabouts Press 2010; HarperCollins India 2011). He currently resides in Mumbai, India.

Choudhury, N. P. (b. —) is the author of *Bali and the Ocean of Milk* (2011). Having studied at IIM Ahmedabad and IIT Kanpur, he left the world of software selling to join an NGO that works in education. He lives in Bangalore.

Da Cunha, N. (b.1934) Nisha da Cunha was schooled in Simla and Delhi, reading English literature at Miranda House, Delhi, before going on to Newham College, Cambridge, to complete an English Tripos. Da Cunha taught English literature at Miranda House for 5 years after which she pursued an extremely successful career at St Xavier's College, Mumbai for 25 years, from where she resigned as head of the department in 1985.

She directed several plays for both of her colleges, including 'The House of Bernarda Alba' and 'The Glass Menagerie' and for Theatre Group Bombay, Chekhov's 'Three Sisters' and Ibsen's 'Wild Luck'. Penguin has published two of her short story collections, *Old Cypress* (1991) and *The Permanence of Grief* (1993) and in 2006 a retrospective collection Vol. 1. Her other two books were *Set My Heart in Aspic* (1997) and *No Black, No White* (2001). Nisha da Cunha currently resides in Bombay.

Das, M. (b.1934) Manoj Das was born in a small coastal village named Shankari in Balasore district, Orissa State. Among other important positions that Das has held are, Member, General Council, Sahitya Akademi, New Delhi, 1998–2002, and Author-consultant, Ministry of Education, Government of Singapore, 1983–85. Das edited a cultural magazine, *The Heritage*, published from Chennai in the 1980s. Das is an Indian award-winning author who writes in Oriya and English. His works include *Amruta*

Phala (1996), *Aakashra Isara* (1997), *Tandralokara Prahari* (2000), *Sesa Basantara Chithi* (1966), *Manoj Dasanka Katha O Kahani* (1971), *The Crocodile's Lady: A Collection of Stories* (1975), *The Submerged Valley and Other Stories* (1986), *A Tiger at Twilight* (1991), *Farewell to a Ghost: Short Stories and a Novelette* (1994), *Samudra Kulara Ek Grama (Balya Smruti)* (1996) and *Tuma Gaan O Anyanya Kabita* (1992).

David, E. (b.1945) is a Jewish-Indian author, an artist and a sculptor. She was born into a Bene Israel Jewish family in Ahmedabad, Gujarat. Her father, Reuben David, was a hunter-turned-veterinarian, who founded the Kamala Nehru Zoological Garden and Balvatika in the city of Ahmedabad. Her mother, Sarah, was a school teacher. As a child, she spent a lot of time in the zoo, watching and communicating with the animals her father nurtured there. She currently resides in Ahmedabad. After her schooling in Ahmedabad, she joined MS University, Baroda, as a student of Fine Arts and Art History. There, she met Sankho Chaudhary, a renowned sculptor, who taught her sculpture and Art History. After her graduation, she returned to Ahmedabad and started her career as a professor in art history and art appreciation. She taught at the CEPT University and NIFT. She started writing about art and became the *Times of India* art critic. Later she became a columnist for *Femina*, a women's magazine, *The Times of India* and other leading national daily newspapers.

Her first book, *The Walled City*, was published in 1997 by East West Books, Madras. It is a story about the forces that unite and divide generations and communities in the walled city of Ahmedabad. It was republished by Syracuse University Press USA and is listed in the library of modern Jewish Literature. Her next book was *By the Sabarmati* (2001), followed by *The Book of Esther* (2002) and *The Book of Rachel* (2006). In August 2007, she wrote her first book for teenagers, titled *My Father's Zoo*. The book was a tribute to her father and contains stories of the animals that lived or still live in the zoo in Ahmedabad. She is the author of *Shalom India Housing Society* (2007) and most recently, *The Man With Enormous Wings* (2010).

Desai, A. (b.1937) was born *Anita Mazumdar* to a German mother, Toni Nime, and a Bengali businessman, D. N. Mazumdar, in Mussoorie, India. She grew up speaking German at home and Bengali, Urdu, Hindi and English outside the house. She first learnt to read and write in English at school and, as a result, it became her literary language. Despite German being her first language, she did not visit Germany until later in life as an adult. She began to write in English at the age of seven, and published her first story at the age of nine. Desai was a student at Queen Mary's Higher Secondary School in Delhi and received her BA in English literature in 1957 from the Miranda House of the University of Delhi. The following year, she married Ashvin Desai, the director of a computer software company and author of the book *Between Eternities: Ideas on Life and the Cosmos*. They have four children, including Booker Prize-winning novelist Kiran Desai. Her children were taken to Thul (near Alibagh) for weekends, where Desai set her novel *The Village by the Sea* (2001). Anita Desai made her debut as a novelist in 1963 with Cry, The *Peacock*. It was followed by *Voices of the City* (1965), a story about three siblings and their different ways of life in Calcutta. Her novel *Fire on the Mountain* (1977) won the Winifred Holtby Memorial Prize. Anita Desai's other works include *Clear Light of Day* (1980), *In Custody* (1984) and *Fasting, Feasting* (1999), each of which was shortlisted for the Booker Prize. *In Custody* was made into a film by Merchant Ivory productions. Her children's book *The Village by the Sea* (1982) won the Guardian Children's Fiction Award. Anita Desai's most recent novel is *The Zig Zag Way* (2004), set in twentieth-century Mexico. Her most recent book is *The Artist of Disappearance* (2011), a trio of linked novellas about the art world, each featuring a different kind of disappearance. Anita Desai currently lives in the United States, where she is the John E. Burchard Professor of Writing at Massachusetts Institute of Technology, Cambridge, MA. Anita Desai is a Fellow of the Royal Society of Literature, the American Academy of Arts and Letters, Girton College, Cambridge and Clare Hall, Cambridge.

Deshpande, S. (b.1938) is the second daughter of the famous Kannada dramatist and writer Sriranga. She was born in Karnataka and educated in Bombay (now Mumbai) and Bangalore. Deshpande has degrees in Economics and Law. When she was living in Mumbai, she did a course on journalism at the Bharatiya Vidya Bhavan and worked for a couple of months as a journalist for the magazine *Onlooker*. While working in the magazine, she began writing and her first short story was published in 1970. Her short stories headed their way in popular magazines like *Femina*, *Eve's Weekly*, etc. Her maiden collection of short stories was published under the title 'Legacy' in the year 1978. Her first novel, *The Dark Holds No Terrors* was published in 1980. Deshpande also won the Sahitya Akademi Award for the novel *That Long Silence* in 1990 and the Padma Shri award in 2009. Shashi Deshpande has written four children's books, a number of short stories and nine novels, besides several perceptive essays, now available in a volume entitled 'Writing from the Margin and Other Essays'. Other works include, *The Dark Holds No Terrors* (1980), *If I Die Today* (1982), *Come Up and Be Dead* (1983), *That Long Silence* (1989), *The Intrusion and Other Stories* (1993), *The Binding Vine* (2002), *A Matter of Time* (2001), *Small Remedies* (2000), *Moving On* (2004) and *In the Country of Deceit* (2008).

Dutt, T. (b.1856–77) was an Indian poetess who wrote in English. Dutt was the youngest girl of Govin Chunder Dutt, a retired Indian Officer. She spent her childhood in Calcutta, her birth town, with her elder sister Arunima and brother Abju.

She remained in Calcutta until November 1869, after which she and her sister Aru travelled to France, Italy and then England. She went to a school in France. After publication of several translations and literary discussions, she published *A Sheaf Gleaned in French Fields*, a volume of French poems she had translated into English, with Saptahiksambad Press of Bhowanipore, India in 1876. Her elder sister Aru translated eight of the poems. This volume came to the attention of Edmund Gosse in 1877, who reviewed it quite favourably in the *Examiner* that year. *Sheaf* would see a second Indian edition in 1878 and a third edition by Kegan Paul of London in 1880, but Dutt lived to see neither of these triumphs. She wrote many poems for the rank and file. At the time of her death, she left behind two unpublished novels – *Le Journal de Mademoiselle d'Arvers* (thought to be the first novel in French by an Indian writer) and *Bianca, or the Young Spanish Maiden* (thought to be the first novel in English by an Indian woman writer) and an unfinished volume of original poems in English, *Ancient Ballads and Legends of Hindustan*. Her father, Govind Chunder Dutt, ensured that these works would be published posthumously: *Bianca* in Calcutta's Bengal Magazine (1878), *Le Journal* by Didier of Paris (1879) and *Ancient Ballads* with Kegan Paul (1882). The poem 'Our Casuarina Tree' is considered as her biography.

Etteth, R. S. (b.1960) Ravi Shankar Etteth is the deputy editor of *India Today* magazine, a political cartoonist and graphic artist. A collection of his short stories has been published in India, and he has written two novels, *The Tiger by the River* (2002) and *The Village of Widows* (2004). He currently resides in New Delhi.

The Tiger by the River is a fictional tale based on a real landscape. It flows in flawless English in the tradition of the Panchatantra, weaving stories within stories. *The Village of Widows* is a fictional story about criminal psychologist Jay Samorin and police commissioner Anna Khan unwillingly joining forces to find the killer of a diplomat in Delhi. Their quest will take them far beyond what is considered normal but as they dig deeper, their search also leads them to the mystery of the village of widows.

Hassan, A. (b.1972) Anjum Hasan was born in Shillong, Meghalaya, where she also studied Philosophy at the North-Eastern Hill University. She moved to Bangalore at the age of 26. This move, as well as the contrast between life in a small Indian town and in a big city, proved to have a great influence on her literary work. Her poetry début came in 2006 with 'Street on the Hill'. Her poems sensitively probe bourgeois life in a small Indian town, referring to childhood observations, memories and secrets, introducing a parade of the town's inhabitants before fleeing from the museum of the past to a joyful festival of travel, love and sensuality.

In 2006, Hasan published her first novel, *Lunatic in My Head*, which made it onto the shortlist of one of India's most prestigious literary prizes, the Crossword Award. The novel is set in Shillong in the 1990s. It is once again a poetic and humorous portrait of a small town that is undergoing great changes, as well as of three of the townspeople trying to break away from their small town fate. In her second novel, *Neti, Neti* (2009), Hasan examines her own move away from a small town. The novel shows the fate of a young woman in an Indian metropolis. *Neti, Neti* was shortlisted for the 2008 Man Asian Literary Prize and shortlisted for The Hindu Best Fiction Award in 2010. Anjum Hasan has also published short prose texts, poetry, travel writing and literary essays in Indian and international periodicals, and she also works as an editor for *The Caravan* magazine. Her poems and short stories have been included in many important anthologies of Indian poetry and short fiction. Anjum Hasan lives in Bangalore.

Jain, S. (b. —) Smita Jain is a trained economist and holds a degree in finance. Having left investment banking, she has written numerous screenplays for television and film. She is the author of *Kkrishnaa's Konfessions* (2008) and *Piggies on the Railway* (2010). She is an avid mountaineer and long-distance runner. Smita Jain lives in Mumbai.

Joseph, A. (b.1978) Anjali Joseph was born in Bombay in 1978. She read English at Trinity College, Cambridge, and has taught English at the Sorbonne, written for the *Times of India* in Bombay and she has been a commissioning editor for ELLE (India). She graduated with an MA in Creative Writing from the University of East Anglia in 2008. Her first novel, *Saraswati Park* (2010), won the Desmond Elliott Prize, the Betty Trask Prize and India's Vodafone Crossword Book Award for Fiction. *Another Country* (2012) is her second novel.

Joshi, A. (b.1939–93) Arun Joshi was born in Varanasi, completed his higher education in the US, and returned to India to become an industrial manager. Arun Joshi kept himself out of the limelight, writing in the pre-Rushdie era when Indian writing in English was something only eccentric people indulged in. His novels delving into existentialism along with the ethical choices a man has to make, won him huge critical appreciation in India, but remained largely unknown in the West. Joshi won the Sahitya Akademi Award in 1982 for *The Last Labyrinth* a story of Som Bhaskar the dichotomy in his character apparent through the name itself: meaning Moon-Suna a 25-year-old who inherits his father's vast industrial wealth. Som is married to Geeta, a pious woman, but is attracted by Anuradha, an alluring woman shrouded in mystery. She is probably married to Aftab, a businessman, but Som finds her so irresistible, that she becomes the prey of his relentless hunt throughout the novel. His first novel *The Foreigner* (1968) is story of a young man, Surinder Oberoi, who is detached, almost alienated – a man who sees himself as a stranger wherever he lives or goes – in Kenya, where he is born, in England and the United States where he is a student and in India where he finally settles. Other works include *The Strange Case of Billy Biswas* (1971), a novel in which the normal and the abnormal, the ordinary and the extraordinary, illusion and reality, resignation and desire, rub shoulders, and *The Apprentice* (1974) about Ratan Rathor an unsophisticated youth, jobless, he comes to the city in search of a career; unscrupulous and ready to prostitute himself for professional advancement.

Kala, A. (b. —) currently lives in New Delhi although she has called three countries and numerous cities 'home'. She enjoys music, sailing, reading and is devoted to her St. Bernard. Her website is www.advaitakala.com.

Kapur, M. (b.1948) Manju Kapur was born in the city of Amritsar in India. She graduated from the Miranda House University College for women and went on to take an MA at Dalhousie University in Halifax, Nova Scotia, and an M.Phil. at Delhi University. Manju Kapur lives in New Delhi, where she is a teacher of English literature at her alma mater Miranda House College. Kapur's first novel *Difficult Daughters* (1998), won the Commonwealth Prize for First Novels (Eurasia Section) and was a number one bestseller in India. Her second novel *A Married Woman* (2003) was called 'fluent and witty' in the *Independent*, while her third, *Home* (2006), was described as 'glistening with detail and emotional acuity' in the *Sunday Times*. Her most recent novel, *The Immigrant* (2008) was being long-listed for the DSC Prize for South Asian Literature. She lives in New Delhi. Her latest novel, *Custody*, was published by Faber & Faber in 2011.

Khan, A. (b.1965) Aamir was born in Bandra's Holy Family Hospital, Mumbai, India, to a Muslim family that has been actively involved in the Indian motion picture industry for several decades. His father, Tahir Hussain, was a film producer while his uncle, Nasir Hussain, was a film producer as well as a director and an actor. His family on his father's side are originally from Herat, Afghanistan. He is a descendant of the scholar and politician Maulana Abul Kalam Azad and a second cousin to former Chairperson of Rajya Sabha, Dr Najma Heptulla. Aamir Khan was first introduced as a child artiste in the 1970s hit *Yaadon Ki Baaraat* (1973), where he was the youngest child in the trio. From the tremendous success of *Qayamat Se Qayamat Tak* (1988), which was released when he was 23, he has become one of India's most famous Bollywood actors. His performances include *Dil* (1990), *Andaz Apna Apna* (1994), *Bollywood Dreams* (1995), *Raja Hindustani* (1996), *Ishq* (1997), *Ghulam* (1998), *Sarfarosh* (1999), *Lagaan* (2001), *Ghajini* (2008) and *Three Idiots* (2009), which is based on Bhagat's *Five Point Someone*. Using classic "method acting", Aamir acts in all genres of Indian films – comedy, action, drama and romance.

Kipling, R. (b.1865–1936) was an English poet, short-story writer and novelist, chiefly remembered for his celebration of British imperialism, tales and poems of British soldiers in India, and his tales for children. Kipling received the 1907 Nobel Prize for Literature. He was born in Bombay, in the Bombay Presidency of British India, and was taken by his family to England when he was five years old. After six months, John and Alice Kipling returned to India, leaving six-year-old Rudyard and his three-year-old sister as boarders with the Holloway family in Southsea. During his five years in this foster home, he was bullied and physically mistreated, and the experience left him with deep psychological scars and a sense of betrayal. Between 1878 and 1882, he attended the United Services College at Westward Ho in north Devon. The College was a new and very rough boarding school where, nearsighted and physically frail, he was once again teased and bullied, but where, nevertheless, he developed fierce loyalties and a love of literature. In 1882, Kipling returned to India, where he spent the next 7 years working in various capacities as a journalist and editor and where he began to write about India itself and the Anglo-Indian society that presided over it. His first volume of poetry, 'Departmental Ditties', which included the poem 'Christmas in India', a poem which exalts the glories of Jesus's birth in the subcontinent was published in 1886, and between 1887 and 1889 he published six volumes of short stories. The first was 'Plain Tales from the Hills', the first of the "Indian Railway Series" set in and concerned with the India he had come to know and love so well. When Kipling returned to England in 1889 via the United States he found himself already acclaimed as a brilliant young writer. The reissue in London of his *Indian Railway Series* titles, including 'Soldiers Three', 'In Black and White' and 'The Phantom Rickshaw', brought him even greater fame, and in 1890 *The Light That Failed*, his first novel (which was only modestly successful) also appeared. By the time 'Barrack-Room Ballads' had appeared in 1892, the year Tennyson died, Kipling was an enormously popular and critical success.

In 1891, he planned a round-the-world voyage, but travelled only to South Africa, Australia, New Zealand, and India, which he would never visit again. In 1892, Kipling married Caroline Balestier, an American. Their honeymoon took them as far as Japan, but they returned, not altogether to Kipling's satisfaction, to live at his wife's home in Vermont, where they remained until 1899, when Kipling, alone, returned to England. During the American years, however, Kipling wrote *Captain's Courageous*, *Many Inventions*, the famous poem 'Recessional', and most of *Kim*, as well as the greater portion of the two Jungle Books, all of which were very successful.

Stalky & Co., which drew heavily upon his experiences at the United Services College, was published in 1899. During the same year, Kipling made his last visit to the United States, and was deeply affected by the death of his eldest child, Josephine. Frequently in poor health himself, Kipling would winter in South Africa every year between 1900 and 1908. In 1902, he bought the house ("Bateman's") in Sussex which would remain his home in England until his death: Sussex itself lies at the center of books like *Puck of*

Pook's Hill and *Rewards and Fairies*, which, though they are ostensibly for children, concern themselves with the ambiguous sense of historical, national and racial identity which lay beneath Kipling's Imperialism. In 1907, Kipling was awarded the Nobel Prize for Literature, but his Imperialist sentiments, which grew stronger as he grew older, put him more and more out of touch with political, social and moral realities. In 1915, his son John was killed in action during World War I, and in 1917 he published 'A Diversity of Creatures', a collection of short stories which included 'Mary Postgate'. Between 1919 and 1932, Kipling travelled intermittently, and continued to publish stories, poems, sketches and historical works. He died in London on 18 January 1936, just after his seventieth birthday, and was buried in Westminster Abbey. His pallbearers included a prime minister, an admiral, a general and the head of a Cambridge college. The following year saw the posthumous publication of the autobiographical *Something of Myself*. Kipling is best known for his works of fiction, including *The Jungle Book* (a collection of stories which includes 'Rikki-Tikki-Tavi'), *Just So Stories* (1902) (1894), *Kim* (1901) (a tale of adventure), many short stories, including 'The Man Who Would Be King' (1888); and his poems, including 'Mandalay' (1890), 'Gunga Din' (1890), 'The White Man's Burden' (1899) and 'If' (1910).

Krishna, R. (b.1982) Rudra Krishna was born in Madras. After entering the Bar at the age of 21, he moved to Cardiff where he completed his Masters in Law, worked in numerous vocations and wrote his first novel, *The Onus of Karma*, before returning in 2008. He has also published a book of poetry, *All I Want Is Everything* in 2004. He is currently working as an editor in a publishing house in Chennai.

Liddle, M. (b.1973) Madhulika Liddle was born in Haflong (Assam, India) to Andrew Verity Liddle and Muriel Liddle. The first 12 years of her life were spent in various parts of India, since her father was an officer in the Indian Police Service (IPS) and was transferred frequently from one town to another. In 1985, Mr Liddle was transferred to New Delhi, and Madhulika finished her schooling in the city, where she went on to study at the Institute of Hotel Management, Catering and Nutrition (IHMCN) in New Delhi.

Madhulika had been writing since childhood, but her first work to be published was a short story named Silent Fear, which won the Femina Thriller Contest in June 2001. She has since written a wide variety of short stories, travel articles, humorous articles and a novel, *The Englishman's Cameo* (2009). In addition, Madhulika maintains a blog on classic cinema. Madhulika's best-known series of works are historical whodunnits featuring the seventeenth century Mughal detective, Muzaffar Jang. *Muzaffar Jang* first appeared in print in a short story, 'Murk of Art', in the anthology, *21 Under 40*, published by Zubaan Books in 2007. Liddle had already begun work on a full-length Muzaffar Jang novel, which was published by

Hachette India in 2009 as *The Englishman's Cameo*. Till now, two books in the series have been published *The Englishman's Cameo* (2009) and *The Eighth Guest & Other Muzaffar Jang Mysteries* (2011). *The Englishman's Cameo* (2009) introduces Muzaffar Jang, a 25-year-old Mughal nobleman living in the Delhi of 1656 AD. Muzaffar ends up investigating a murder of which his friend, a jeweller's assistant, is accused. The book became a bestseller in India, and was published in French by Editions Philippe Picquier, as *Le Camée Anglais*. Liddle's latest collection of black humour short stories, 'My Lawfully Wedded Husband and Other Stories' was published in 2012.

Markandaya, K. (b.1924–2004) was born in Chimakurti, India. She studied at the University of Madras and then worked as a journalist. In 1948, she settled in England and later married an Englishman. Her first novel, *Nectar in a Sieve* (1954), an Indian peasant's narrative of her difficult life, remains Markandaya's most popular work. Her second novel, *Some Inner Fury* (1955) is set in 1942 during the Indian struggle for independence. It portrays the troubled relationship between an educated Indian woman, whose brother is an anti-British terrorist, and a British civil servant who loves her. Marriage provides the setting for a conflict of values in *A Silence of Desire* (1960), in which a religious middle-class woman seeks medical treatment, without her husband's knowledge, from a Hindu faith healer rather than from a doctor.

In Markandaya's fiction, Western values typically are viewed as modern and materialistic and Indian values as traditional and spiritual. She examined this dichotomy in *Possession* (1963), in which an Indian shepherd-turned-artist is sent to England, where he is nearly destroyed by an aristocratic British woman. Later works by Markandaya include *A Handful of Rice* (1966), *The Coffer Dams* (1969), *The Nowhere Man* (1972), *Two Virgins* (1973), *The Golden Honeycomb* (1977), and *Pleasure City* (1982).

Menon, A. (b.1912–89) Salvator Aubrey Clarence Menen was born London to Irish and Indian parents. After attending University College, London, he worked as a drama critic and a stage director. During World War II, he was in India where he organized pro-Allied radio broadcasts and edited film scripts for the Indian government. After the war ended, he returned to London to work with an advertising agency's film department, but the success of his first novel, *The Prevalence of Witches* (1947), induced him to take up writing full-time. Aubrey Menen's writings are often satirical, exploring the nature of nationalism and the cultural contrast between his own Irish–Indian ancestry and his traditional British upbringing. Apart from his novels and non-fiction works, Menen wrote two autobiographies entitled *Dead Man in the Silver Market* (1953) and *The Space within the Heart* (1970). Other notable works include *The Prevalence of Witches* (1947), *The Stumbling-Stone* (1949), *The Duke of Gallodoro* (1952), *The Ramayana, As Told by Aubrey Menen*

(1954), *The Fig Tree* (1959), *A Conspiracy of Women* (1965), *The Space within the Heart* (1970), *Cities in the Sand* (1972), *The New Mystics and the True Indian Tradition* (1974) and *Four Days of Naples* (1979).

Naidu, S. (b.1879–1949), also known by the sobriquet *The Nightingale of India*, was known as something of a child prodigy, Indian independence activist and poet. Naidu was the first Indian woman to become the President of the Indian National Congress and the first woman to become the Governor of Uttar Pradesh state. She was the daughter of Aghorenath Chattopadhyaya. He was a scientist and philosopher, and founder of the Nizam College, Hyderabad. Sarojini Naidu's mother Barada Sundari Devi was a poetess baji and used to write poetry in Bengali. Sarojini Naidu was the eldest among the eight siblings. One of her brothers, Birendranath, was a revolutionary and her other brother, Harindranath, was a poet, dramatist and actor.

At the age of 12, Sarojini Naidu attained national fame when she topped the matriculation examination at Madras University. Her father wanted her to become a mathematician or scientist but Sarojini Naidu was interested in poetry. She started writing poems in English. Impressed by her poetry, Nizam of Hyderabad gave her scholarship to study abroad. At the age of 16, she travelled to England to study first at King's College London and later at Girton College, Cambridge. There she met famous laureates of her time such as Arthur Symons and Edmond Gosse. It was Gosse who convinced Sarojini to stick to Indian themes – India's great mountains, rivers, temples and social milieu – to express her poetry. She depicted contemporary Indian life and events.

Sarojini Naidu's three volumes of verse *The Golden Threshold* (1905), *The Bird of Time* (1912) and *The Broken Wing* (1917) were published in 1916 and 1917. The three books were combined in *The Sceptred Flute* (1928) and included the poems 'Songs of My City' (1912) and 'Song's of Radha The Milkmaid' (1912). Some later poems are included in 'The Feather of the Dawn' (1961). The most detailed biography of Sarojini Naidu is Padmini Sengupta, *Sarojini Naidu: A Biography* (1966).

Narayan, R. K. (b.1906–2001) Rasipuram Krishnaswami Narayanswami, who preferred the shortened name R. K. Narayan, was born in Madras, India. His father, an educator, travelled frequently, and his mother was frail, so Narayan was raised in Madras by his grandmother and an uncle. His grandmother inspired in young Narayan a passion for language and for people. He attended the Christian Mission School. Narayan graduated from Maharaja's College in Mysore in 1930. In 1934, he was married, but his wife, Rajam, died of typhoid in 1939. He had one daughter, Hema. He never remarried. Narayan wrote his first novel, *Swami and Friends*, in 1935, after short, uninspiring stints as a teacher, an editorial assistant and a newspaperman. In it, he invented the small south Indian city of Malgudi, a literary microcosm that critics later compared to William Faulkner's Yoknapatawpha County. More than a dozen novels and many short stories that followed were set in Malgudi. Narayan's second novel, *Bachelor of Arts* (1939), marked the beginning of his reputation in England, where the novelist Graham Greene was largely responsible for getting it published. His fourth novel, *The English Teacher*, published in 1945, was partly autobiographical, concerning a teacher's struggle to cope with the death of his wife. In 1953, Michigan State University published it under the title *Grateful to Life and Death*, and along with his novel *The Financial Expert*, they were Narayan's first books published in the United States. Subsequent publications of his novels, especially *Mr Sampath*, *Waiting for the Mahatma*, *The Guide*, *The Man-eater of Malgudi*, and *The Vendor of Sweets* established Narayan's reputation in the West. Many critics consider *The Guide* (1958) to be Narayan's masterpiece. Told in a complex series of flashbacks, it concerns a tourist guide who seduces the wife of a client, prospers, and ends up in jail. The novel won India's highest literary honour, and it was adapted for the off-Broadway stage in 1968.

At least two of Narayan's novels, *Mr Sampath* (1949) and *The Guide* (1958) were adapted for the movies. Narayan's stories begin with realistic settings and everyday happenings in the lives of a cross-section of Indian society, with characters of all classes. Gradually fate or chance, oversight or blunder, transforms mundane events to preposterous happenings. Reviewing Narayan's 1976 novel *The Painter of Signs*, Anthony Thwaite of the *New York Times* said Narayan created 'a world as richly human and volatile as that of Dickens'. His next novel, *A Tiger for Malgudi* (1983), is narrated by a tiger whose holy master is trying to lead him to enlightenment. This and his fourteenth novel, *Talkative Man* (1987), received mixed reviews.

In his eighties, Narayan continued to have books published. He returned to his original inspiration, his grandmother, with the 1994 book *Grandmother's Tale and Other Stories*, which *Publishers Weekly* called 'an exemplary collection from one of India's most distinguished men of letters'. Donna Seaman of Booklist hailed the collection of short stories that spanned over 50 years of Narayan's writing as 'an excellent sampling of his short fiction, generally considered his best work' from 'one of the world's finest storytellers'. Narayan once noted: 'Novels may bore me, but never people'.

Perrin, A. (b.1867–1934) Alice Perrin was born in India, the daughter of Major General John Innes Robinson, of the Bengal Cavalry, and Bertha Beidermann Robinson. After her education in England, Perrin married Charles Perrin (d.1931), an engineer in the India Public Works Department, in 1886, and the couple returned to India for the next 16 years. They had a son, Lancelot Charles Perrin (born c.1889), who later worked in the Irrigation Branch of the Indian Public Works and married Vera Alexandrina St. John in November 1913. After the Perrins' return to England, Charles worked for the London Water Board and the Ministry of Health. Perrin's career as a popular Anglo-Indian novelist and short-story writer began with the two-volume novel *Into Temptation*, published in 1894. Her first collection of short stories, 'East of Suez' appeared in 1901. She continued publishing novels every two to three years until her last novel, *Other Sheep*, was published in 1932, two years before her death in Vevey, Switzerland, in 1934. In total, she published 17 novels, many of which focus on the British colonial experience in India, such as *The Spell of the Jungle* (1902), *The Anglo-Indians* (1912), *The Happy Hunting Ground* (1914), *Star of India* (1919) and *Government House* (1925).

Rajendra, R. (b. —) Rajiv Rajendra is a corporate consultant and writer. He also directs and writes for stage. Rajiv has travelled and worked across four continents, through natural and concrete jungles, and currently divides his time between Singapore and India. His first novel *Doosra* (2011) is a fictional story about the 2011 World Cup where hot favourites India are playing their penultimate group match. Amidst this, Tarun's world comes crumbling down with allegations of assault, numerous affairs and match-fixing.

Rao, R. (b.1908–2006) Raja Rao was born in Hassan, in the state of Mysore (now Karnataka) in South India, into a well-known Brahmin (Hoysala Karnataka) family. He was the eldest of nine siblings – two brothers and seven sisters. His native language was Kannada. Rao's post-graduate education was in France and all his publications in book form have been in English. His father taught Kannada at Nizam College in what was then Hyderabad State. The death of his mother, when he was four, left a lasting impression on the novelist – the absence of a mother and orphanhood are recurring themes in his work. Another influence from early life was his grandfather, with whom he stayed in Hassan and Harihalli.

Rao was educated at Muslim schools, the Madarsa-e-Aliya in Hyderabad and the Aligarh Muslim University, where he became friends with Ahmed Ali. He began learning French at the University. After matriculation in 1927, Rao returned to Hyderabad and studied for his degree at Nizam's College. After graduating from the University of Madras, having majored in English and history, he won the Asiatic Scholarship of the Government of Hyderabad in 1929, for study abroad.

Rao moved to the University of Montpellier in France. He studied French language and literature, and later at the Sorbonne in Paris, he explored the Indian influence on Irish literature.

Returning to India in 1939, he edited with Iqbal Singh, *Changing India* an anthology of modern Indian thought from Ram Mohan Roy to Jawaharlal Nehru. He participated in the Quit India Movement of 1942. In 1943–1944 he coedited with Ahmed Ali a journal from Bombay called *Tomorrow*. He was the prime mover in the formation of a cultural organization, *Sri Vidya Samiti*, devoted to reviving the values of ancient Indian civilization; this organistion failed shortly after inception. In Bombay, he was also associated with *Chetana*, a cultural society for the propagation of Indian thought and values. Rao's involvement in the nationalist movement is reflected in his first two books. The novel *Kanthapura* (1938) was an account of the impact of Gandhi's teaching on non-violent resistance against the British. The story is seen from the perspective of a small Mysore village in South India. Rao borrows the style and structure from Indian vernacular tales and folk-epic. Rao returned to the theme of Gandhism in the short story collection 'The Cow of the Barricades' (1947). In 1998, he published Gandhi's biography *Great Indian Way: A Life of Mahatma Gandhi*. In 1988, he received the prestigious International Neustadt Prize for Literature. *The Serpent and the Rope* was written after a long silence during which Rao returned to India. The work dramatized the relationships between Indian and Western culture. The serpent in the title refers to illusion and the rope to reality. *Cat and Shakespeare* (1965) was a metaphysical comedy that answered philosophical questions posed in his earlier novels.

Rao, R. R. (b.1955) R. Raj Rao was born in Bombay, India. He earned a Ph.D. in English from the University of Bombay in 1986 and received the Nehru Centenary British Fellowship for his post-doctoral research at the Centre for Caribbean Studies, University of Warwick, UK. He attended the International Writing Program, Iowa, in 1996. His works include 'Slide Show'. He has edited Ten Indian Writers in Interview and co-edited *Image of India in the Indian Novel in English (1960–80)*. He works as a professor of English at the University of Pune. Rao is openly gay. On the recurring themes of homosexuality in his works, Rao says: 'I am myself a poet, novelist, playwright and writer of non-fiction. Similarly, my teaching and research interests in queer theory and queer literature are a direct and natural outcome of my being gay and imaginatively tackling the subject in my fiction, poetry and plays'.

His 2003 novel *The Boyfriend* is one of the first gay novels to come from India. Rao was one of the first recipients of the newly established Quebec-India awards. Rao published the non-fiction work *Whistling in the Dark* in 2009 and the novel *Hostel Room 131* in 2010. His next book, provisionally titled *Lady Lolita's Lover* is also a novel. His other works include *Sildeshow* (1992), 'One Day I Locked My Flat in Soul City' (2001), 'The Wisest Fool on Earth and Other Plays' (2003) and *Whistling in the Dark: Twenty-One Queer Interviews* (2009).

Roy, A. (b.1961) Arundhati Roy was born in Shillong, Meghalaya, to a Keralite Syrian Christian mother and a Bengali Hindu father, a tea planter by profession. She spent her childhood in Aymanam, in Kerala, schooling in Corpus Christi. She left Kerala for Delhi at age 16, and embarked on a homeless lifestyle, staying in a small hut with a tin roof within the walls of Delhi's Feroz Shah Kotla and making a living selling empty bottles. She then proceeded to study architecture at the Delhi School of Architecture, where she met her first husband, the architect Gerard Da Cunha.

She won the Booker Prize in 1997 for her first novel *The God of Small Things* (1997). Since winning the Booker Prize, she has concentrated her writing on political issues. These include the Narmada Dam project, India's Nuclear Weapons, corrupt power company Enron's activities in India. She is a figurehead of the anti-globalization/alter-globalization movement and a vehement critic of neo-imperialism.

In response to India's testing of nuclear weapons in Pokhran, Rajasthan, Roy wrote *The End of Imagination* (1998), a critique of the Indian government's nuclear policies. It was published in her collection *The Cost of Living* (1999), in which she also crusaded against India's massive hydroelectric dam projects in the central and western states of Maharashtra, Madhya Pradesh and Gujarat. She has since devoted herself solely to nonfiction and politics, publishing two more collections of essays as well as working for social causes. Roy was awarded the Sydney Peace Prize in May 2004 for her work in social campaigns and advocacy of non-violence. In June 2005, she took part in the World Tribunal on Iraq. In January 2006, she was awarded the Sahitya Akademi award for her collection of essays, *The Algebra of Infinite Justice* (2002), but declined to accept it. Her other works include *Power Politics* (2002), *War Talk* (2003), *An Ordinary Person's Guide to Empire* (2004), *Public Power in the Age of Empire* (2004) and *Listening to Grasshoppers: Field Notes on Democracy* (2009).

Sanghi, A. (b.1969) Ashwin Sanghi was born and raised in Mumbai, Maharashtra, India. His schooling was at the Cathedral and John Connon School. After graduating from Cathedral in 1985, Sanghi attended St. Xavier's College, Mumbai. He attended the Yale School of Management, receiving an MBA in 1993. After graduating from Yale, Sanghi joined his family's business enterprise while continuing to write thriller fiction part-time. Sanghi's first novel *The Rozabal Line* was originally published in 2007 under his pseudonym Shawn Haigins. The revised edition of *The Rozabal Line* was published by Westland Ltd. & Tranquebar Press in 2008 under his own name Ashwin Sanghi. *The Rozabal Line* deals with the subject of Jesus having survived the crucifixion and having settled down and died in India, eventually being buried in Roza Bal. His second novel *Chanakya's Chant* (2010) is a fictional retelling of the life of Chanakya the great political strategist of ancient India. The novel relates two stories in parallel, the first of Chanakya and his machinations to bring Chandragupta Maurya to the throne of Magadha; the second that of a modern-day character called Gangasagar Mishra who makes it his ambition to position a slum child as the prime minister of India. *Chanakya's Chant* was released in 2011 and entered all major Indian national bestseller lists within two months. It reached number 1 on *India Today*'s bestseller list in April 2011.

Singh, K. (b.1915) Khushwant Singh was born in Hadali District Khushab, Punjab in a Sikh family. His father, Sir Sobha Singh was a prominent builder in Lutyens' Delhi. He was educated at Modern School, New Delhi, Government College, Lahore, St. Stephen's College in Delhi and King's College, London, before reading for the Bar at the Inner Temple. Singh has edited *Yojana*, an Indian government journal, *The Illustrated Weekly of India*, a newsweekly and two major Indian newspapers *The National Herald* and the *Hindustan Times*. During his tenure, *The Illustrated Weekly* became India's pre-eminent newsweekly. After Singh's departure, it suffered a huge drop in readership. From 1980 through 1986, Singh was a member of Rajya Sabha, the upper house of the Indian parliament. He was awarded the Padma Bhushan in 1974 for service to his country. In 1984, he returned the award in protest against the siege of the Golden Temple by the Indian Army. In 2007, the Indian government awarded Singh the Padma Vibhushan. His works include *The Mark of Vishnu and Other Stories* (1950), *Train to Pakistan* (1956), 'The Voice of God and Other Stories' (1957), 'A Bride for the Sahib and Other Stories' (1967), 'Black Jasmine'(1971), 'The Collected Stories' (1989), *Delhi: A Novel* (1990), *The Company of Women* (1999) and *Truth, Love and a Little Malice* (2002).

Sundar, G. (b. —) is a medical doctor by profession and she currently has a consultancy practice where she lives, in Pune and also an online health counsel for a leading insurance brokerage firm. She has followed cricket and enjoyed it since her childhood, her first fiction is a narrative of cricket: *The Premier Murder League* (2010).

Swaminathan, K. (b.1958) Kalpana Swaminathan is a surgeon and writer based in Mumbai, India. She is a paediatric/neonatal surgeon who lives in Mumbai. Her works include books for children *The True Adventures of Prince Teentang* (1993), *Dattaray's Dinosaur* (1994), *Ordinary Mr Pai* (2000) and detective fiction *Cryptic Death* (1997) featuring her detective Aunt Lalli. She has authored more than 12 novels, short stories and children's books. She also occasionally writes in a pseudonym Kalpish Ratna along with fellow surgeon Ishrat Syed. They write on science, arts and literature. Kalpana Swaminathan has also won the 2009 Vodafone Crossword Book Award (Fiction) for *Venus Crossing: Twelve Stories of Transit* (2009). Kalpana deals with complex subjects in her novels. For instance, her novel *Bougainvillea House* (2006) is a psychological thriller where she touches on subjects like adultery, sex and death. In her novel *Ambrosia for Afters* (1997), she spoke about how emotionally demanding a natural process like growing up could be. Her other works include *Jaldi's Friends* (2003), *The Page Three Murders* (2006), *Bougainvillea House* (2006), *The Gardener's Song* (2007) and *The Monochrome Madonna* (2010).

Swarup, V. (b. —) Vikas Swarup was born in Allahabad (India) in a family of lawyers. After his schooling, Vikas attended Allahabad University and studied History, Psychology and Philosophy. He also made his mark as a champion debater, winning national level competitions. After graduating with distinction, he joined the Indian Foreign Service in 1986, motivated by an interest in international relations and a desire to explore different cultures. In his diplomatic career, Vikas has been posted to various countries such as Turkey (1987–90), the United States (1993–97) Ethiopia (1997–2000), the United Kingdom (2000–03) and South Africa (2006–09). Since August 2009, he is the Consul General of India in Osaka-Kobe, Japan.

He penned his first novel, *Q&A* (2005), in two months, when he was posted in London. Published in 2005 by Doubleday/Random House (UK & Commonwealth), Harper Collins (Canada) and Scribner (US) it has been published in 42 languages. It was shortlisted for the Best First Book by the Commonwealth Writer's Prize and won South Africa's Exclusive Books Boeke Prize 2006 as well as the Paris Book Fair's Reader's Prize, the Prix Grand Public, in 2007. It was voted the Most Influential Book of 2008 in Taiwan, and winner of the Best Travel Read (Fiction) at the Heathrow Travel Product Award 2009. Harper Collins brought out the audio book, read by Kerry Shale, which won the award for Best Audio Book of the Year 2005. The BBC produced a radio play based on the book, which won the Gold Award for Best Drama at the Sony Radio Academy Awards 2008 and the IVCA Clarion Award 2008. The film version of *Q&A*, titled *Slumdog Millionaire*, directed by Danny Boyle, took the world by storm, winning more than 70 awards including four Golden Globes, 7 BAFTAs and a staggering 8 Oscars, including Best Adapted Screenplay and Best Picture. Swarup's second novel, *Six Suspects* (2008), was released in the UK by Transworld in August 2008. Published by Harper Collins in Canada and St Martin's Press in the US, it has sold translation rights in 30 languages. Radio 4 commissioned a radio play based on the novel. It has been optioned for a film by the BBC and Starfield productions and John Hodge, who wrote the script for films like Trainspotting, Shallow Grave and The Beach, has been commissioned to write the screenplay. Swarup has written for *TIME*, the *Guardian*, the *Telegraph* (UK), the *Financial Times* (UK), British Airway's in-flight magazine *HighLife*, *DNA* (India), *Outlook* (India) and *Liberation* (France).

Taseer, A. (b.1980) was born in London to Salman Taseer and Tavleen Singh. They were unmarried, and separated shortly afterwards. Taseer grew up in New Delhi, before going off to a residential school in Kodaikanal. Later, he graduated in French and Political Science at Amherst College, Massachusetts. Taseer has worked for *TIME* magazine, and as a freelance journalist has also written for *Prospect* magazine, the *Sunday Times*, the *Sunday Telegraph*, the *Financial Times*, *TAR* magazine and *Esquire*. Taseer lives between New Delhi and London and his works include *Stranger to History: A Son's Journey Through Islamic Lands* (2009), *Translated from the English: Terra Islamica* (2009), *The Temple-Goers* (2010) and *Noon* (2011).

Tennyson, A. (b.1809–92) Alfred Tennyson was born in Somersby, Lincolnshire, the fourth of the twelve children of George Tennyson, clergyman, and his wife, Elizabeth. In 1816, Tennyson was sent to Louth Grammar School, which he disliked so intensely that in later life he refused even to walk past the school. From 1820, he was educated at home, mainly by his father, who introduced him to such works as *The Arabian Nights*, *The Koran* and other books of folklore and myth. He joined his brothers, Frederick and Charles, at Trinity College, Cambridge, in 1827 and with his brother Charles, published *Poems by Two Brothers* in the same year.

In 1830 he published *Poems Chiefly Lyrical*, which was attacked by Professor John Wilson writing in *Blackwood's Magazine* as Christopher North, who complained of the infantile vanity and painful striving after originality of the poems, though he did add that he had good hopes of Alfred Tennyson. Tennyson published *Poems* in 1832, having benefited from Hallam's assistance in choosing and negotiating with the publisher, and in proof reading and editing the manuscript. The volume received generally unfavourable reviews, though Hallam continued to promote it, himself writing a review that appeared in Moxon's *The Englishman's Magazine* together with one of Tennyson's sonnets. A new version of *Poems* appeared in 1842 in two volumes, the first volume containing revised versions of the poems from the previously published works, and the second volume new works, including 'The Lady of Shallot', 'The Lotus Eaters',' Morte d'Arthur' and 'Ulysses'. The publication established his reputation, receiving praise from both Carlyle and Dickens, followed by an influential essay by R. H. Horne in the New Spirit of the Age. 'The Princess, a Medley' was published in 1847, and sold well, running to 5 editions by 1853. In 1850, he succeeded Wordsworth as the Poet Laureate, and married Emily Sellwood. The same year, he published *In Memoriam*, substantially a memorial to his friend Arthur Hallam, on which he had been working intermittently since 1833, and which addressed the high Victorian interests in death, remorse and spiritual growth. The book was a critical and commercial success, and went to a three further editions in the same year.

He continued to write and publish until his death in 1892. Other works include: *Idylls of the King* (1859), *Enoch Arden and Other Poems* (1864), *The Holy Grail and Other Poems* (1869), *Harold* (1876), *The Falcon* (1877), *Ballads and Other Poems* (1880), *The Promise of May* (1882), *Beckett* (1884), *Tiresias and Other Poems* (1885), *Locksley Hall Sixty Years After* (1886), *Demeter and Other Poems* (1889), *The Death of Oenone and Other Poems* (1892) and *The Foresters* (1892).

Tharoor, S. (b.1956) was born in London to Lily and Chandran Tharoor, both from the state of Kerala. Tharoor studied at Montfort School in Mumbai. He attended high school at St Xavier's Collegiate School in Kolkata and obtained his Bachelor of Arts degree in history from St. Stephen's College, Delhi. Tharoor went on to win a scholarship to study at The Fletcher School of Law and Diplomacy at Tufts University and earned three degrees in three years – a Ph.D. and two master's degrees. Tharoor is the youngest person in the history of the Fletcher School to be awarded a doctorate. His doctoral thesis, 'Reasons of State', was a required reading in courses on Indian foreign-policy making. In 2000, Tharoor was awarded an honorary Doctor of Letters degree by the University of Puget Sound and in 2008 he received an honorary doctorate degree by the University of Bucharest.

Tharoor has written numerous books in English. Most of his literary creations are centered on Indian themes and they are markedly 'Indo-nostalgic'. Perhaps his most famous work is *The Great Indian Novel*, published in 1989, in which he uses the narrative and theme of the famous Indian epic Mahabharata to weave a satirical story of Indian life in a non-linear mode with the characters drawn from the Indian Independence Movement. His novel *Show Business* (1992) was made into the film 'Bollywood' (1994). The late Ismail Merchant had announced his wish to make a film of Tharoor's novel *Riot* shortly before Merchant's death in 2005. Tharoor has been a highly regarded columnist in each of India's three best-known English-language newspapers, most recently for the *Hindu* newspaper (2001–08) and in a weekly column, "Shashi on Sunday," in the *Times of India* (January 2007–December 2008). Following his resignation as Minister of State for External Affairs, he began a fortnightly column on foreign policy issues in the "Deccan Chronicle". Previously he was a columnist for the *Gentleman* magazine and the *Indian Express* newspaper, as well as a frequent contributor to *Newsweek International* and the *International Herald Tribune*. His Op-Eds and book reviews have appeared in the *Washington Post*, the *New York Times* and the *Los Angeles Times*, among other papers. His monthly column, 'India Reawakening', distributed by Project Syndicate, appears in some 80 newspapers around the world. Tharoor began writing at the age of six and his first published story appeared in the 'Bharat Jyoti', the Sunday edition of the 'Free press Journal', in Mumbai at age 10. His World War II adventure novel *Operation Bellows*, inspired by the Biggles books, was serialized in the *Junior Statesman* starting a week before his 11th birthday. Each of his books has been a best-seller in India. *The Great Indian Novel* (1989) is currently in its 28th edition in India and his newest volume. *The Elephant, the Tiger and the Cellphone* (2007) has undergone seven hardback reprintings there.

Tripathi, A. (b.1974) Amish Tripathi is an author from Mumbai, India. Tripathi is an alumnus of the Indian Institute of Management, Calcutta. He worked in the financial service industry for nearly 14 years before turning to writing. Although he originally wanted to be a historian, he chose a career in finance because he couldn't afford the former. Tripathi's debut work *The Immortals of Meluha* (2010) was a surprise bestseller, breaking into the top seller charts within a week of its launch. *The Immortals of Meluha* was the first in the Shiva Trilogy. The trilogy is a fictionalized biography of the Indian deity Shiva. It narrates how Shiva was 'just a man, 4000 years ago but is today remembered as the Mahadev (the God of Gods).' The second book in the trilogy *The Secret of the Nagas* was released in August 2011.

Trivedi, A. (b. —) Anish Trivedi is a former investment banker who gave up Wall Street to host radio, anchor television and run a media company. He is the writer of two plays, 'Still Single' and 'One Small Day', and a regular contributor to magazines that include *GQ* and *Elle*. His acting credits include the stage, Hollywood and Bollywood. He lives in Mumbai, but writes all over the world. His first novel *Call me Dan* (2009) explores urban India through the life of Gautam Joshi, occasionally known as Dan. Thirty–year-old Gautam works at a call centre and is a part of a new generation that is still coming to grips with money (having it) and morals (losing them).

Usha, K. R. (b. —) has been writing fiction for over two decades, beginning with short fiction, which were published in various Indian magazines. Her short story 'Sepia Tones' won the Katha Award for short fiction in 1995. *Sojourn*, her first novel, was published in 1998 and the second, *The Chosen*, in 2003. *A Girl and a River* (2007) is her third novel. Usha lives and works in Bangalore.

Vadukut, S. (b. —) Sidin Vadukut was born in a small village near Irinjalakuda. He spent the most part of his childhood in Abu Dhabi and came back to India to pursue his higher education. An engineer from National Institute of Technology, Tiruchirappalli, Sidin says his father bought him his MBA from IIM Ahmedabad. He subsequently worked with the management consulting firm AT Kearney before quitting and writing 'Dork'. He currently lives in London, UK.

He is currently the managing editor of Livemint.com. In January 2010, Sidin's debut novel *Dork: The Incredible Adventures of Robin 'Einstein' Varghese* was published. This is the first part of the 'Dork Trilogy' and takes a satirical dig at the management consulting industry.

INDEX

The index numbers in bold represent where the topic is covered substantially.